ELOQUENT WITNESSES

Frontispiece. Detail from Giovanni Mansueti's painting 'De Verschijning van de H. Hieronymus aan de H. Augustinus'. Reproduction courtesy of the Bonnefantenmuseum, Maastricht.

ELOQUENT WITNESSES

BOOKBINDINGS AND THEIR HISTORY

A volume of essays dedicated to the memory of Dr Phiroze Randeria

Edited by Mirjam M. Foot

THE BIBLIOGRAPHICAL SOCIETY

THE BRITISH LIBRARY

OAK KNOLL PRESS

MMIV

© The Bibliographical Society 2004

ISBN 0 948170 14 X (BIB. SOC.)
ISBN 0 7123 4827 1 (BL)
ISBN 1 58456 117 3 (OKP)

CIP catalogue records for this book are available
from the British Library and the Library of Congress

Published by the Bibliographical Society of London

The British Library, 96 Euston Road,
London NW1 2DB, England

Oak Knoll Press, 310 Delaware Street,
New Castle, Delaware 19720, U.S.A.

Printed in Great Britain by Henry Ling Ltd

Designed and typeset by Paul W. Nash

CONTENTS

LIST OF CONTRIBUTORS

Giles Barber was on the staff of the Bodleian Library from 1954 to 1970 and Librarian of the Taylor Institution, Oxford, until retirement in 1996. He has written extensively both on bookbinding and on the history of the French booktrade. His catalogue of the books and bookbindings at Waddesdon Manor is in the process of production.

Carmen Blacker is the great-granddaughter of the binding collector John Blacker. She was Lecturer in Japanese at the Faculty of Oriental Studies at Cambridge from 1958 to 1991, and is the author of various books and articles on Japanese religion and folklore.

Christian Coppens is Curator of Manuscripts and Rare Books at the Katholieke Universiteit, Louvain, and has written on bookbinding history, the history of the booktrade and private libraries.

Mirjam Foot is Professor of Library and Archive Studies at University College, London. She was formerly Director of Collections and Preservation at the British Library. She has written several books and numerous articles on the history of bookbinding, and on a variety of preservation and conservation topics. She was the 2003 Sandars Lecturer at Cambridge.

David Pearson is Director of the University of London Research Library Services. His publications include *Provenance research in book history* (1994) and *Oxford bookbinding 1500–1640* (2000); his handbook on *English bookbinding styles 1450–1800* is due to appear in 2004.

Nicholas Pickwoad is a freelance book conservator who is in charge of the St Catherine's monastery library project at the Camberwell School of Arts and is adviser on book conservation to the National Trust of Great Britain. He also teaches courses both in Europe and the USA on the history of European bookbinding structures and has written several articles on this subject.

Nicholas Poole-Wilson has been managing director of Bernard Quaritch Ltd for the past twenty-five years.

Esther Potter is an independent scholar with a special interest in the structure and development of the nineteenth century bookbinding trade. She was co-author (with Graham Pollard) of *Early bookbinding manuals* (1984).

Jan Storm van Leeuwen is Curator of Bookbindings at the Koninklijke Bibliotheek in The Hague, and has written several books and articles on bookbindings of the Netherlands and elsewhere. His next book will focus on eighteenth century bookbinding in The Netherlands.

Marianne Tidcombe is the author of *The Bookbindings of T. J. Cobden-Sanderson* (1984), *The Doves Bindery* (1991), *Women Bookbinders 1880–1920* (1996), and *The Doves Press* (2002). Her next book, with Peter Corley, is on the life and work of Katharine Adams.

INTRODUCTION

I N 1990 Dr Phiroze Randeria, wishing to honour the memory of his
elder brother who, after the death of their parents, had devoted
his youth to bringing up his younger siblings, established a series
of lectures. Dr Randeria's own interest in the history of bookbinding,
the literature of which he collected with great enthusiasm and
persistence, suggested the theme for such a series. His generous
endowment has enabled the Bibliographical Society to organise,
since 1991, an annual lecture on a bookbinding topic. Dr Randeria
who was a somewhat shy and unassuming man, but of great charm
and kindness, invariably sat in the first row of the Gustave Tuck
Theatre of University College, London, on these occasions, in later
years accompanied by his son.

Several years ago, the Council of the Bibliographical Society
decided that these Randeria lectures should be published as a way of
showing gratitude to the donor.[1]

Alas, on 7 May 2001 Dr Randeria died, aged 76, after a long
illness. The Society will remain grateful for his generosity and this
volume is dedicated to his memory.

It is a wide-ranging book, opening with a general statement on the
pitfalls and possibilities of binding research, an essay that raises
several questions that have been addressed in those that follow. The
next essay shows what paintings of bindings can tell us about the
people for whom books were bound and what the bindings themselves can reveal about their owners. This is followed by a lengthy
account of a specific type of book, the school prize, demonstrating
what a knowledge of binding history can teach us about approaches
to education. More detailed discussions of types of bindings and
specific styles of decoration also address broader issues, such as the
purpose of certain bindings and why they were made, as well as the
political and economic circumstances that made their production
possible.

Structural, as well as decorative, features provide evidence for
how the binding trade was organised and how binders adapted
themselves to a changing and demanding clientele. Studies of the
bindings in two particular collections show how much can be learnt
from accurate and detailed observation both of structure and design,
and how work-practices in the sixteenth and eighteenth centuries can

be derived from such observation, combined with the scarce surviving archival and contemporary written evidence. There is more written and printed evidence for the rapid developments that took place in the nineteenth century and Benjamin West was clearly in the fore-front of adopting new techniques to cater for an expanding trade in attractive bindings.

How a collector's passionate obsession can be taken advantage of by a less than scrupulous provider and what role women played in the binding trade, especially from the 1880s onwards, are shown in the last two essays.

This book demonstrates clearly that bindings can tell us much about themselves, about how they were made, by whom and for whom, but that they can also explain a great deal about the cultural and social circumstances in which they were produced; that they are eloquent witnesses of their time.

Mirjam M. Foot   August 2002

1. Several, but by no means all, lectures have been published elsewhere. Most have been rewritten or revised for this volume. By request of their authors the lectures of Anthony Hobson and Vanessa Marshall have not been included.

ACKNOWLEDGEMENTS

The Council of the Bibliographical Society is indebted to the following for permission to reproduce slides and photographs from their collections: The Master and Fellows of Balliol College, Oxford; The Bancroft Library, University of California, Berkeley; The Bayerische Staatsbibliothek, Munich; The Bibliothèque Chiroux-Croisiers, Liège; The Bibliothèque municipale, Troyes; The Bibliothèque nationale de France; The Bodleian Library, University of Oxford; Bonnefantenmuseum, Maastricht; The British Library Board; Dansk Skolemuseum; Gebr. Douwes Fine Art, Amsterdam; Duke University Library; Durham University Library; The Master and Fellows of Emmanuel College, Cambridge; the late Sir Paul Getty KBE, Wormsley Library; Groeningen Museum, Bruges; The University Library, Louvain; Konrad Meuschel; Park Abbey, Heverlee, Louvain; The Pierpont Morgan Library; Röhsska Konstslöjdmuseet, Göteborg; The Royal Library, Brussels; The Royal Library, The Hague; Rijksmuseum, Amsterdam; John Rylands University Library, Manchester; The Board of Trinity College, Dublin; The Board of Trustees of the Victoria and Albert Museum (National Art Library, V&A Picture Library); Waddesdon, The Rothschild Collection (The National Trust, photographer: Eost & Macdonald).

The editor wishes to record her gratitude to David Chambers and Paul Nash for all their work in getting this book into printable form.

LIST OF COLOUR PLATES

Frontispiece. Detail from Giovanni Mansueti's painting 'De Verschijning van de H. Hieronymus aan de H. Augustinus'. Bonnefantenmuseum, Maastricht.

1. Binding by Albert Magnus, Amsterdam, 1679. I. Cats, *Werelts begin, midden, eynde, besloten in den trou-ringh*, Dordrecht, Matthias Havius, 1637. The Hague, Royal Library, 1791 B 1.

2. Binding by the First Stadholder Bindery, the Hague, *c.* 1730. Paulus Merula, *Politijck handboexken, van de Staet van 't Nederlandt*, Leyden, Abraham van Geer-Vliet, 1650. The Hague, Royal Library, 138 G 29.

3. Paris mosaic binding by Lemonnier. M. Bandello, *Novelle*, London, 1740 (lower cover). Waddesdon Manor, B1/24/4.

4. Paris mosaic binding, *c.* 1746. *Ordinaire de la messe*, MS 1725 (lower cover). Waddesdon Manor, B1/22/9.

5. A Dublin binding, *c.* 1772. Sallust, *The Cataline and Jugurtine Wars* (transl. H. Maffet), Dublin, 1772. British Library, C. 67.e.15.

6. A Dublin binding by William Hallhead's binder, *c.* 1775. *The Holy Bible*, Cambridge, 1763. Trinity College, Dublin, Armoire.

7. A binding by Hagué. *Epigrammata antique urbis*, Rome, Iacobus Mazochius, 1521. British Library, C.48.h.10.

8. Embroidered binding by May Morris, bound by T. J. Cobden-Sanderson, 1891. William Morris, *Love is enough*, London, 1873. Bancroft Library.

11

BOOKBINDING RESEARCH
Pitfalls, Possibilities and Needs
Mirjam M. Foot

WHEN THE Bibliographical Society celebrated the first fifty years of its existence with *Studies in retrospect,* published three years after the event because of the war, E. P. Goldschmidt, in his inimitable ironic manner, characterised the history of bookbinding as 'A humble auxiliary discipline, rather childish to some, attractive to others, not entirely useless and undoubtedly innocuous'.[1] Fifty years later, a critic of its historiography, with none of Goldschmidt's mellow wisdom, judged 'The study of bookbinding [to be] a branch of scholarship that has suffered from a conspicuous lack of elementary scholarly principles for a very long time', continuing: 'this discipline is vitiated by its traditional association with an ephemeral and name-fetishistic sensationalism where a fascination with questions of attribution is much in evidence and today's extolled truth is the lie of tomorrow.'[2]

Goldschmidt, though milder in tone, had already expressed the same reservation, when he described the study of bookbinding in the 1880s and nineties as 'too exclusively preoccupied with the artistic charm of their chosen objects, ... too beglamoured with the reputed ownership of lovely queens and royal mistresses', but, Goldschmidt concluded that it was 'not for those reasons valueless'.[3] Our critic on the other hand dismissed the 'discoveries' in the field of binding research as 'sensationalistic and pretentious ... insignificant from a scholarly perspective'.[4]

Goldschmidt, comparing the history of bookbinding to the history of costume, encapsulated in a single phrase the state this subject had reached by the 1940s, its lack of status and its incompleteness. Did the following fifty years do nothing to lend the subject greater academic respectability? The history of bookbinding is still a relatively young academic discipline; it lacks an established and generally agreed vocabulary, and its methodology is still in its infancy. It has to a large extent limited itself to the observation and description of physical objects and in many cases, both observation and description leave a great deal to be desired. It has drawn conclusions from an insufficiently large sample. Especially the study of Coptic, Anglo-Saxon and early medieval bindings suffered from a lack of surviving evidence. According to Professor Janos Szirmai, we are basing our conclusions on no more than 0.01% of the probable total output, the rest having perished.[5] It is also true to say that speculation and wishful thinking have from time to time got the better of scepticism and caution. Nevertheless, during the past century or so, a great deal of useful and valuable work has been done and the subject has moved from the aestheticism of the arts and crafts, 'the cult of Beauty and Good Taste' as Goldschmidt called it,[6] into the field of bibliography. As early as 1905, Strickland Gibson began a paper to the Bibliographical Society on the 'Localization of books by their binding' with the words: 'It is my intention in this paper to treat bindings from a purely utilitarian point of view, considering them simply in the nature of clues and to suggest the method by which they may be made to throw light on the history of the books they contain'[7] – a distinct move away from 'name-fetishism' and the fascination with royal mistresses. Goldschmidt himself, in his *Gothic and Renaissance bookbindings* (London, 1928), was one of the first, at least in England, to treat the subject in a scholarly way and to take it out of the domain of the amateur and the connoisseur.

The debt we owe him and other early scholars[8] is incalculable. Nevertheless, with a very few exceptions (Berthe de Regemorter and Graham Pollard are notable ones), they occupied themselves largely with the observation and interpretation of binding decoration, with the attempts to identify decorative tools, to postulate groups of tools into workshops and to attribute these workshops to binders, real men and women with names and addresses.

It is not surprising that the study of decorative tools proved both the most attractive and the most fruitful way to further the subject and increase our knowledge of this aspect of the booktrade. Its attraction needs no explanation, for anyone with an eye for colour and form will be struck by the brilliance of gold on glowing leather, by the elegance of line of arabesque or intricate interlace, by the variety and often comical effect of picturesque ornament. Moreover, the scholar can isolate facts by painstaking comparison, can identify tools and groups of tools, in an attempt to create order out of aesthetic pleasure. The study of tools and combinations of tools is the surest way to identify individual workshops and it is this aspect of binding research that has been most successfully pursued over the past fifty years.

This kind of work takes time and patience, but it can be done and – provided the raw material is extensive – it is complex but not difficult. Or is it? How solid are the facts? The tool itself, hand-engraved in brass, is a fact, but are all tools quite such incontrovertably identifiable individuals as we once thought? Staffan Fogelmark in his *Flemish and related panel-stamped bindings* (New York, 1990) argues, with convincing force, that panels at least were cast and not engraved, thereby throwing doubt on the validity of earlier literature on the subject. Cast panels would have existed in multiple, identical copies and can therefore not be used to identify the work of an individual binder or binder's shop. Anthony Hobson in *Humanists and bookbinders*[9] describes plaquettes found on Renaissance bindings as cast from a mould, so that different shops could and indeed did use identical copies of the same original. Can Fogelmark's arguments be extended to the manufacture of corner- and centre-blocks? So far, no positive evidence in favour of such a supposition has been presented, but the opposite has not been proven either.[10]

There is no evidence that small hand tools were cast and there is a certain amount of evidence that they were engraved. The few binder's tools from the twelfth century onwards that have survived are certainly engraved. Small tools, as impressed on bindings, turn up over limited periods of time in specific locations. There is one exception: an opening bud tool that belonged to Wotton's binder B, who used it in Paris on bindings belonging to Marie Mauroy and Marie Gryolay.[11] A tool which appears to be identical with this open bud was also used in London by the MacDurnan Gospels binder.[12] A great many small hand tools look at first glance much alike, but careful inspection soon shows small but perceptible differences.[13] Even if the hand-engraved tool is a fact (and one possible exception is not enough to cast serious doubt on a great deal of positive evidence), what do we know about its maker, its use and its life?

Very little is known about tool cutters at work before the nineteenth century. They were metal workers who cut dies for seals, coins and medals, as well as bookbinders' finishing tools and printers' ornaments, and even punches for typefounders; they may also have made clasps and metal corner- and centre-pieces for bindings, but exactly what their business consisted of and how widely their skills ranged we do not know, nor do we know where they got their patterns from. It is thought that much ornament derives from a common source. Some binders' tools have close links with manuscript illuminations, book illustrations or title-page designs, even with carvings, sculpture, ceramics and architecture. Some finishing tools have close affinity with printers' ornaments and with patterns for embroidery, but who specified the design for these tools? In the eighteenth and nineteenth centuries tool cutters issued pattern books or pattern sheets for binders to choose from.

The philanthropist, Thomas Hollis, who gave away large quantities of books, had them bound in bindings with emblematic tools. Most of these tools were designed for him by Giovanni Battista Cipriani, probably in 1758 or early 1759. We do not know who cut the first set of these tools, but, when after a fire in Matthewman's bindery in 1764 a duplicate set of tools had to be cut, Hollis commissioned Thomas Pingo, the medallist and later assistant engraver at the Royal Mint, to do this.[14] Roger Payne took great interest in the design of his tools and may well have specified them. When he bound a set of Dugdale's works for Sir Richard Colt Hoare in 1796, he wrote: 'Sir Richard Hoare Order'd me to make the Pattern for Finishing the Sides of Dugdale I propose to Finish all the Dugdale uniform. But to make a difference in the English History by using Acorns & Oak Leaves which I think would not be so proper in the Monasticon as those flowers & Leaves I have done for the Monastic part'.[15] The legend that Roger Payne cut his own tools has no firm basis, on the contrary, in a letter of 16 May 1796 he talks about the necessity of getting tools cut and the time it takes to get this done.[16] Both G. D. Hobson and Anthony Hobson have attempted to trace tool designs to their source of inspiration, and Anthony Hobson has studied the meaning of certain Italian emblematic tools with most interesting results,[17] but more work is needed in this field, both to establish the connection between binding tools and other forms of ornament, and to discover more about the makers of these tools.

We know a little more about the use of finishing tools and their life span, but here too problems abound. We know for instance that by the seventeenth century and most probably earlier, in France the binding trade was divided into forwarding and finishing and that consequently books bound by a variety of forwarders could be finished in the same shop and *vice versa*. The question then arises whether the man called *relieur du roi* was the finisher, or the forwarder, or whether he was the mastermind directing both operations. Whatever the nature of his involvement, are we right to link the names of the successive *relieurs du roi* with the tools found on royal bindings? Evidently not, as it has been shown that tools that occur on French royal bindings made when Gommar Estienne was *relieur du roi* turn up later when Claude Picques held the office.[18] I am inclined to think that it is perfectly possible that both Estienne and Picques, once they had become royal binders, were too grand to work at the bench themselves and that instead they organised the work and used the best Paris forwarders and finishers available at the time. If one assumes that the *relieur du roi*, the man responsible for the binding of the king's books, was the man who specified the designs, it would explain why these tools, although they are the same, were used to such different effect during the reigns of successive kings.

The same problem arises in France in the eighteenth century. Is the name on the binder's ticket that of the entrepreneur, the forwarder or the finisher? Only in a few cases is the ticket specific, for example that of Dubuisson who is clearly stated to be the *doreur*. Claude Devers called himself *relieur, doreur sur tranche et sur cuir*.[19] But Antoine-Michel Padeloup, *relieur du roi,* is known to have given work to Dubuisson for tooling in gold, although it is apparent from a trade card and from the inventory made after his death in 1758 that he owned both forwarding and finishing tools. He was obviously over-loaded with work and several bindings with Padeloup tickets can clearly be attributed to other ateliers.[20] Binders' tickets on their own can never be conclusive evidence for attribution. It is after all perfectly easy to remove a ticket from a binding or to paste one in. A signature tooled on the binding itself, usually on the spine, sometimes on the cover hidden among the tooling, and later often on the turn-in, suggests, but does not prove, that the signer was the finisher.

In England the problem of responsibility seems less acute, since the trade was organised differently, and forwarding and finishing were carried out by the same person or, at least, in the same shop.[21] But were tools borrowed? Did they on occasion belong to the publisher or, even, to the owner of the book? Were they given out with the unbound books to a number of shops? There are bills for bindings supplied to the library of Henry, Prince of Wales, by John Norton and Robert Barker, both important booksellers and printers, but we do not know whether they had their own binderies or employed someone else. From the evidence provided by the bindings themselves, it appears that the greater part of the Prince of Wales's library was bound in a standard style *c.* 1610. The disposition of royal insignia on these bindings suggests that the blocks belonged to a central source, possibly Norton or Barker, but were allocated, with the books, to a number of binders.[22]

Tools were inherited and sold. They could move from binder to binder and from shop to shop. Their life span would have been dependent on how often they were used and how carefully they were treated. It is not unusual to find the same tool occurring over a period of thirty to fifty years, sometimes in combination with different sets of other tools. When Jean de Planche left England *c.* 1575, he must have left some at least of his finishing tools behind, as several tools that occur on his earlier bindings continue to turn up on English bindings that cover books printed between 1577 and 1645.[23]

Therefore, if we cannot draw conclusions from single tools, are groups of tools more reliable indicators of the work of a specific bindery? In many instances this is indeed the case, but there is some evidence that in the seventeenth, eighteenth and nineteenth centuries journeymen-finishers, with their own sets of tools, travelled round the country looking for work. Some were employed in country houses to gild the backs of the books in the library. The result, uniformly decorated spines lining the walls, can be seen in several large houses, but it could be dangerous to link the tooling of the covers with that of the spines, as the two operations may have been carried out by different binders at different times.[24]

And even when groups of tools can be identified, when they turn up in the same combination over a period of thirty or forty years, when the provenance of the books they decorate points to the same place of origin, and the bindings can with some confidence be attributed to a locatable and datable workshop, the question then arises how to link such groups of bindings with the men (and occasionally women) who produced them? Finding their names in archival sources is hard work, needing perseverance and devoted pursuit, but it can be done on occasion as Pollard, Nixon, and more recently Paul Christianson have proved.[25] But to link these names with the products for which they were responsible needs more than perseverance; it needs insight as well as luck. To hit on an inventory or bill where the books listed can be identified as individual copies, to find a contemporary inscription linking a specific copy with its binder, to quarry from extant accounts specific dates and specific products, needs luck, but also the knowledge and insight necessary to use it.

One example will have to suffice. Humfrey Wanley, Lord Harley's learned, scrupulous and sometimes pernickety librarian, noted in his diary whenever he sent a particular book or a batch of books from his Lordship's library to be bound.[26] Several of the bindings from the Harleian library, now in the British Library, match Wanley's descriptions and their binder can be identified. On 27 June 1721 Wanley wrote: 'Mr Elliot begun to work about the CODEX AVREVS, in Order to the New Binding of it, the Cover it had in the Second Binding of it perhaps about 90 years ago, being worn out, and the whole sewing gone to decay.' On 13 July, this most valuable and precious book, a manuscript of the four Gospels written in gold, *c.* 800, for the court of Charlemagne, was covered and the diary records: 'Mr Elliot having clothed the CODEX AVREVS in My Lords Marocco-Leather, took the same from hence this day, in Order to work upon it with his Best Tools; which he say's he can do with much more Conveniency at his house than here.' From Elliott's bill it is clear that the tooling took three days and on 22 July he made the box, lined with '2 yards of Persian Silk'. The total cost, without the leather – this having been supplied by Wanley – came to £7.4s.6d. and Elliott was paid for this and other work on 26 April 1722.[27] This is very convenient, but it is rare to have a sufficiently detailed bill or a diary and the book or collection it refers to close together.

Linking a named binder with his output is satisfying, but what does it tell us about the booktrade at a particular point, or about social and cultural history, of which the production of a book is but a small part? How does the binder fit into the chain of author, patron, scribe or printer, publisher, bookseller, buyer and reader? The relationship between the binder and all others involved in the production and marketing of books, as well as that between him and the owners of the books, has changed over the centuries, but our knowledge of the exact nature of these relationships, and how and when they altered, lacks precision. What was the relationship between binders and other decorative artists, how did they relate to leather-workers, for example? Before the end of the eighteenth century, divisions between branches of similar crafts were not so distinct, and finishers would not have limited their skills to the decoration of bindings only. They also tooled boxes, containers, covers and cases for telescopes and other instruments, and furniture, in the same way as cut-leather artists applied themselves not only to the decoration of chests and instrument cases, but also from time to time to book covers. What exactly was the binders' role outside the booktrade? How were they regarded in the arts, crafts and business hierarchies? The majority of binders were no doubt craftsmen who played a useful, even an indispensable role in the production of a book, but some were artists and some were businessmen. On the whole their social status was fairly humble, even within the booktrade, but some moved in exalted circles: Charles Lewis went round London 'wearing tassels to his half boots'[28] and ran a large business; Samuel Kalthoeber was much in demand and had to resist being lured away by Catherine the Great of Russia; Cobden-Sanderson moved among the intellectual aristocracy and had many influential friends who also incidentally were clients. The role of the binder in society over the centuries deserves more attention that it has received so far.

What was the connection between the binder and the person who ordered the binding and who was this? Frequently the owner of the book would commission its binding, or ask his bookseller to arrange this, but in some cases the publisher or the printer did so, either for presentation to the patron or dedicatee of the book, or to some other suitable grandee, or the bookseller might have a limited number of a readily-saleable title bound up for stock. In 1542/3 Thomas Berthelet, the King's printer, was paid for supplying bindings to King Henry VIII.[29] Berthelet himself was not a binder and presentation copies of books he printed appear to have been bound in at least three different shops: King Henry's bindery, the Greenwich bindery and the King Edward and Queen Mary bindery.

Authors and editors also ordered presentation bindings: Lord Herbert of Cherbury must have believed that a glittering exterior would draw the attention to the brilliance of the argument inside the covers. The presentation copies of his treatise on truth, *De veritate* (1633), translated into French as *De la vérité* (1639), were all bound in the same London shop in gold-tooled goatskin.[30]

Lavish presentation bindings could indicate the esteem in which the recipient was held by the donor and might hint at the *noblesse* that obliged the granting of preferment in return. Clement Adams, the schoolmaster to the King's pages, subtly flattered his royal master by commissioning the Flamboyant binder to tool a presentation inscription in Latin on the binding of Luther's *Ennaratio Psalmorum* (Strasbourg, 1538) which reads in translation: 'The wealthy, Sire, give their friends golden gifts, but this book contains something better than gold. Your Adam, who is your devoted servant, hopes that you will be as pleased to receive this as he is to give it.'[31] The printer Christopher Barker gave Queen Elizabeth as a new year's gift in 1584 a folio Bible (1583) bound in embroidered red velvet. He received in return a piece of gold plate, weighing 11 1/8 ounces: a royal reward for a gift fit for a queen.[32]

Samuel Pepys was known to appreciate the charm of a fine binding and several handsomely bound copies reached him in his capacity as

Secretary to the Admiralty and a powerful wielder of Admiralty patronage. *The Whole Art of navigation* (London, 1685) bound by Charles Mearne in gold-tooled and black painted red goatskin was presented to Pepys the 'Saviour of the Navy' by its author, Daniel Newhouse.[33] And *An Account of several late voyages & discoveries* of Sir John Narborough (London, 1694) handsomely bound by Robert Steel was dedicated and presented to Pepys by the publishers, Samuel Smith and Benjamin Walford.[34] Bindings as gifts were not always inspired by ulterior motives and there are many instances of finely bound books passing between friends, between relations or between husband and wife, such as Nicholas Bacon's gift of the works of Saint Basil in Greek (Basel, 1551) to his wife Anne in 1553.[35] As well as ordering books to be bound for presentation, most collectors ordered bindings for their own libraries. The products of such commissions varied widely, from the relatively simple serviceable bindings for personal use, to the bindings that were both useful and a pleasure to the eye roving along the gold-tooled spines lining the walls, such as those that Pepys ordered for his library, to the outright luxurious objects of art that brought such aesthetic satisfaction to men like Jean Grolier and Thomas Mahieu. The condition of many of the most splendid bindings made for famous collectors leaves one with the sense that these books were enjoyed rather than read. Private libraries are apt to reflect the taste, both in content and in form, of their owners. Thomas Wotton preferred to have his books bound in Paris, while Robert Dudley, Earl of Leicester, patronised his own countrymen. It would be interesting to know more about the individual collector's degree of involvement in the specification for and production of the bindings they acquired.[36] We know that Sir Robert Bruce Cotton went to considerable detail in telling his binders what to do. On the original paste-downs of a manuscript on parchment *Evangelia* [and] *Nomina benefactorum Dulmensis ecclesia* (*c*. 840) bound in gold-tooled red turkey, is written: 'Bind this book as strong as you can and very fair in the read leather / let it be shewed [sewed] withe 3 double threds waxed and when it is backed and sewed send it me and I will mark wher you shall cutt it / gett it as euen at the head as you can'. He continued at the end of the manuscript, presumably after he had seen it sewn and covered: '[cut it] as I have marcked and [round] it not to muche in the back for fear you put som leaves so forward that the[y] may be in danger of Cutting / sett flowers of gold on the back and corners and mak it very fayre and lett me have it ready this night when [I] send about 5 c in the afternoone'.[37] There are quite a number of Cotton manuscripts with such detailed instructions to his binders, but, although we know that one binder was called 'mr Hil [Hal?]' and two others lived in Paternoster Row and Warwick Lane, we do not know anything more about them.

The famous collectors who had their names, mottoes or armorial bearings tooled on their bindings can be identified with greater or lesser ease, although caution is needed in attributing bindings with royal arms to royal owners, as so many of these were either made for other members of the royal household, or were trade bindings. Those whose devices are less explicit, at least for later historians, are more difficult to trace. One example is the well-known and much discussed Apollo and Pegasus device, which was subsequently attributed to the non-existent 'Mecenate, Physician to the Pope', to 'Canevarius' and more specifically to 'Demetrio Canevari', to 'Cangiani', and again to 'Raphaelis Mecenate, Physician to Pope Urban', to Pier Luigi Farnese, to Ottavio, second Duke of Parma, to Cardinal Alessandro Farnese, and to 'Petrus Ludovicus, Duke of Castro'. Anthony Hobson brought an end to this unsatisfactory series of speculations[38] and concluded that the owner of the bindings with this device was Giovanni Battista Grimaldi (c. 1524–c. 1612), a Genoese patrician and banker. Is this simply a process driven by 'name-fetishistic sensationalism where ... today's extolled truth is the lie of tomorrow'? Is it no more than exchanging one name for another, a process that 'has not added one iota to our knowledge of the bindings'?[39]

In many instances where attributions of bindings, both to owners and to binders, have merely produced a string of names without materially altering our view of how the bindings were made, when, where and under what circumstances, or without leaving us with any greater understanding of the person for whom they were made and of the historical and cultural context of their creation, the exercise of name swapping is indeed futile, but some scholars, in particular Anthony Hobson in several recent books,[40] have both asked and answered a far wider range of questions. The names themselves are less important than the light shed on the formation and history of specific libraries, the cultural background against which the books and manuscripts were produced, the reasoning behind the use of certain devices, the sources of inspiration for specific ornaments, and the ways in which designs developed.

Much of this work has focused on binding decoration and much has been accomplished in this field over the last fifty to sixty years in particular. However, more recently, there has been a change in direction, an attempt at extending research into areas beyond the study of decoration. There is more interest in a detailed study of the whole bound book, the materials that have been used and its structural features. There has also been a branching out into wider fields, into social history, into the history of education, of learning, of the intellectual development of mankind. The humble aspect of the booktrade, the history of bookbinding has much to contribute here.

A detailed study of materials and techniques needs to be based not only on the surviving objects, but also on written evidence. Over the past thousand years or so binders – and sometimes observers – have described, more or less accurately and explicitly, the technical processes involved in the binding of books. These manuals, whether they served as *aides mémoires* or as a set of instructions, were largely written by and for craftsmen. They present the practice at a given time in a particular place and they can be of great use to the historian, however frustrating and incomprehensible they often turn out to be. A list of *Early bookbinding manuals* was compiled by Graham Pollard, continued by Esther Potter and published by the Oxford Bibliographical Society in 1984, and several early manuals, such as those by Anshelmus Faust (1612), Dirk de Bray (1658), J.-V. Capronnier de Gauffecourt (1763), Hendrik de Haas (1806), and the pseudonymous *Bibliopegia; or, the art of bookbinding* (1835) have been re-published over recent decades.[41]

The retrospective, historical observation and detailed description of the nature and the use of materials and of the changes in technical practice, is something else. Only in the past three decades or so, a few scholars, such as Roger Powell, Bernard Middleton, Christopher Clarkson, Nicholas Pickwood, and Michael Gullick in the U.K., and Jean Vezin, Janos Szirmai, Guy Petherbridge and others on the continent and in America, have started to study the materials that constitute a binding and the techniques that were employed to create it. They observed, with attention to minute detail, all the constituent parts of a binding or, where the original structure was defective, such traces of it as remained, and they have begun to explain how binders worked, how they used their instruments, in some cases what those instruments were, and how they obtained the results we now have before us. In most, though not all instances, this work has concentrated on the earlier periods. An initiative, started in Cambridge, to compile a census of medieval bookbindings in Britain, began with a description of their structure. Similar initiatives are taking place in Italy and

France. In due course, these ambitious projects will provide us not only with lists of remaining specimens, but with a much greater knowledge of medieval techniques and materials. So often, well-meaning attempts at replacing or repairing older binding structures have destroyed evidence that would have been of great value to the binding historian.

The pioneer work of Graham Pollard, who published in *The Library* for 1956[42] an influential article on 'Changes in the style of bookbinding, 1550–1830', was followed by Middleton and Pick-woad.[43] They have shown that not only medieval binding structures are of interest, and their work on the history and development of the use of materials and the practice of techniques during the sixteenth, seventeenth, eighteenth and nineteenth centuries has encouraged the study of trade bindings, a subject that had hitherto received far too little attention. Yet it was the simple, plain trade binding that provided the binder's daily bread. It was the trade binding that was ordered, produced and used in quantity, and that formed the solid foundation on which the trade was built.

In the study and description of binding structure, materials and technique, we are hampered by the lack of an agreed and generally understood vocabulary. Most disciplines in the humanities have developed their terminology alongside their subject. The history of bookbinding suffers from a lack of an explicit, unmistakable, gen-erally-understood and generally-accepted terminology. This termin-ology is most sorely needed when technical processes are described, although the lack of a common vocabulary for the description of the decorative aspects of a binding means that literature without illustra-tions is of little use. Several attempts have been made – in America, on the continent and in Britain – to establish a terminology, but so far with limited success.[44] Terms are often vague and open to a multiplicity of interpretation, or so inflexible that only their author fully understands their meaning. Matters are complicated further due to different technical practices in different countries, which means that there are frequently no direct equivalent terms for certain structural details. Nevertheless, a multi-lingual, internationally-agreed vocabulary, including descriptive terms for the component parts of a binding, as well as terms for every step of the various binding processes, elaborately illustrated, written by binders, conser-vators and historians is urgently needed. An attempt at systematising decorative binding tools so that they can be classified, coded, ordered, and ultimately retrieved, was published in a lengthy article in the *Archives et bibliothèques de Belgique* (1991). The system was designed for Dutch and Flemish binding tools from the fifteenth, sixteenth and eighteenth centuries. The fondness for vast ranges of *pointillé* and solid, curving and curling, floral and fleuron-type ornamental tools during the seventeenth century must have defeated even this impressive and energetic team of scholars.[45] It is a laudable and very interesting exercise, but I doubt whether it would have been intelligible without the large number of illustrations. Moreover, the tools have been classified according to different categories, such as heraldry, human, animal, plant, object, letter/cypher, and geometrical form, and have not been described further. Description of ornament without illustration is highly subjective and time would be spent better in compiling illustrated tool catalogues for individual binders or groups of bindings. Much good work of this kind has already been done, but more is needed, however tiresome it is to compile accurate same-size reproductions of a binder's stock of tools.

Standards of description also vary with each author and each publication. Guidelines on how bindings should be described, what should be observed, which elements recorded, to what degree of detail and in what way, could usefully be developed alongside the compilation of an agreed terminology, remembering that what needs to be described varies with the binding under consideration and with the purpose of the description. Complex records for their own sake are a luxury that can be ill afforded.

It is tempting to let the study of the specific become an aim in itself. The questions how books were bound, with what materials, which techniques were employed, what tools were used and in what way, when and where materials, instruments and methods were used first and last, by whom and for whom, are all fascinating and crying out for solution, but this is not enough. The history of bookbinding can do more than explain itself. The development and change, both in binding decoration and in binding structure can tell us much about the history of book production and the history of the booktrade; it can also contribute to a better understanding of the history of culture and civilisation.[46]

Changes in the style of trade bindings, their structure and their decoration, reflect changes in methods of book production and its continuous growth. This in turn is a consequence of the spread of learning, increased education for a different and wider public, and changes in readership. There are various periods in the history of bookbinding when a greater demand for books led to changes in binding technique as well as in binding decoration. The post-Roman-esque revival of stamped bindings on the continent follows hard upon the monastic revival of the first half of the fifteenth century. The religious reform movement among the Benedictine and Augustine monasteries in Italy and Germany, and the establishment of religious communities in the Netherlands, brought with it an increased emphasis on study, on reading and writing, stimulated the formation of libraries and necessitated the binding of books. These bindings were decorated with blind lines and individual hand tools. The increase in book production following the invention and spread of printing caused a further increase in the production of blind-tooled bindings. Soon a cheaper and quicker way of decorating bindings was developed at the end of the fifteenth century with the introduction first of rolls and then of panels. At the same time binders started to look for ways in which to speed up the actual binding process and to cut the cost of production. From the beginning of the sixteenth century one can observe a change to cheaper materials and less time-consuming practices.[47] The industrial revolution in Britain in the second half of the eighteenth century gave a further impetus to increased book production and accelerated binding methods, resulting in a re-organis-ation of binders' shops and practices, and culminating in the gradual mechanisation of binding processes in the 1820s and 1830s.

The search for cheaper covering materials goes back a long way. Already in the fourteenth century we find limp vellum bindings used for account books, and limp vellum bindings for school books and classical texts were popular, especially in the Low Countries and Germany, but also in Spain, Italy and France, in the sixteenth and seventeenth centuries. Attempts at using sheepskin, rather than the more expensive calf or hide, came in for censure from the Stationers' Company in London in the sixteenth and seventeenth centuries. Paper covers for thin pamphlets were used all over Europe, and in the eighteenth century we find canvas used instead of leather to cover school books, to be followed by various kinds of book cloth in the nineteenth century.

Who owned these simpler and cheaper bindings? Were they made to order or were they offered for sale in quantity by the publishers and booksellers? Until the nineteenth century, publishers and book-sellers would, as a rule, offer their wares unbound in sheets, or sewn, put into boards, or in bindings of limp vellum or paper. But copies of easily-saleable texts could be bound up for stock. One finds popular devotional books, books of religious tracts, school books and editions of the classics in early retail bindings tooled in blind with a roll or a panel, sometimes containing the publisher's or bookseller's initials or device. The presence of sizeable quantities of historical, classical and religious books, grammars, law books, and scientific works, in blind-tooled bindings that originated in Oxford and Cambridge is not surprising. University dons and students alike needed books and, if they could afford to, had their books bound locally. During the seventeenth century the books most frequently offered bound for sale in England were still Bibles and Prayer books, devotional works, works by popular classical authors, herbals, and, later in the century, dictionaries and history books. During the eighteenth century, this pattern remains, but we now also find that travel books, books on architecture, poetry and some fiction are sure enough of a sale to be offered at a fixed price ready bound. Even women's magazines, such as the *Miss's magazine* and the *Young lady's magazine* could be had in 1760 bound in sheep at 5*d.* per volume, reflecting clearly a broadening of the reading public during the second half of the eighteenth century.[48]

This aspect of the history of bookbinding, what it tells us about the books themselves, their production, their dissemination and their readership needs to be developed further and for this more work should be devoted to the simple, plain, run-of-the-mill trade bindings that have so far managed to escape both the restorer's knife and the attention of most historians.

A better-defined methodology, backed up by a more precise and internationally-usable terminology; further research into the sources of binding ornament; more knowledge of the tool cutter and of his relationship with the binder and the patron; a greater understanding of the binder's place in society and his interaction with the printers, publishers, booksellers, and owners of his work, will lead to a better understanding of the history of the book and of its place in the history of society.

NOTES

1   E. P. Goldschmidt, 'The study of early bookbinding' in: *Studies in retrospect: the Bibliographical Society 1892–1942*, Cambridge, 1945, p. 175.
2   S. Fogelmark, 'Hobson's magnum opus: wary walking recommended', *Text: Svensk tidskrift för bibliografi*, vol. 4, no. 4 (1991), p. 204.
3   Goldschmidt, *op. cit.*, p. 177.
4   Fogelmark, *op. cit.*, p. 205.
5   Professor Szirmai himself has done a great deal to bring all available evidence to light. See J. A. Szirmai, *The Archaeology of medieval bookbinding*, Aldershot, 1999.
6   Goldschmidt, *op. cit.*, p. 175.
7   *Transactions of the Bibliographical Society*, VIII , London, 1907, pp. 25–38.
8   Such as W. H. J. Weale, G. D. Hobson, J. B. Oldham, G. Pollard, and H. M. Nixon, to name only a few of those who are no longer with us.
9   Cambridge, 1989, p. 96.
10   See below: D. Pearson, 'English centre-piece bookbindings 1560–1640', pp. 119–21.
11   See *Fine bindings 1500–1700 from Oxford libraries*, Oxford, 1968, nos 34 and 35.
12   E.g. on the MacDurnan Gospels at Lambeth Palace, see H. M. Nixon, 'Elizabethan gold-tooled bindings' in: *Essays in honour of Victor Scholderer*, Mainz, 1970, p. 254, no. 1, pl. 7, and pp. 269–70, note 38.
13   For some examples see M. M. Foot, 'Influences from the Netherlands on bookbinding in England during the late 15th and early 16th centuries' in: Foot, *Studies in the history of bookbinding*, Aldershot, 1993.
14   W. H. Bond, *Thomas Hollis of Lincoln's Inn: a Whig and his books*, Cambridge, 1990. For tools cut for John Evelyn, see M. M. Foot, 'An Englishman in Paris: John Evelyn and his bookbindings' in: Festschrift for Michel Wittock (forthcoming).
15   Letter from Roger Payne to Sir Richard Colt Hoare, 15 June 1796. See: M. M. Foot, *The Henry Davis Gift: a collection of bookbindings*, vol. I, London, 1978, pp. 105–6.
16   *Ibid.*
17   A. R. A. Hobson, *Humanists and bookbinders*, Cambridge, 1989.
18   Foot, *Henry Davis Gift*, I, pp. 171–82. Hobson, *Humanists and bookbinders*, pp. 207–12. See also M. M. Foot, 'Un grand Duc, immortel à la posterité' in: D. E. Rhodes (ed.), *Bookbindings and other bibliophily*, Verona, 1994, pp. 123–4.
19   P. Culot, 'Les reliures françaises signées du xviiie siècle', *Bulletin du bibliophile*, 2 (1988), p. 191.
20   L. Gruel, *Manuel historique et bibliographique de l'amateur de reliures*, 2 vols, Paris, 1887–1905, vol. I, p. 141. E. Thoinan, *Les Relieurs français*, Paris, 1893, pp. 361–7. Foot, *Henry Davis Gift*, I, pp. 196–8.
21   This changed in the nineteenth century when larger numbers of books and the emergence of the publisher forced the binders to organise their work differently and the various processes would be carried out by different workmen, but still usually in the same shop.
22   H. M. Nixon, *Twelve books in fine bindings from the library of J. W. Hely-Hutchinson*, Oxford, 1953, pp. 11–2. For Prince Henry's library see: T. A. Birrel, *English monarchs and their books*, London, 1987, pp. 30–9.
23   M. M. Foot, 'A London binding, c. 1638', *The Book Collector*, XXXI (1982), pp. 482–3; reprinted in Foot, *Studies*, pp. 190–1.
24   For some examples see M. M. Foot, *The History of bookbinding as a mirror of society*, London, 1998, pp. 107–8.
25   P. Christianson, *A Directory of London stationers and book artisans, 1300–1500*, New York, 1990.
26   C. E. Wright and R. C. Wright (eds.), *The Diary of Humfrey Wanley 1715–1726*, 2 vols, London, 1966, and for quotations below.

27   H. M. Nixon, 'Harleian bindings' in: *Studies in the book trade in honour of Graham Pollard*, Oxford, 1975, pp. 168–9.

28   T. F. Dibdin, *The Bibliographical Decameron*, vol. II, London, 1817, p. 522.

29   British Library, Add MS. 28196; printed by C. Davenport, *Thomas Berthelet*, Chicago, 1901, pp. 35–48. But see: H. M. Nixon, 'Early English gold-tooled bookbindings' in: *Studi di bibliografia e di storia in onore di Tammaro de Marinis*, Verona, 1964, pp. 283–306.

30   Six presentation copies of the Latin edition and fourteen of the French translation are known. See Foot, *The Henry Davis Gift*, I, pp. 51–8.

31   H. M. Nixon, 'Early English gold-tooled bookbindings', p. 299.

32   Bodleian Library, Oxford, Douce Bib. Eng. 1583 b.1, illustrated in: *Fine bindings 1500–1700 from Oxford libraries*, no. 163 (frontispiece).

33   H. M. Nixon, *Catalogue of the Pepys library*, vol. VI, *Bindings*, Woodbridge, 1984, p. XXIX, pl. 49.

34   *Ibid.*, p. XXIX, frontispiece, pl. 52.

35   H. M. Nixon, *Sixteenth-century gold-tooled bindings in the Pierpont Morgan Library*, New York, 1971, pp. 105–8.

36   See also M. M. Foot, 'Scholar-collectors and their bindings' in: R. Myers and M. Harris (eds.), *Antiquaries, book collectors and the circles of learning*, Winchester, 1996, pp. 27–43; Foot, *The History of bookbinding as a mirror of society*, pp. 93–112.

37   British Library, Cotton MS Domitian A VII, fols. 1, 84^v. For Cotton's library, see: C. G. C. Tite, *The Manuscript library of Sir Robert Cotton*, London, 1994.

38   A. R. A. Hobson, *Apollo and Pegasus*, Amsterdam, 1975, where previous attributions have also been discussed.

39   Fogelmark, *op. cit.* (*Text*), pp. 204–5.

40   *Apollo and Pegasus. Humanists and bookbinders. Renaissance book collecting*, Cambridge, 1999.

41   A. Faust, *Beschrijvinghe ende onderwijsinghe ter discreter ende vermaerder consten des boeckbinders handwerck* (ed. G. Colin), Brussels, Bibliotheca Wittockiana, 1987. D. de Bray, *Kort onderweijs van het boeckenbinden* (ed. K. van der Horst and C. de Wolf), Amsterdam, Nico Israel, 1977. J. V. Capronnier de Gauffecourt, *Traité de la relieure des livres* (trans. C. Benaiteau, ed. E. B. Smyth), Austin, Texas, W. T. Taylor, 1987. H. de Haas, *De Boekbinder* (intro. W. G. J. Callenbach; J. Storm van Leeuwen), Utrecht, HES, 1984. [J. A. Arnett], *Bibliopegia; or, the art of bookbinding, in all its branches* (ed. J. Bidwell), New York/London, Garland, 1980.

42   Fifth series, vol. XI, no. 2.

43   B. C. Middleton, *A History of English craft bookbinding technique*, 4th revised ed., London, 1996. N. Pickwoad, 'Onward and downward' in: R. Myers and M. Harris (eds), *A Millennium of the book*, Winchester, 1994, pp. 61–106; *Bucheinbände in der Bibliotheca Augusta*, Wolfenbüttel, 1999; 'Tacketed bindings' in: D. Pearson (ed.), *For the love of the binding*, London, 2000, pp. 119–68; and 'The Interpretation of bookbinding structure', below, pp. 127–70.

44   E.g. W. K. Gnirrep, J. P. Gumbert and J. A. Szirmai, *Kneep en binding*, The Hague, 1992.

45   E. Cockx-Indestege, J. Storm van Leeuwen, W. G. H. Barends, W. van Dongen, J. M. M. Hermans, and R. Top, 'Boekbandstempels', *Archives et bibliothèques de Belgique*, LXII, nos 1–2 (1991), pp. 1–98.

46   For an attempt at demonstrating this see: M. M. Foot, *The History of bookbinding as a mirror of society*, London, 1998.

47   For examples see: N. Pickwoad, articles quoted in note 43 above.

48   See M. M. Foot, 'Some bookbinders' price lists of the seventeenth and eighteenth centuries' in: Foot, *Studies in the history of bookbinding*, pp. 15–67.

1. Portrait of Marritge Vooght Claesdr, by Frans Hals, 1639. Amsterdam, Rijksmuseum, C 139. Reproduction by courtesy of the Rijksmuseum.

BOOKBINDINGS

Their Depictions, their Owners
and their Contents

Jan Storm van Leeuwen

THE SEVENTEENTH-CENTURY Dutch painter Frans Hals (*c.* 1583–1666), next in fame only to Rembrandt, confined himself, unlike Rembrandt, to the painting of portraits. Even his genre-pieces look like portraits. Hals was a sharp observer and his works seem to give a true reflection of what his sitters looked like. He did not depict with a love of detail, especially seen from close by, objects are painted with fluent brushstrokes, not paying attention to detail, but seen from farther away they clearly show the components they are made of. Let us take as an example the portrait of Marritge Vooght Claesdr in the Rijksmuseum in Amsterdam, painted in 1639, when she was 62 years old.[1] She wears the clothes we would more or less expect of a lady of her age, in many shades of black – she was a member of the Dutch Reformed Church – but pretty luxurious and expensive, according to her husband's status. He was Pieter Jacobsz Olycan, mayor of Haarlem and member of the Dutch States General. The book in her hands shows Hals' eye for the construction of objects (fig. 1). It is generally described as a Bible and shows gilt fore- and tail-edges, gauffered in a diaper pattern and a black binding with what was called silverware in Holland at the time. One can clearly discern the almost square corner-pieces mounted over the edges of the boards and the centre-piece in the form of a coat of arms. The catch plates of both the silver clasps are wide at the edge and taper to a point at the other end, while the catches have an oval in the middle. A plate to which a chain was attached can be seen at the top of the binding. The chain, which would be similarly attached to the back cover and allowed the book to be carried by it, is not shown. It would probably draw too much of our attention away from the stern face of Marritge.

The binding was by no means an invention of Hals's. Several of these pieces are known, in the same format and made of a very strong black leather with a marked grain – it is usually called shagreen or sharkskin, but cannot come from a fish, because it shows

2. Binding in black shagreen, with silver clasps and furniture, with the
name of Janniken de Mans van Heemskerck, *c.* 1625. Edges gilt and gauffered,
in a symmetrical pattern with leaves and flowers. *Biblia, dat is: de gantsche Heylige
Schrifture*, Amstelredam, Paulus van Ravesteijn, 1624, 8vo [and] [*De Psalmen des
propheten Davids*, n.p., n.d.], 8vo. The Hague, Royal Library, 345 G 14.

hair follicles and must come from a mammal. Bindings with flat silver clasps and corner-pieces with engraved decoration, as in Marritge's portrait, are most common in the sixteen-twenties. They cover 'Church books', octavo editions of the Bible, together with the Psalms with musical notation and sometimes the Hymns. A binding that can be called the twin of the one depicted by Hals, is in the Royal Library in the Hague (fig. 2).[2] According to an inscription on the clasps this piece originally belonged to a certain Janniken Jans de Mans van Heemskerck. I have not been able to make out whether the engraved coat of arms in the centre is hers or that of her husband. The book is a Dutch Bible edition of 1624, together with the Psalms. The endleaves show many manuscript annotations concerning Janniken's family. The binding cannot be dated much later than the Bible itself. I think it was given to Janniken by her husband at their wedding.

The special use of these chained Bibles can be learned from an old Dutch children's song, set to the tune of 'Ah, vous dirai-je, Maman', for which Mozart composed twelve lovely variations.[3] Roughly translated the song goes 'Shortjacket is always ill, in the middle of the week, but not on Sundays. On Sunday she goes to church with her book full of silverware'. I will not discuss the weekly business of this woman, but concentrate on her church-going Sundays. She went with her book full of silverware, which must mean clasps, centre- and corner-pieces and a chain for carrying. In our mind's eye we can see them go to church, these women clothed in black and white, with their expensive Bibles in black and white, to listen to the preacher in black and white. While staying within the terms of sobriety of the Dutch Reformed Church, they could display their wealth nonetheless.

Back to Frans Hals: Marritge Vooght was proud of her Bible. It may have been a gift from her husband in 1620, 1625, or 1630, on the 25th to 35th anniversary of their wedding. As mentioned earlier, this type of binding is mainly known from the 1620s. It is unlikely that her binding was made long before or after that time and it certainly cannot have been a wedding present for her in 1595. I consider the painted binding as an object that actually existed and indeed, I think that Marritge was depicted with a 'portrait' of her own Bible, as a display of piety and a nice gesture towards her husband, who figures in the companion piece, as well as a display of the wealth of the family. Thus the knowledge of what book and binding were and what function they had, gives insight into the meaning of Hals's beautiful portrait.

Books in paintings can be interesting, as is shown by several portraits Frans Hals also painted of clergymen, which are not all of them preserved in the orginal, but in early copies. Yet, these are sufficiently accurate to draw conclusions from the books in the clergy's hands, which are described in the literature as Bibles and have the same type of binding. These are the portraits of Michiel van Middel-hoven of 1626, Samuel Ampzing of c. 1630, Henrik Swalmius of c. 1645 and Herman Langelius of c. 1660. The sitters are caught in the act of reading. They hold their book in one hand, with their index finger in the volume, as if to mark the opening where they were reading when the painter interrupted them. These portraits are also known as engravings, made shortly after the painting, with the aim of furthering the name and fame of the sitters.

The largest portrait is that of Michiel Jansz van Middelhoven, who was a preacher in Voorschoten near Leyden (fig. 3).[4] The binding is clearly made of vellum with laced-in thongs and yapp edges. I have never seen the portrait itself and am not certain about the colour of the edges of the leaves, but I assume it to be brick red as is the case in the other portraits, like the one of Samuel Ampzing of c. 1630.[5]

The vellum binding with laced-in thongs, with or without yapp edges and with ties, is used pre-eminently in the Dutch United Provinces in the seventeenth century for scholarly books and not for Bibles and Psalm- or Hymnbooks. The many bindings of this type on Dutch scholarly books that still exist are in themselves sufficient proof for this hypothesis, but the fact that when the Dutch painter Gerrit Dou (1613–1675) painted a still life with books as attributes of *Studium* he choose this type of binding, is also significant.[6]

Obviously these four men did not want to be portrayed as preachers, but as scholars. Obviously they wanted to be known as such, not only among family and friends but also in a larger circle. Unlike the preacher Van Middelhoven, his wife, Sara Hessix, wanted to be depicted as a devout person.[7] Her portrait, the companion piece to that of her husband, shows her with a book in her hand of the same type as that of Marritge Vooght, but smaller and simpler. It is in black shagreen over wooden boards and has silver clasps. She holds the book towards the spectator, even more than Marritge Vooght does, as if to stress the value of the Bible with Psalms and the Calvinist Songbook.

As indicated, the vellum binding sewn on thongs laced through the covers and with a hollow back was much in favour in the seventeenth century with scholars for their own library, which does not mean

3. Portrait of Michiel van Middelhoven, early copy after an original
by Frans Hals, 1626. Present whereabouts unknown.

4. Portrait of Lucas van Rijp, by Willem van Mieris, 1696.
Reproduction by courtesy of Gebr. Douwes Fine Art, Amsterdam.

that it was not used for other people or purposes. The reason can be easily understood: these bindings were relatively cheap. The supple and sturdy vellum could stand handling very well and the yapp edges and green silk ribbons protected their contents from insects and dust. As long as the scholar's study did not become too hot and dry – of which there was little chance in this damp country – these bindings could survive for a long time. The type was extensively used for books in small formats, up to small quarto, but less for large quartos and rarely for folios and larger. For the larger formats a structure with a tight back and raised cords was preferred, as we find in the calf or morocco bindings then prevalent. This type of vellum binding is sometimes called a 'Dutch binding'.

The Dutch prize binding, given to the future scholar, was made of the same material and has the same structure. Therefore the type of binding with laced-through thongs was used for small-size prize books, and remained in use until well into the nineteenth century, although it was no longer used for any other purpose. Not much will be said here about these bindings, which were given away in the Netherlands twice a year in the Latin school as an encouragement for diligence to the best pupil in each class. They are dealt with by Chris Coppens in detail elsewhere in this volume.[8] But it is appropriate to show an interesting example in the context of this article.

A man's portrait, in a private collection and painted by the Leyden painter Willem van Mieris in 1696, remained anonymous until a short time ago (fig. 4).[9] The man's clothes and wig show him to be a scholar. His left hand rests on a table with two books, while his right points towards them. Like Dou, Van Mieris was adept at the detailed way of depicting, which is known by the term of 'Feinmalerei'. We can clearly see that both books are bound in gold-tooled vellum with a flat spine and ribbons at the fore-edge, of the type just described. The uppermost binding, on an octavo, is lying with the lower cover towards us; two thirds are visible. The ribbons are red and white; the edge is sprinkled red. The covers show a frame of blind lines, while the rest of the tooling is in gold, showing a small tool in the corners and a large block in the centre. The combination of gold and blind tooling points to Leyden as the place where the binding could very well have been made, but anyone familiar with this block does not need that hint. It represents Athena, belonged to the Leyden Latin school and was used from at least 1677 onwards. The example illustrated is in the collection of the Royal Library in the Hague and dates from around 1735 (fig. 5). It is in practically every respect the

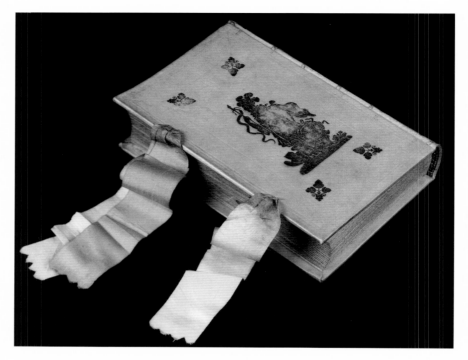

5. Prize binding in white vellum, tooled in blind and gold, with the coat of arms of Leyden on the covers. M. Tullius Cicero, *Epistolarum ad quintum fratrem libri tres ... cum ... commentario Valerii Palermi*, Hagae-Comitum, apud Isaacum Vaillant, 1725, 8vo. The Hague, Royal Library, 489 J 13.

same as the binding in the portrait, with blind and gold tooling on the covers, red and white ribbons and a red sprinkled edge, red and white being the colours of Leyden's coat of arms. The binding in the Royal Library has two frames made with blind-tooled lines and the painted binding only one, but this difference is not significant; there are such bindings too in the Royal Library, but they have lost their ties. The decoration of the binding on the quarto below is less easily recognisable.

This example was discovered by Jan Spoelder, who defended a thesis on prize bindings in June 2000.[10] He showed that this man had himself portrayed with two prize bindings, not because he was a proud prize winner in his youth – dozens of fellow pupils will have done so during his time in his Latin school – but because he was the rector of the school, the man directly responsible for the distribution of the prizes. The portrait therefore can only depict Dr Lucas van

Rijp, rector of the Leyden school from 1685 to 1716. It is known from archival material that Van Mieris painted him. Here the knowledge of bindings was essential for the identification of the portrait.

This, however, must not lead to the conviction that every binding depicted in a portrait can tell us something about the person portrayed. This can only be true if the painter had the ability and wanted to keep close to nature in his works. Rembrandt's books, for instance, usually large folios, tell us little that is specific, but underline the painterly effect of the depiction. I even think that Rembrandt liked his books disbound rather than bound, because they have more effect like that.

To finish this discussion of what bindings in paintings can teach us, there is a much earlier example by the famous Flemish painter Jan van Eyck. In his Van der Paele-alter panel (fig. 6), the donor of the painting, Canon Van der Paele, is seen in piety, kneeling before the Virgin Mary (1436).[11] In his hands he holds a small book, immediately recognisable as a girdle book, bound in reversed leather.[12] It looks very much like the girdle book kept in the Göteborg Art Museum (fig. 7), but the chemise is larger.[13] I think this has been exaggerated by Van Eyck, because he did not want there to be any uncertainty about what he depicted. Only a few girdle books in original bindings have been preserved, of which several small, leather-bound ones contain religious texts. The type is far better known, however, because of the many works of art from the late Middle Ages and early Renaissance in which they are depicted. Thus it is known that they were often carried by pilgrims, who could take them along on their pilgrimage.[14] They would hang upside-down from their girdle, with the protrusion of the leather at the tail – like Van Eyck painted it – in order to be used at any time, while still fastened at the girdle. I think that Van der Paele was aware of this. The girdle book in its binding tells us that Van der Paele wanted to show himself not only as an important devout Canon, who donated a chapel and everything belonging to it to Saint Donaas in Bruges, but also as a pilgrim.[15] Old, sickly and rich, he may have come to see life as a permanent pilgrimage towards Christ and the Virgin Mary and have wanted to make that clear in Van Eyck's painting, which originally served as an epitaph to Van der Paele in his own chapel.

Girdle books and other kinds of binding from the Middle Ages cannot be shelved in the standing position of today. At the time of their production the small number of books possessed by private

6. Canon Van der Paele, detail of the so-called Van der Paele Madonna,
by Jan van Eyck, 1436. Bruges, Groeningen Museum.

7. Girdle binding in off-white chamois leather, early 14th century.
Isidore of Seville, *Synonyma*, manuscript on parchment, *c.* 1300.
Göteborg, Röhsska Konstslöjdmuseet, RKM 519–15.

people, religious houses and institutions, were not shelved in this
way, but lying on a table, a shelf, or a lectern, or kept in a chest.
Many prints, paintings and miniatures from the end of the fifteenth
century and the beginning of the sixteenth prove this. When libraries
grew larger, the books could no longer be laid down next to each
other and the upright standing position became the prevalent one.
Yet, at first, they were not placed with the spines towards the
beholder, but with the fore-edges, which could then be titled. In many
libraries in the Netherlands the books maintained this position until
well into the seventeenth century. Prints from that time show two
horizontal strips, which are often held to represent the raised cords

41

8. Engraving showing a steward, receiving payment. Joost de Damhouder, *Practycke in civiele saecken,* 's Graven-hage, de Weduwe, ende Erfgenamen van wijlen Hillebrant Iacobssz van Wouwe, 1626, p. 55.

on the spine, but are in fact the clasps on the fore-edge (fig. 8). The engraver would, of course, know that spines of books in his own time did not have two raised cords, but usually, four or five. In the more or less public libraries of the sixteenth century the spines were turned towards the thick walls and were susceptible to damp and therefore a second covering of reversed leather was added, held by strips of brass along the joints, as can be found on a binding in the Royal Library, which was probably made in Alkmaar in the second half of the sixteenth century.[16] In the course of the seventeenth century in Holland the libraries would be 'turned round', whereby the books started to show their spine. Spine titling became the custom.

To my knowledge the richly gold-tooled bindings made by Dutch binders during the last thirty-five years of the seventeenth century, such as the famous Amsterdam master bookbinder Albert Magnus, have never been depicted in contemporary paintings. But these too can tell us something about a person who commissioned them. Twenty years ago I bought a book by Jacob Cats, a famous Dutch poet, called 'The beginning, middle and end of the world, as enclosed in the wedding ring', in a luxurious red morocco binding (colour plate 1).[17] On the strength of the tools used, this binding must be attributed to Magnus, who lived from 1642 to 1689.[18] The binding has an almost entirely decorative design on the covers, with open crowns in the corners and a larger crown in the centre, under which we find the letters 'G. P.' and 'A. E. V. U.' on the upper cover and 'Anno 1679' on the lower.

At first I had no idea what these letters could stand for, but the edge decoration was helpful in this respect. It is gauffered and painted and shows symbols relating to spiritual and physical love, such as the Phoenix, Amor shooting his arrows, two hands connected by a locked chain, two doves and a cock upon a hen. Linked with the content of the book, the edge and date can very well refer to a marriage. This suggests that a certain G. P. married A. E. V. U. in 1679. While reading an article by Herman de la Fontaine Verwey on Magnus, it occurred to me that the pretty uncommon initials V. U. could stand for Van Uchelen,[19] for Verwey showed the Amsterdam merchant Paulo van Uchelen, who was born in 1641 or 1642 and died in 1702, to have had financial dealings with the famous binder. An investigation in the Amsterdam City Archives was successful; Gilles Pelgrom was betrothed to Anna Elisabeth van Uchelen on 1 June 1679; book and binding clearly were a gift to the couple, possibly from the bride's uncle, Paulo van Uchelen.

After Van Uchelen's death an auction of his 'splendid collection of art and books' was held in 1703 by Hendrik Wetstein, whose wife was a sister of Van Uchelen's son-in-law.[20] An introduction to the auction catalogue gives a portrait of the bibliophile and his collection. It appears that the collector knew exactly how his books had to be bound. 'All folios (with the exception of some ten) and all quartos (some 70 excepted) are neatly bound in horn [i.e. vellum], nicely gilt on the spine and the covers and all so similar, that one may rightly state that the like of it has never been seen in our country'. All books were bound according to Van Uchelen's instructions. He must have had a permanent binder to do this. It would not be surprising, Herman Verwey stated in his article, if this had been Albert Magnus.

This was the state of affairs until a short time ago. But some gold-tooled vellum bindings in the collection of the Royal Library, which have the same crown that is also found on the marriage binding, at the corner of the second frame on the covers, could be those about which Verwey was speculating. Because, with the exception of prize and atlas bindings, gold tooling on vellum was not at all common in Holland at the time and these bindings, on books in large formats, from quarto to broadsheet format, had to be attributed to Magnus on the strength of the tools used. The titles of the Royal Library books in bindings with this crown on the covers had to be compared with Van Uchelen's auction catalogue, which, fortunately, is available on micro-fiche. The catalogue does not lend itself very well to a comparison, because many titles are incomplete and often contain mistakes. Moreover the cataloguer states that in each division he brought together not only books that belong to the same subject, but also those he found appropriate to it, or that were written by the same author as books that do belong in a particular division. Contrary to what was normal at the time, the division by format was not strictly observed. So, if one does not find a certain title in the catalogue, this does not necessarily mean that it is not there. Nevertheless I found the titles of eight books among the thirteen 'crown-bindings' the Royal Library possesses. This in itself is a good score. Van Uchelen had children, so one might expect not all his books to have been sold after his death and some books may have left his collection before he died. Yet, the percentage of books found seemed a little too low for absolute certainty.

Apparently, according to the foreword to the catalogue, Van Uchelen's larger bindings had raised cords and the titles were tooled in black and not written as was normal at that time. Three bindings with crowns could be discarded, for they have a flat spine or a manuscript title and, to be sure, their titles were not found in the catalogue. Ten remained, eight of which were found in Van Uchelen's catalogue (fig. 9). Their titles are tooled in ink or soot, a fact I did not at first realise. This is unique in the Netherlands and points to one collector who knew exactly what bindings he wanted. The match with Van Uchelen's catalogue is the most perfect one could ever expect, especially when the wide variety of books is taken into account.

Of these eight, three are genealogical works:

> Du Bouchet. *Histoire genealogique de la Maison Royale de Courtenay* ... A Paris, Chez Iean du Puis, 1661. Fol. (RL 38 F 7)

> *Les Marques d'honneur de la Maison de Tassis.* A Anvers, En l'imprimerie, Plantinienne de Balthasar Moretus, 1645. Fol. (RL 52 B 9)

> C. Segoing. *Armorial universel contenant les armes des principales maisons estatz et dignitez des plus considerables royaumes de l'Europe* ... A Paris, Chez N. Berey, 1654. Fol. (RL 3193 C 9).

The other books cover all sorts of subjects:

> [Iacobus Franquart]. *Pompa funebris optimo potentissimiq[ue] principis Alberti pii, archiducis Austriae* ... Bruxellae, 1623. Oblong fol. (RL 2102 A 8). A work consisting of prints depicting the burial of Archduke Albert of Austria in Brussels

> Aesop[us]. *Fables with his life: in English, French and Latin. Newly translated. Illustrated with ... sculptures ... added, thirty one new figures ... by Francis Barlow.* London, Printed by H. Hills jun. for Francis Barlow, 1687. Fol. (RL 488 B 17)

> *Const-thoonende iuweel, by de loflijcke stadt Haerlem, ten versoecke van Trou moet blijcken, in 't licht gebracht* ... Tot Zwol, By Zacharias Heyns, 1607. 4to. (RL 789 H 30). A work in Dutch about a contest of rhetoricians in Haarlem, 1607

> *Der Stadt Hamburgt Gerichtsordnung und Statuta.* Gedruckt zu Hamburg, In verlegung M. Frobenij, Durch Paul Langen, 1605. 4to. (RL 375 H 17). A legal work in German, of 1603

> Isaac Vossius. *Variarum observationum liber.* Londini, Prostant apud Robertum Scott, 1685. 4to. (RL 2104 B 12). A miscellany.

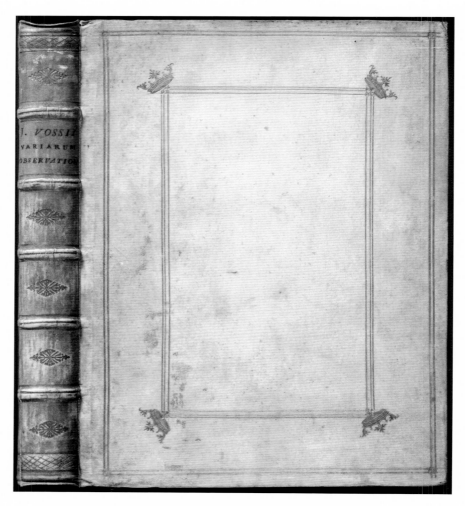

9. Binding in white vellum, from the workshop of Albert Magnus, *c.* 1695.
Isaac Vossius, *Variarum observationum liber*, Londini, Robertus
Scott, 1685, 4to. The Hague, Royal Library, 2104 B 12.

The ten books mentioned came from the library of Paulo van
Uchelen and the various tools used on their bindings show that they
come from Magnus's shop, but they cannot have been bound by the
master binder himself. In the first place, one would expect him to
have given at least part of the work to his apprentices or workmen
during his life time and secondly, Magnus died before the most recent
of them was bound, in fact he died long before Van Uchelen and there
seems not to have been any break in the binding activities.

Another example of an owner who can be identified by his bindings (and not by his arms or cipher) tells a nice, slightly romantic story, which at the same time shows how data from different sources can give insight into book collecting in Holland in the eighteenth century. The Royal Library possesses fifty bindings with, in the centre of the covers, a lion in a laurel wreath or in a composition of decorative tools, made by the same anonymous Hague bindery, that I have given the nickname 'First Stadholder Bindery'. Some fifteen more are to be found in other collections around the world.[21] A family of Hague binders called Stofvoet would perfectly fit the large production of this shop, of which some 250 fine bindings are known, but so far any proof that this family can definitely be linked with the First Stadholder Bindery is lacking.[22]

Most of the lion bindings are in sprinkled calf (colour plate 2) and look very similar; they cannot be dated easily on the basis of the contents which date from the sixteenth and seventeenth centuries, and they must stem from the beginning of the earliest period of the bindery, c. 1725 to c. 1735. Some are in mottled calf and can be dated c. 1730–40, whereas a small group of bindings on six different works is of red morocco and shows a wider variety of tooled designs. Four morocco bindings were made between 1734 and 1749 at the latest. Two others, with tell-tale differences when compared to the rest, must stem from the end of the seventeen-fifties and will not be taken into account in what follows.

In my book on Hague bindings of the eighteenth century, I proposed that all or most of the lion bindings were made for one collector, without knowing who that could be.[23] The lion is found in the coats of arms of several provinces of the Dutch Republic, like Holland, but these books did not come from their official libraries. The owner might have been someone with 'lion', 'lions' or 'of lions' in his name, but that is looking for a needle in a haystack, since such names were and are popular in the Netherlands. In 1976 the knowledge that I did not and could not know the answer had to suffice.

Most of the lion bindings entered the collection of the Royal Library *en bloc* in 1807 as part of the collection of Joost Romswinckel.[24] This important Leyden book lover and his collection will not be dealt with here, but I want to discuss an annotation he used to make on one of the flyleaves at the end of his books, near the joint, which shows the books to be his, for the catalogue of his library is lost. The annotation usually contains some numbers and letters and a number in a circle, but it is usually partly erased and can only be read with difficulty, if at all. The number in the circle was formerly supposed to represent the amount of money Romswinckel paid for the book in pennies – by now this is known not to be true – and the rest was considered to be arbitrary. Yet a number of these annotations look like 89 followed by '9 ail' or 'gail', where 'gail' could perhaps stand for 'gaillard' and 89 for 1789. The Royal Library possesses a catalogue of a book auction by the Hague dealer Johannes Gaillard of 23 to 28 November 1789, in which the titles of the books with the annotation 'gail 89' were found, actually under the numbers, that often appeared above Romswinckel's 'gail 89'. So Romswinckel bought most of his lion books at this sale. It is not known which collection was sold at this date, although the catalogue mentions the unfinished name 'Crev' as that of the owner, and Gaillard obviously wanted his clients to think of the famous Pieter Anthony Bolognaro-Crevenna.[25]

In the Royal Library in Brussels there are ten large, identical red morocco volumes bound by the First Stadholder Bindery. They contain works by Gerard van Loon, his *Aloude Hollandsche histori* (1734), his *Hedendaagsche penningkunde* (1732) and his *Beschryving der Nederlandsche historipenningen* (1723–31).[26] The books are printed on very large paper of a superb quality. In his time Van Loon was a famous connoisseur of coins and medals and these works deal with this subject. The volumes have a lion in a laurel wreath in the centre of the covers and thus belong to the lion group (fig. 10). This set was mentioned in a report dated 1817 by Pierre Lammens to William I, then King of Holland and Belgium.[27] Lammens had visited the National Library in Paris, in order to discover which books looted by French soldiers from libraries in the Low Countries were still to be found there. Next to an Ovid edition of Colard Mansion, he only found this set of Gerard van Loon's works, described as (translated from the French) 'Royal folio format, bound in red morocco, gilt on the edge and covers. This is the copy the author donated to the university library of Louvain as a mark of gratitude towards the university where he had studied.' Obviously the set was not returned to Louvain, but remained in Brussels, which is just as well, for otherwise it would almost certainly have been destroyed by fire in World Wars I or II.

In the University Library in Louvain is a letter of 1752 in which Van Loon addressed Professor Rega of Louvain University about his wish to donate his own copies of his most important works to his *alma mater*, where he had studied fifty years ago, and about the way

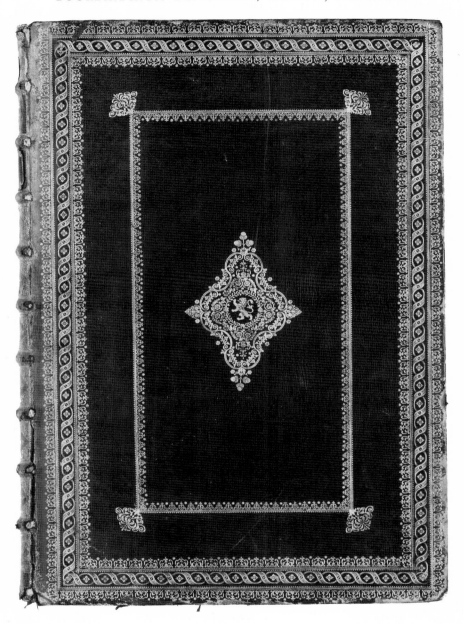

10. Binding in red morocco, by the First Stadholder Bindery, the Hague, 1734–40.
Gerard van Loon, *Hedendaagsche penningkunde*, 's Gravenhaage, Pieter
van Thol, 1732, fol. Brussels, Royal Library, VB 10. 107 E 2 RP.

in which he wanted to send the volumes to Louvain.[28] Since this particular set of lion bindings had belonged to Van Loon himself, the logical supposition is that the others had been his as well. One of the other reasons is that several books in lion bindings have extra engravings, among which are proofs of some prints in Van Loon's *Nederlandsche historipenningen*. Who else could have had proofs at his disposal, except the printmaker, the publisher and the author, of whom the author is the only logical person to have possessed the books in lion bindings? The books deal almost exclusively with the history and geography of Holland in the strict sense of the word, and those of the Netherlands in the wider sense.

Gerard van Loon was born in 1683; he studied law in Louvain between 1700 and 1702 and then continued his studies in Leyden. As a Catholic he could not occupy official positions in the Republic and he devoted himself to his love, the history of the Netherlands and to coins and medals, exactly the subjects of the works mentioned. To this end he built up an extensive book collection. In the beginning he was successful as a writer, but after having published an old rhyme chronicle in 1745, which appeared to have been a forgery, he was accused of having Catholic viewpoints, and he ended his historical studies in order to concentrate on religion. In one of his biographies there is a vague mention of a sale of his books at that time, but this could not be substantiated. As shown, he gave his own works beautifully bound to the university of Louvain in 1752. At the same time he intended to give his manuscripts to Leyden university, which in the end did not happen. He died in 1758, without offspring, and his unmarried sister inherited his possessions. His library was auctioned in 1759; the catalogue is preserved. This catalogue has far fewer mistakes and wrong arrangements than that of Van Uchelen's books, but a disadvantage is that especially the small books are often brought together in lots and not described separately. Many lion bindings are on books in small formats. Unfortunately not many books in lion bindings can be found in Van Loon's catalogue. Even when we ignore those whose description is unclear, out of the sixty that remain, only sixteen, or 27%, can be found. This is more than can be found normally when one tries to trace books of one collection in the catalogue of another, but far less than is desirable, and it makes the identification of the lion bindings with Van Loon less certain than I would like. But it does not make it unlikely. Van Loon had a generous nature and it is possible that he gave a large part of his historical collection away when he stopped his studies in this field.

After all, he was unmarried and had no offspring. Moreover there is this reference to a possible sale in the seventeen-forties or early fifties. We may never be sure, yet I believe that it was Van Loon who commissioned the lion bindings, or at least the majority of them.

In her 1997 Panizzi lectures, Mirjam Foot discussed what the study of bindings can reveal about the history of the book, of collecting and of culture.[29] Here I have tried to demonstrate in more detail several points she touched upon, while using examples from my own experience, showing that the cultural surroundings in which these bindings came into existence are important. The study of bindings can have an important role for the study of books and especially of former owners. Bookbinding is an integral part of book production and distribution and the bindings themselves reflect the ideas and wishes of their first owners and the skills of their makers.[30]

NOTES

1   Seymour Slive, *Frans Hals*, 3 vols, New York, 1970–74, cat. 129.
2   Jan Storm van Leeuwen, 'Beschermen, vormen, versieren: observaties over de boekband', *Jaarboek van het Nederlands Genootschap van Bibliofielen 1999*, Amsterdam, 2000, pp. 66–8.
3   KV 265.
4   Slive, *op. cit.*, cat. 38.
5   Slive, *op. cit.*, cat. 76.
6   Ronni Baer, *Gerrit Dou 1613–1675: master painter in the age of Rembrandt*, London, New Haven, Washington, 2000, cat. 18.
7   Slive, *op. cit.*, cat. 39.
8   C. Coppens, 'The prize is the proof', pp. 53–105 (below).
9   J. Spoelder and R. J. A. te Rijdt, 'Een portretidentificatie op grond van prijsboeken: Lucas van Rijp door Willem van Mieris, 1696', *De Boeken wereld*, 15 (1999), no. 3, pp. 226–30.
10 Jan Spoelder, *Prijsboeken op de Latijnse school: een studie naar het verschijnsel prijsuitreiking en prijsboek*, Amsterdam, Maarsen, 2000.
11 Bruges, Groeningen Municipal Museum; Max J. Friedländer, *The van Eycks – Petrus Christus* (with a preface by Erwin Panovsky), Leyden, 1967, p. 42 (*Early Netherlandisch painting*, vol 1).
12 For girdle books, see among others: Ursula Bruckner, 'Das Beutelbuch und seine Verwandten: der Hüllenband, das Faltbuch und der Buchbeutel', *Gutenberg-Jahrbuch*, 1997, pp 307–24.
13 Thomas Baagøe, *Skrift, tryck och band: om bokkonst i Röhsska Konst-slöjdmuseet*, Göteborg, 1980, p. 21.
14 Lisl and Hugo Alker, *Das Beutelbuch in der Bildende Kunst*, Mainz, 1966.

15 A. Dewitte, 'De kapelanie-stichtingen van kanunnik van der Paele', *Biekorf: Westvlaams archief voor geschiedenis, oudheidkunde en folklore*, 72 (1971), pp. 15–20; A. Viaene, 'Het Grafpaneel van kanunnik Van der Paele voltooid in 1436 door Jan van Eyck (Groeningen Museum Bruges)', *Biekorf: Westvlaams archief voor geschiedenis, oudheidkunde en folklore*, 66 (1965), pp. 257–64.

16 Jan Storm van Leeuwen, 'Beschermen', *op. cit.* (note 2), pp. 63–6. This type of binding is also found in England, and also on Bibles in large formats.

17 Jan Storm van Leeuwen, 'Beschermen', *op. cit.* (note 2), pp. 68–71.

18 Mirjam M. Foot, *The Henry Davis Gift: a collection of bookbindings*, vol 1: *Studies in the history of bookbinding*, London, 1978, pp. 230–58.

19 H. de la Fontaine Verwey, 'The binder Albert Magnus and the collectors of his age', *Quaerendo*, 1 (1971), pp. 173–6.

20 *Catalogus nitidissimorum & equisitissimorum librarum & iconum viri spectatissimi Pauli van Uchelen ... publica fiet auctio a.d. 1. Octobris 1703. & seqq. in aedibus defuncti ...*, Amsterlaedami, Ex Officina Wetsteniana. A copy is kept in the Amsterdam University Library.

21 Jan Storm van Leeuwen, 'De leeuw-banden, Gerard van Loon en het exemplaar van drie van zijn werken in de Brusselse Koninklijke Bibliotheek' in: Claude Sorgeloos (ed.), *Mélanges d'histoire de la reliure offerts à Georges Colin*, Brussels, 1998, pp. 199–238.

22 Jan Storm van Leeuwen, *De Achttiende-eeuwse Haagse boekband in de Koninklijke Bibliotheek en het Rijksmuseum Meermanno-Westreenianum*, 's-Gravenhage, 1976, pp. 59–60.

23 Jan Storm van Leeuwen, *De Achttiende-eeuwse Haagse boekband*, p. 58.

24 J. A. G[ruys], 'Joost Romswinckel' in: *Collectors and collections: Koninklijke Bibliotheek 1798–1998*, Zwolle, 1998, pp. 36–40.

25 Jos van Heel, 'Bolognaro Crevenna: een Italiaans koopman en bibliofiel in Amsterdam', *Jaarboek voor Nederlandse boekgeschiedenis*, 5 (1998), pp. 73–93.

26 *Exposition de reliures II, du XVIIe siècle à la fin du XIXe*, Brussels, 1931, cat. 393 (Exh. Royal Library Brussels).

27 I am grateful to Bart Op de Beeck of the Brussels Royal Library for alerting me to this.

28 I am grateful to Dr Christian Coppens for drawing my attention to this letter.

29 Mirjam M. Foot, *The History of bookbinding as a mirror of society*, London 1998 (Panizzi Lectures 1997).

30 I am grateful to Dr Anna Simoni for her help with translating this essay into English.

THE PRIZE IS THE PROOF

Four Centuries of Prize Books

C. Coppens

WHEN ONE EXPLORES the literature on prize books, it is noticeable that book historians have only rarely tackled this subject and, when they have, they have produced mostly detailed or descriptive studies, often repeating received wisdom and thereby limiting the view in a field that calls for a broadening of perspective. Historians of education in their turn see the prize book more as a piece of folklore and never did any systematic research, although a few authors have tried to explain the phenomenon of the prize distribution itself. However, both approaches have the potential to connect with and help each other. This article is certainly not the last word about prize books, it is an exploration of a field which invites us to enlarge our view.[1]

I – A BOOK AS A PRIZE

1. The Prize Book

I prefer to talk about prize *books* instead of prize *bindings*, as I want to consider the book that was given as a prize as a whole. Most of the time the binding indeed plays an important role, but a binding does not always identify a book as a prize book. Usually the binding for a prize book was specially made for it, but sometimes it was not, when an old book in its original binding was simply recycled to serve as a prize. But even when it was made for the occasion, it is no longer always possible to see whether it was made for a prize distribution. One can be fairly sure that a vellum binding with the coat of arms of a city or a small town from the Northern Netherlands is a prize binding, though the arms may be deceptive, certainly when the binding is made of leather, as the arms could also represent an owner's mark of the city council or of the town library. This is even more often the case in France and the Southern Netherlands.

A survey of the constituent elements of a prize book can make clear what we are talking about. First of all there is the binding. This can be made of leather, vellum or paper. The leather can be sheepskin or calf; it is rarely goatskin, only a few examples from the end of the nineteenth century are recorded. However rich the donor may have been, the amount of money was always limited and this was spent rather on rich gilding, on what caught the eye, than on good quality material, which nobody noticed. On the contrary, low quality was often hidden under some form of decoration, be it gold tooling or marbling.

Apart from a few examples known from Germany and Liège, prize bindings in vellum almost only occur in the Northern Netherlands, certainly when specially made for a prize distribution. Before the nineteenth century a prize book is seldom, if ever, bound in paper. With the evolution of the publishers' binding in the nineteenth century, many prize books were covered in paper, sometimes blocked in gold with the arms of the city or the school. In the Southern Netherlands and also in France many newly made half leather prize bindings were covered with embossed paper, in imitation of book cloth.

Prize bindings are mostly decorated simply on the sides with gold tooled fillets, or with arms blocked in the centre, or richly tooled; the latter are sometimes seen as the archetypal prize bindings. Rich decoration may be a feature of prize bindings that have been illustrated in the available literature, mainly French prizes, but on the whole these are the minority, if not the exception, certainly in some regions. The municipality may normally have paid for the binding of prize books, it rarely did so for extra gilding except sometimes when its name could be associated with the gift, and the same was the case with private sponsors.

Secondly there is the *ex-praemio* or prize dedication. This can be a hand-written inscription, short, long, dry, or with some imagination, usually on the recto of the flyleaf. Or it can be printed on a label, with the details supplied in manuscript, tipped in, mostly on the pastedown, or sewn in and sometimes folded to fit into the format of a smaller book, as a frontispiece in front of the title-page. Sometimes the *ex-praemio* was a loose leaf, just inserted in the book and mostly now lost, or it was just a kind of diploma without direct connection with the book. Sometimes the *ex-praemio* was tooled on the binding, with or without a written or printed *ex-praemio* inside the book.

The *ex-praemio* definitely identifies a book as a prize book, but unfortunately it has often been removed by the heirs, when they sold off, or just wished to get rid of, the dusty books of a member of the family, or by somebody who may not have felt completely comfortable with his or her ownership of the book. Sometimes there are some traces left, such as the corners or the top of the tipped in label, remains of the sewn or pasted-in leaf, or even just a missing flyleaf; all these may arouse some suspicion, certainly in combination with a typical prize binding.

Thirdly there is the book itself. If one can speak of a typical prize book, it is usually an edition of one of the classics. This is true before 1800, and in general for Holland and Britain until the beginning of the twentieth century. From the end of the sixteenth century onwards, under influence of the Jesuits and the Counter Reformation, many devotional and other religious works found their way in to prize distributions, certainly in France and in the Southern Netherlands. From the seventeenth century onwards contemporary secular, neo-Latin and vernacular poetry was given in Holland, and during the nineteenth century it seems that the same happened in Britain, but, for so far as we know, rarely in other countries.

During the nineteenth century prize books became quite a profitable market in French-speaking regions. French and Belgian publishers, mostly Roman Catholics, started to publish huge series, from small octavos to large quartos, especially as prize books, though they were also available separately. During the first half of the twentieth century, in Holland and Belgium some normal series or single editions of books for young people were announced as especially appropriate for, or even recommended as, prize books. As a provisional conclusion on the general appearance of prize books, we can say that after 1800 in a large part of continental Europe one can see a broadening of the subjects of books given as prizes, though the religious divide in schools, meant that ideologically history and nature became the most favoured subjects. The classical appearance of the prize binding disappears gradually to make way for the publishers' binding, but some publishers try to do something with it. The *ex-praemio* survived, and still does in some schools.[2]

2. *The Schools*

The most characteristic and the most widespread kind of school where prize books were given, is of course the grammar school, the so called Latin school, where classical languages and literature, mainly Latin, were and remained for a long time the main subjects of the curriculum, even after Latin had lost its main position as the *lingua franca* of the learned western world. Prize books of classical authors were in their right place there. Grammar schools could be run by the city or have their own government, or they could be run by religious orders in regions under Roman Catholic rule, or by the local churches in those under the influence of the Reformation; both were most supported in one way or another by the city or town government, or by universities, or by private enterprise.

Prize books were also given in Sunday schools, founded in England in 1780 by the journalist and methodist philanthropist Robert Raikes (1734–1811), and introduced in Holland in the 1830s. After the foundation of the Dutch Association for Sunday Schools in 1865, there was obviously quite a profitable market for some publishers. They were also given in primary schools from some time during the nineteenth century onwards, but maybe also earlier, in the 'small schools' in the city, which were often private schools, as well as in the country, where the schools were more often parish schools, and in the Sunday schools which were mainly held in the city long before Raikes had started with his movement, and which mainly dealt with religious and moral education. They were given during the nineteenth and part of the twentieth centuries on the occasion of regional examinations at certain ideological kinds of schools, and they were given at training colleges, at art academies and at universities. They were given on other occasions in which competition in one way or another played a part, even if not directly in a school-like context. A prize book was a metaphor for honour.

It started in the sixteenth century when European society saw an acceleration of the transition from a mainly oral, spoken culture to a culture dominated by a practice of writing and silent reading. The commercialisation of the printed book became its manifestation and its instrument. From then onwards those who could not readily read and write stood outside the economical, social and political dynamism.

This phenomenon translated itself into an increased demand for a new type of school education, while the traditional educational system was in crisis. A new social class was longing for moral and material emancipation by claiming the most important means of social control, writing and reading. As this evolution went together with the Reformation on the one hand and the Counter Reformation on the other, in one part of Europe schooling was taken over by the protestant authorities, in another part by the Jesuits, both based on the *modus parisiensis*, the model created by the education of the *Devotio moderna*, of the Brethren of the Common Life.

3. The Educational Background

Competition and the Jesuits

The distribution of prize books in schools and elsewhere cannot be dissociated from education itself, nor can education be dissociated from its socio-cultural background, from social, political or ideological history. It is in any case a characteristic aspect of the history of five centuries of West European schools.

While the distribution of prizes spread quickly during the sixteenth century, the idea certainly was not new. It is well known that Verrius Flaccus, the educator of the emperor Augustus's grandsons, gave his pupils prizes for their achievements. Marcus Fabius Quintilianus, a Spaniard and a contemporary of Flaccus, recommended in his influential *Institutio oratoria* the distribution of prizes on the occasion of monthly competitions to reward the deserving pupils. This approach might have been new in the western history of education, however the idea on which it was based had already been formulated by Aristotle in his *Rhetoric*. Emulation was, he wrote, a hallmark of the virtuous, and is the opposite of envy, a characteristic of mean people. The virtuous man is striving by emulation for good things he wishes to acquire, without of course keeping his neighbour from them, or envying him if he achieves them. He who plans for himself a better future, tries to reach this goal by emulation when he finds he is entitled to it and he can share it with others.[3]

Already in Quintilian the much broader idea of *emulatio* which Aristotle had formulated was narrowed to *competitio*, to rivalry. From the sixteenth century onwards, both concepts got entwined in the context of education, in the way that emulation often meant competition. Competition indeed played an important role in schooling as developed from the sixteenth century onwards and it was no coincidence that it was inspired and stimulated by the humanist movement. The prize here was much more a stimulus for emulation than a reward. The child should learn to act from duty and should not be deviated by a reward from his pure motives nor be strengthened in his self-conceit.[4]

The first to integrate prize distributions systematically in their educational system and give them their definitive form and wide diffusion, were the Jesuits. Francis Bacon (1561–1626) wrote in his *Advancement of learning* (1605): 'They are so good that I wish they were on our side'.[5] When they were founded in 1540 by Ignatius of

Loyola (1491–1556) as vanguard of the Counter Reformation, education was not at all their aim. This, however, did not last long. In 1546 they began their own schools. In little more than ten years they ran almost forty colleges, an overwhelming start of a successful career, however not without a break. In 1773 the order was abolished and was only able to start again in 1814 to continue in the same tradition as if nothing had happened.

It was obviously due to the energy of the order and its founder, supported by his secretary Juan de Polanco (1516–1577), that a real educational system could be established. Jerónimo Nadal (1507–1580) worked out the concept in a coherent way and applied it for the first time in the college of Messina, founded in 1548. He formulated the first statement of the intention, principles and organisation of the Jesuit schools and laid in this way the foundation for the *Ratio studiorum*, prepared in 1581–82 and printed for the first time in Rome in 1586. The editions of 1591 and 1599 were extended versions and this text stayed almost unchanged for three centuries and laid down in detail all actions in a Jesuit college.[6]

In the 1591 edition the prize distribution was recorded. The text confirms that the practice was already in use from 1558 onwards in Messina, Coimbra and Rome. For rhetoric, six prizes were provided in the first or top class: two for Latin oratory, two for Latin verse, and two for Greek. In the second class also six prizes were provided. The third class, called grammar, received four prizes, two for prose and two for verse. In the fourth class at least two prizes for prose were reserved, but there could be more if the class was large enough. Spread over the years there were for every form one or more prizes for Christian doctrine. Roughly, in these Jesuit schools at least twenty-two books varying from folio format to octavo or duodecimo, were given yearly on the occasion of the prize distribution.[7]

Apart from its strict organisation the main contribution of the Jesuits to the prize distribution was certainly its staging, the pomp and circumstance, which made it the high day in school life, for the pupils and not least for all others concerned. A theatrical performance soon became an essential item in the programme. School theatre certainly was not a Jesuit invention, but they succeeded nonetheless to make Jesuit drama a household word, that knew then how to fascinate (or bore) a full house and to attract scholars from all over the world. Much energy was spent on the performance; it must not fail to impress. A strong element of propaganda was connected with it. It had to endear the school to the public who brought pupils and money to the college, and in the competition with other schools it was not unimportant to steal the show.[8]

The World

Evidently there was also an educational foundation. The performance gave the pupils not only the opportunity to make a public appearance, rhetoric played an important role indeed, but it enabled them to demonstrate their gifts and to enjoy themselves. The preparation lasted almost the whole year and channelled a lot of energy. Undoubtedly a strong element of competition was connected with it, between schools, between forms, and between the pupils themselves. This competition, of which the performance was part, fitted in with the educational theory of emulation. The emulation was there to stimulate the closed school-like life and to channel the energy, to regularise it.

In a school, and pre-eminently in a boarding school, the pupil was literally and even more figuratively cut off from the world, which spread a pestilential infection and where the devil was abroad to get the child in his clutches, ideas still current in the middle of the twentieth century. Evil was immanent in the world and the child had to be protected from it. It was not only the world which was experienced as fundamentally bad, but also the nature of the child, of man himself. The world was hereby seen only as the opportunity for a much deeper-rooted evil to manifest itself. Therefore the child was cut off from the world and was constantly watched, to prevent that it would be attracted by the depth of evil in itself. This went from physical control, for which fellow pupils were sometimes used, to selection and expurgation of classic and contemporary literature, bowdlerization, with occasionally the interpolation of edifying quotations, *ad usum Delphini*.[9]

In this way of thinking, it is obvious that the child became isolated from the world, but it was cut off also from its own spontaneity. Naturally with this process it was necessary to stimulate the child, who was then driven in other ways, and to motivate it with rewards to feel more comfortable. This artificial world which was created and in which precisely antiquity played a prominent role, this channelling, was the world of emulation. Study itself was an exercise in compliance and modesty, an idea not only proper to the Society of Jesus but also to other religious orders. Study moreover was work that had to be carried out as expiation and as a token of honour to God, rather than an initiation into knowledge.[10]

This stock of ideas that was shown in different shades by various educators was not unique to the Jesuits, any more than the whole educational system was, which they so successfully developed. Ignatius himself had studied at the universities of Alcalá, Salamanca and Paris and so had the nucleus of the later Society. Through this group, the so-called Parisian method of education, the *modus parisiensis*, was adopted in the Jesuit schools as their structural element.[11]

Modus parisiensis

The Parisian educational system had developed during a couple of centuries and consisted of a complex of educational standards and school-like practices. The division into six or seven forms, or classes, certainly is one of the most characteristic structural elements. The word *classis* itself was a sixteenth century rediscovery of a concept already used by Quintilian. The class system required *promotiones*, tests to assess the transition from one form to another. This required that pupils were inscribed on the *rotulus*, the roll, the list of pupils.[12]

The normal method of education in medieval schools was the *lectio*, in the course of which the schoolmaster read an author and added glosses. The pupil noted these and read the author for himself. From the Renaissance onwards the reading of an author was called, according to Quintilian, *praelectio* or *expositio*. The schoolmaster gave a thorough analysis of the text as a whole and of its parts. Afterwards there were *questiones*, questions raised by the master, which had to be argued and defended by the pupils in a hypothesis and its antithesis. This was a direct preparation for the *disputationes*, the weekly or monthly disputes when the students had to defend given hypotheses and antitheses in public. The *emulatio* was inherent in this system. Quintilian already knew that ambitious pupils have the intention to win. According to Erasmus this was indeed the best method to stimulate a child, to teach him to win and to lose, and particularly to teach him to conquer himself. Rewards and prizes were connected with it.[13]

All these constituent elements were not new, but they formed a system of their own, which was however not the only educational system in Europe. Bologna had its own method, which spread all over Italy, Spain and the South of France. In parallel with this was an educational movement, which was not based on the methods of Bologna or Paris, but in the sixteenth century the Parisian colleges contributed to it. This was the educational method of the Brethren of the Common Life, of the *Devotio moderna*, which originated in the Northern Netherlands where someone like Erasmus went to school. Jan Standonck (d. 1504) of Mechelen in the Southern Netherlands, who had studied with the Brethren in Gouda, introduced in *Montaigu* all sorts of reforms. With the reform in the Parisian *Collège de Montaigu* all kinds of uses characteristic for the schools of the Brethren made their appearance in Paris and they soon spread widely. Through *Montaigu*, Ignatius, who had known the *Devotio moderna* earlier, was influenced by the Brethren. The influence of *Montaigu* explains the spread of the form system, of the division of classes in *decuriae*, groups of ten pupils who among other things played a role in the discipline of the school population. It explains the transitional examinations and the promotions in grammar schools, it explains the *rapiaria*, note books where the pupils noted striking sentences, a kind of *loci communes*, common place books. Lastly, the influence of *Montaigu* explains the distribution of prizes for the best pupils.[14]

This new approach spread over western Europe mainly through the influence of the Jesuits. Moreover, the emphasis on religious education must not be underestimated. This too was particular to the *Devotio moderna* and was common property in the Paris colleges. School life was given rhythm by religious exercises. In fact, in the proper lessons little time was spent on religious education and though Basil, Gregory of Nazianzus, Chrysostom or Jerome were recommended by the *Ratio*, mainly pagan literature, such as Virgil and Cicero, was studied. But classical texts were sterilised and Christianised, as if the authors were forerunners of Christianity, or already almost real Christians and their works pious tracts. Besides this the classics not only had the advantage that they could be used as a foundation course for Christian doctrine, they certainly wrote very good Latin in a clear style and that could not always be said of the Church Fathers or other ecclesiastical authors.[15]

Antiquity as fiction

Through the language and its grammar the child obtained access to the world of ancient Rome, or rather, to a completely fictitious world, constructed by the educators and imposed as a moral alternative to the pernicious contemporary world and to his own passions. The French historian and influential educator, Charles Rollin (1661–1741),

UN PREMIER PRIX,

1. 'A first prize', wood-engraving by J.-J. (Jean-Ignace-Isidore-Gérard) Grandville (1803–1847), engraved by Auguste(?) Leloir (1809–1892). Louis Reybaud, *Jérome Paturot à la recherche d'une position sociale*, Paris, 1846, before p. 425.

who published an edition of Quintilian (2 vols, Paris, 1712), wrote in his *Traité des études* (4 vols, Paris, 1726–31) that the contemporary world only aimed at wealth, luxury and easy satisfactions, or as Baudelaire (1821–1867) would have written it, *luxe, calme et volupté*. To counter the attractions of these to the child, a lesson of morality was not enough. The child should be 'carried away to other countries and other times. The flood of empty slogans should be opposed by the sayings and the example of the great characters of Antiquity'. The authority granted to Antiquity was accompanied with a world view where innovation or original ideas were seen as harmful. A world without division or turmoil was, if not the best, at any rate the easiest preparation for respect for the established authority, whether political, social or religious.[16]

These ideas are reflected directly in the literature given as prize books. It is not true that the content did not matter and that only the nicely tooled binding had to astound the public at large and the competitors, even after the role it had to play in the shows was finished. Instead, for the most part the content was part of this role. The classics, the majority of the prize books before 1800, and in some regions even afterwards, had their place in this artificial world of which the whole construction of the *emulatio* was the merry-go-round.

4. *The Prize Distribution*

The oldest known representation of the moment of the distribution of prize books is dated 1683 and was made in the Jesuit college of Brussels. The coloured drawing belongs to a surviving series of *affixiones* from 1630 until 1685. The *affixiones* were exhibitions of the best compositions of the pupils in verse and prose, in Latin, Greek and Hebrew, held once or twice a year in the courtyard of the school. This custom had started already during the earliest days of the Jesuit schools in the sixteenth century, and the rules for it are laid down in the definitive version of the *Ratio* (Rome, 1599). One of the rules points to a creative imitation and emulation of hieroglyphs, Pythagorean symbols, devices, emblems or riddles. These *affixiones* are closely connected with the Jesuit drama. While the theatre tried to initiate the child in religious and moral life, to educate him to a sense of public responsibility, to impart in him love of his country by depicting the life of national heroes, it certainly was also meant to demonstrate to the public what fair results education by the Fathers could lead to.[17]

The aim of the emblematic setting was in essence rhetorical. Emblems make authoritative statements. By means both of nature, especially fauna and flora, and tradition, mythology, the Bible, history and literature, as well as of human experience, they offer norms and arguments for correct behaviour in an attractive combination of word and image. It should not be a surprise that printing and binding are several times present in this series. Well known as it was, prize distribution could hardly be absent from the rhetorical display of a Jesuit college, such as that in the *affixiones*. The yearly exhibitions were arranged around a fixed theme, and the theme of the year 1683 was piety and learning, *pietas et doctrina*. According to Jesuit educational philosophy, reason strives by its very nature after virtue and piety, while the virtuous person strives after wisdom and knowledge. The former theme, *pietas*, was developed by the pupils of Rhetoric, in the final year or first class, the latter, *doctrina*, by those of Poetics, in the second or penultimate year. They chose the book as *locus communis* around which to build their statements. The very last of a long series of thirty eight emblems is the prize distribution. The acquisition of much learning is the true reward of much labour. This prize is the greatest of all desires, attested by a statement of Juvenal (V, 18), *Votorum summa*.

The representation, though obviously not made by a first class painter, is very interesting as it gives a lively view of the ceremony of a prize distribution in a Jesuit college in the Southern Netherlands, and probably, according to the strict prescriptions of Jesuit organisation, in all these institutions all over Europe. The books are put in a small bookcase placed on a table and serving as a real showcase. There are three shelves, obviously meant for the prizes for the three upper forms. It is nice to see that they are arranged according to format, from the large ones, the folios or quartos, to the small ones, the octavos or duodecimos. A priest speaks and gives a book to a pupil. The show has just started, the first book is being presented, the audience is listening with excitement.[18]

The next representation, or rather series of representations, of a prize distribution that exists, dates from about fifty years later and comes from the Northern Netherlands. On the occasion of the biannual prize distributions the best pupil of the last form before going to the academy, or the university, made a speech in Latin which was in some schools printed for the occasion. On the title-page of these printed orations from Leiden and Delft in Holland, dating from at least 1713 to 1749, there is an engraving representing this ceremony. As usual it is taking place in a church with the necessary pomp and circumstance. The bewigged curators, usually a few regents of the city or town and one or two clergymen, who were responsible for the smooth running of the school, are sitting behind the table, while before them is a pile of books. The rector, as master of ceremony, calls from the pulpit the name of the pupil to receive his prize from the president-curator. Some pupils have already received it, they carry the book under their arm, others are waiting impatiently. Proud members of their families are watching expectantly from the pews. Each pupil has to declaim a *gratiarum actio* or *gratias*, a short word of gratitude in verse, sometimes written next to the *ex-praemio* on the flyleaf of the book, which closes the circle.[19]

The third representation dates from the very end of the eighteenth century and is a close-up of a prize distribution in post-Revolutionary France. Instead of the organ in the Dutch church, a brass band trio dressed in fashionable clothes, is playing on a platform to give the same pomp and circumstance to the show as in the centuries before. There are the masters of ceremony, there is the seated dignitary who is placing a laurel crown on the head of one of the children. And, again, the proud family is watching curiously. The language may have changed a little, the rhetoric stays the same.[20]

It is striking that, though symbols may have changed in appearance, essence and show stayed the same throughout several centuries, from the Jesuits in the Southern Netherlands, through the Protestant city and town schools in Holland, to a French *lycée* after the Revolution which announced a reform of education and schooling, and has even survived all these changes to remain in existence until the second half of the twentieth century.

II – PRIZE BOOKS IN EUROPE

1. France

The French prize book in the seventeenth century is roughly characterised by a lavishly tooled binding. The design followed the prevailing fashion dictated by Paris. In the centre there is usually the coat of arms of the donor on a field *semé* with armorial motifs and/or his initials, or the armorial centre-piece is framed by a more or less

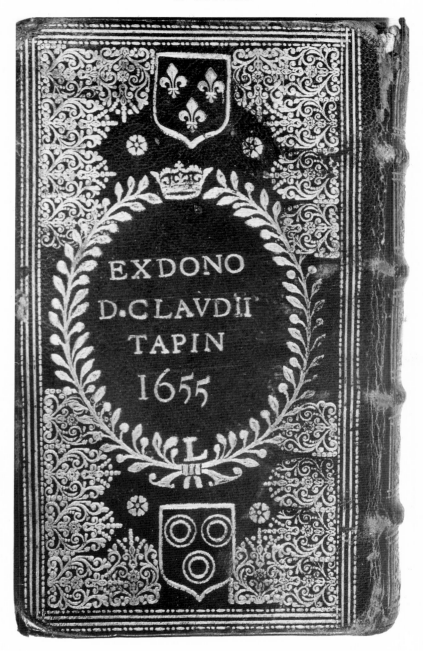

2. Prize book of 1655, typical for the college of Chalon-sur-Saône, donated by
Claude Tapin by a foundation in his will of 1631. Marcus Aurelius Antoninus,
De vita sua libri XII. Graecè & Latinè, Lyon, for François de La
Bottière, 1626, 12°. Heverlee, Park Abbey, Pr FIII/14.

elaborate dentelle, sometimes enriched with fan motifs. The edge is usually gilt. The rich decoration of the bindings was directly connected with the social class of the donors, *les agonothètes* as they were called in France (from the Greek ἀγωνοθετέω, to organise competitions, ἀγών τίθημι, and ἀγωνοθέτης, the one who organises a competition and distributes the prizes), ranging from the King himself, the Court, all possible worldly and religious dignitaries and institutions, to local noblemen, or rich burghers, and the city or town Council. During the eighteenth century decoration became more austere and was mostly limited to the arms in the centre and fillets along the borders, usually tooled on marbled leather, the marbling having sometimes caused damage by progressive acidification.

The *ex-praemio* is either completely hand-written on the flyleaf, sometimes enriched with decorative penwork, or there is a printed prize dedication bound in where the details have been filled in by hand. This seems not to occur before 1680, though too often the dedication has been removed and there is no systematic research available to prove this. There is a variant where the *ex-dono* is fully printed and the *ex-praemio* written on the opposite flyleaf. Both hand-written and printed prize inscriptions are often provided with a paper seal or a seal in red wax to attest authenticity.

The books were mostly works of the classics, the Fathers, or other early Christian authors, though humanistic treatises seem also to have been appreciated. In Jesuit schools books by members of the Order were presented as well. The language was almost always Latin, sometimes Latin and Greek, though from the eighteenth century onwards religious and learned literature in French was also given.

Prize books in France could be recent publications, or they could be second or third hand books, sometimes printed one, or two, or even more centuries before the prize was given and put in a new binding. True, classical texts stayed the same, though they were updated by new commentaries, but the main reason certainly was the financial state of the school and the poor support of the magistrates or the private benefactor. Indeed some prizes prove that brand new books were bought for the distribution, while in other cases it is clear that old material was recycled, from the second hand book market, from one or other private collection, sometimes re-using a former prize book, or even from a Jesuit library itself.[21]

With the Revolution, and the changes in education in the nineteenth century, came a greater variety in content and in binding. The nationalisation of schooling, with the strong centralisation that characterises French policy, led to much prize-book binding becoming quite uniform, greatly resembling the basic scheme of the Old Regime.

The impetus for change came with the Enlightenment and with the Encyclopaedists who criticised the unworldly education shaped by the Jesuits. D'Alembert (1717–1783) wrote in the *Encylopédie* (Paris, 1753) under the entry *Collège*: 'A young man after having spent the ten nicest, most precious years of his life in a college, leaves it when he has used his time for the better, with a very imperfect knowledge of a dead language, with the rules of rhetoric and philosophical principles he must try to forget; often with a moral corruption of which the corruption of his health is the least consequence; sometimes with wrongly understood religious principles; but most usually with such a superficial knowledge of religion that it succumbs to the first wicked conversation, to the first immoral reading'.[22] Already in

3. A Latin crammer: 'On pratiqua sur les élèves le système suivi sur les bœufs et les moutons, ou, si l'on veut, sur les boxeurs et les jockeys: on les dressa en vue d'un résultat donné et spécifié', engraving by J.-J. Grandville. Louis Reybaud, *Jérome Paturot à la recherche d'une position sociale*, Paris, 1846, p. 422.

4. Prize book given at the Paris 'Pension Regnauld' (Boulevard des Batignolles) for geometry in 1841. Jean-Baptiste Rousseau, *Œuvres choisies*, Paris, 1829, 12°. Private collection.

1685 Claude Fleury (1640–1723), a priest and a critical historian of education, had suggested that at the right time a break should be made with the traditional and dominant system and that the natural curiosity of the child for its surrounding world ought to be satisfied. This naturally curious child grew eighty years later into Jean-Jacques Rousseau's (1712–1778) *Emile* (Amsterdam and The Hague, Jean Néaulme, 1762).[23]

This was the dawn of educational revolution. As soon as the nature of the child itself was no longer a pit of iniquity into which it could fall any minute, and the world no longer a menacing pestilence, the child could touch the world and be led by its interest in its world and its time. New educational concepts argued that nothing is as instructive as knowledge of the real world and concern for contemporary events and that the child should no longer be referred to an artificial world to be approached in a foreign language. As the exact sciences were freeing themselves more and more from philosophy, the teaching of both should take this into account. Moreover La Chalotais (1701–1785), Attorney General of the Breton parliament, anti-Jesuit and one of the most important minds on education before the French Revolution, wrote that foreign languages should be taught, English because of its importance for science and trade and German because of its importance for war. In any event, greater diversification had to be brought into education. These ideas were very influential, but, though education was broadened, much remained as it had been.[24] This evolution, whichever direction it took, can be recognised in the prize books, or, *vice versa*, recognition of this development is necessary to understand prize books.

At the end of the eighteenth century central schools were set up, the *Ecoles centrales*, but they were unable to compete with private schools. In 1808 Napoleon created the *Université de France*, which was not so much a university as a sort of ministry to coordinate secondary and higher education. That is the reason why many inscriptions in nineteenth-century prize books name the *Université de France*, with the name of the school underneath.[25] Until the middle of the century and in some schools even later, prize books bound in leather, if only cheap sheepskin, were given, although the decoration is at times of poor quality. Meanwhile machine binding had begun which on the whole allowed larger and better, standardised production, such as a combination of blind- and gold-tooled decoration applied with a blocking press.

5. A typical French publishers' binding for prize and other gift books, by Mame in
Tours, with a block designed and engraved by Auguste D. Souze (1829–after 1892).
Antoine Ricard, *Christophe Colomb*, Tours, Alfred Mame et Fils, 1892, fol.

During the eighteen-forties large series were published, mainly by Catholic publishers such as Alfred Mame (1811–1893) in Tours and the Barbou family in Limoges, first and foremost intended as prize books for the enormous range of primary and secondary schools which had been established next to the Jesuit and other traditional schools. It is noticeable that the latter schools obviously did not make use of them, perhaps because they considered them inferior. These series testify to the polarisation of education. They usually contain moralising or devout stories, sometimes drawing on well-known stories from world literature, or on romanticised and ideologically coloured, and therefore bowdlerised and manipulated, historical events. Nor does their design always testify to good taste and they are often rather cheap, both literally and metaphorically. Even today, the better produced books of this kind, in formats from small folio to small octavo, if in good condition, are still attractive collectors' pieces.[26]

Besides primary and secondary schools, in which the habit of the presentation of prize books was generally wide-spread, there was at least one French university where in the second half of the nineteenth century prize books were also handed out: the University of Caen in Normandy. This is quite exceptional in the prize book tradition. Prize books of 1873, 1874 and 1889 are known and there may of course still be others hidden in public or private collections. They are bound either in full sheepskin or in half leather with the boards covered in cloth. Like many French prize bindings of the nineteenth century, one kind has a laurel wreath on the upper cover, but instead of an heraldic motif it here encloses the name of the faculty. There is no printed or manuscript *ex-praemio*, but prize and student are identified on the spine. The other kind has the *ex-praemio* on the upper cover as it were. These are from the Law Faculty and seem to fit in with an attempt to enhance the scholarly and professional qualities of the training. Surprisingly the prize books known are all second prizes. This may be sheer coincidence, but it could well be that the first prize was a sum of money and/or a medal. There were indeed private foundations at Caen to support different courses in the Law Faculty and these continued until the 1960s, though maybe they only awarded a sum of money with a medal as a token of honour.[27]

There is quite a large amount of material available for the French prize book which, with all that belongs to it, is almost paradigmatic for many prize givings on the continent. It can be used as a point of reference for the further study of this phenomenon because the ideas of the Enlightenment and of the Revolution had such a great influence.

2. *The Iberian Peninsula and Italy*

Unfortunately, information on prize givings is almost completely lacking for southern Europe, for the Iberian Peninsula and for Italy. As we have seen, it was there that the Jesuits started their colleges and introduced prize distributions as focal points in their educational system. The first prize distribution in Coimbra for instance was in 1558, in Rome it took place in 1565 in the presence of Cardinal Alessandro Farnese (1520–1589). An interesting detail is that it was emphasised that the books should be well bound. It seems unlikely that the Jesuits would not have continued there what they did in the rest of Europe. We can only confirm that in northern Italy, Piedmont, Lombardy and Tuscany, from at least the beginning of the nineteenth century until the First World War, prize book distribution was in general very similar to that in France. As Piedmont was part of France from 1797 to 1814, this was certainly not mere coincidence. A striking characteristic is that the *ex-praemio* is very often impressed on the binding, which identifies the book unmistakably as a prize book. This applies to the books bound by hand and it applies to a certain degree also to the publishers' bindings. For the latter, great French publishing houses, like Hachette and Mame, found an outlet there even after 1814, although publishers in Turin, Milan and Florence clearly also targeted this market. The inference from this is that princely personages supported the prize givings with books and/or with their presence at the ceremony. Such publishers' bindings could also be personalised, with the whole *ex-praemio* or with a reference to the patron-prince printed on them, or they were *passe-partout* bindings with the word 'premio' on them, which could be put around any book of the same format. The content might be one of the classics, French literature of the seventeenth century like Racine (1639–1699), or contemporary Italian literature, whether or not specially written for the young, or the whole gamut of rubbishy moralising and devotional tracts. One striking item is certainly Roberto Bellarmino's (1542–1621) *Dell'arte di ben morire* (as a sixth prize for piety), quite a cynical gift for a young school leaver.[28]

6. DAT PROSPER NATUS. 1785. Louis-Englebert, Duke of Arenberg (1750–1820), had an occasional tooled binding made after the birth of his son. Given as a prize in Enghien/Edingen, the residential place of the dukes, 24 August 1785. Roeland van Leuve, *Doorlugte voorbeelden der Ouden*, Amsterdam, Hendrik Bosch, 1725, 4°. Heverlee, Park Abbey, W I5.

3. The Southern Netherlands and Prince-Bishopric of Liège, Belgium

a. The Southern Netherlands

The Southern Netherlands are even today difficult to understand without a minimal knowledge of their chaotic history. They border France, were for a time at least in part ruled by France, in part incorporated into France, and they were already since the late Middle Ages strongly influenced by France in language and customs, through links with Burgundy. Continuous rule by different peoples could not fail to leave its mark on mentality and culture, the positive result of which may well have been a great suppleness and intense cultural diversity; slanderers may call this a lack of identity and absence of civilisation, but they are not necessarily always right. If during the late Middle Ages the Southern Netherlands were a centre of trade, art and culture, the religious wars, the separation of the Northern Netherlands in 1585 and the reign of the Counter Reformation, signified a break, economically and culturally. Many intel- lectuals and craftsmen fled to the North. With Rubens (1577–1640) and Van Dyck (1599–1641) as the last flowering in the fine arts and the successors of Plantin (c. 1520–1589) in the world of the book, there was afterwards apparently, roughly speaking, no longer the potential in craftsmen and patrons to guarantee quality – at least in the craft of bookbinding, let alone the ability to produce lavishly decorated luxury bindings. This does not mean that there were none at all, but that they are rather rare. The prize book of course reflects this. The magnificent prize book donated in 1605 by the Regents to the Jesuit College in Brussels, from the Otto Schäfer collection in Schweinfurt, must be seen as a true exception.[29]

Compared with the often richly tooled French prize binding, the prize book in the Southern Netherlands distinguishes itself by its heterogeneity, also due to the variety of institutions running the schools and, in many cases, the inferiority of the materials used together with weak execution. In so far as these bindings received any special decoration, it was the application of the stamp of a coat of arms. These could be the arms of the patron, the town, the religious order which conducted the school or of the authority which patronised the grammar school, for example, a faculty of the University of Louvain to which a school in the town was directly linked. There is one instance of a book which has the arms of the donor abbey impressed on the covers and which has also a folding frontispiece once more bearing the arms. This custom is known from dedicatory copies or special donations, but is uncommon in a prize book. It does of course emphasise again the generosity and above all the power of the donor.[30]

The *ex-praemio* was always handwritten, but shows a peculiarity not usually found in neighbouring countries. In quite a few schools it was obviously customary for the rector or the form master, when writing the *ex-praemio* onto the flyleaf, also to write some verses alluding to the pupil's name or an anagram or Latinisation of it. The very detailed instructions for the Jesuit schools in the Southern Netherlands provided a strict number of prizes for each form, the first three for instance receiving a book, the next seven a print, and this was certainly a widespread custom which continued until late in the twentieth century.[31]

Here too the works of classical and early Christian authors were often given as prize books and in Jesuit schools the authors of that Order were also represented. Next to classical and early Christian authors, any learned, historical or pious book seemed suitable to be given as a prize to a pupil, such as Vopiscus Fortunatus Plemp's (1601–1671) *Fundamenta medicinae* (Leuven, 1664), a prize for good writing given in a Brussels private school in 1741. Other examples are a tract volume with three Lyonese editions of 1621–26, two of Giovanni Pierio Valeriano (1477–1558), his *Pro sacerdotum barbis ... declamatio* (1621) and his *Hieroglyphicorum collectanea* (1626), and one of Louis de Caseneuve (fl. 1620–26), *Hieroglyphicorum et medicorum emblematum dodekakrounos* (1626), a commentary on Thomas Aquinas (1225–1274), the complete works of Fénelon (1651–1715), a kind of handbook for priests for a boy of fifteen, a tract volume with texts on the history of relics in a Salzburg monastery for a child of fourteen in some provincial grammar school in 1778, and a folio 1616 Lyon confessors' manual, given to another boy in 1765. Though the influence of the Enlightenment can occasionally be felt here too in the kind of book given, it seems evident that at least for some of the schools the content of the book did not matter and that any book that could be found, as long as it was not offensive of course, was good enough to embellish the show.[32]

b. The Prince-Bishopric of Liège

The Prince-Bishopric of Liège flourished from the sixteenth century onwards, and until the end of the eighteenth century comparative peace and prosperity reigned there. In 1815 it came with the rest of the Southern Netherlands under the Dutch King, William I (1772–1843), and with the formation of Belgium became part of it.

The relative prosperity and, until the abolition of the Order in 1773, easy cooperation between the city authorities and the Jesuit school find expression in the care bestowed on the prize books. During the seventeenth century the bindings, made of leather or vellum, are very carefully decorated and the pupil's name, his rank, his form and sometimes also the date are often tooled on the binding within a decorative frame. The binding is often decorated with corner-pieces and a central armorial block with the arms of the city, or that of the Jesuits, or with a more general religious representation, such as the Crucifixion. The *ex-praemio* is not always repeated in manuscript on the flyleaf. In the eighteenth century the decoration is usually simplified to a block with the arms of the city on both covers and the general quality has deteriorated. In many cases the *ex-praemio* has been divided. There is the *ex-dono*, often ready printed, with the names of the two burgomasters who sponsored the prizes with money from the municipal treasury, pasted onto the pastedown, while the *ex-praemio* proper is written by hand on the facing flyleaf. Here too some verses alluding to the pupil's name were sometimes included. Later in the century at least some of the prize books are characterised by bearing the arms and names of the two burgomasters, one on each cover. There is at present too little material to judge whether this has anything to do with the disappearance of the Jesuits. It is noticeable that of the available material, Liège editions figure quite often as prize books and that the dates of these editions are not all that much earlier than that of the prizegiving, which is a confirmation of financial means and good organisation.[33]

c. Belgium

With the foundation of an independent state in the nineteenth century, the return of the Jesuits in 1814, the extension of the school system and the establishment of innumerable congregations dedicated to various facets of instruction, a veritable explosion of the prize book took place, as it did in France. The classics still played a prominent part, above all in the Jesuit schools, but revised views on child rearing and education resulted in a wide range of literature specially written for the young and suitable for children.

7. Both covers of a prize book of the Jesuit college of Liège given in 1613 to Renier de Saint Vith. Louis Richeome, SJ, *Peregrinus Lauretanus* (transl. Johann Haickstein), Cologne, Johann Crith, 1612, 8°. Liège, Bibliothèque Chiroux-Croisiers, Fonds Capitaine 7784.

The improvement in quality which can be found from roughly the second half of the eighteenth century onwards shows also in the overall quality of the bindings, although clearly there were not the

8. The oldest recorded prize book. Given to Emanuel Duensis in 1577.
Augustin, *Meditationes*, Dillingen, Sebald Mayer, 1571, 8°.
Antiquariat Konrad Meuschel, cat. 87, no. 4.

means for handing out luxuriously bound books. As was the case in France, from 1840–50 specialised production comes to the fore, largely marketed by French publishers. But for a long time quite a high standard was maintained in prize books given by the Belgian state. The decoration of the bindings made specially for these occasions testifies here also to a standardisation, both in confessional, and in state or municipal schools. It appears that after the First World War only books were given which were on general sale in local bookshops, although, until the 1960s at least, there were evidently savings banks or similar enterprises which had special dust jackets printed for the prize giving in which publicity undeniably played the chief part.[34]

4. Germany

a. The regions under Roman Catholic influence

In the regions under Roman Catholic influence education was mainly directed by the Jesuits. The Cologne *Gymnasium Tricoronatum* is the oldest Jesuit school in Germany. It became renowned soon after its foundation in 1557, attracting pupils from the Southern Netherlands, Switzerland, Hungary and Scotland. In 1560 there were 560 pupils, by 1600 already almost double that number. The Jesuits' presence was prominent in Catholic regions, for instance in Paderborn where the college grew to a university in 1614, Dillingen where the order took over the university in 1563 and Ingolstadt where they gradually 'invaded' the university from 1548 onwards.[35]

The bindings seem always to have been made specially for the occasion, but the books inside could be much older. The binding is usually of sheepskin, sometimes plain, or tooled with fillets or rolls along the edges, and with a Jesuit tool or an armorial block in the centre; sometimes they are more elaborately decorated with a double frame of rolls linked at the corners. At times the lower cover has the Jesuit emblem with the text stamped on the leather. Sometimes the binding is in vellum with tooling in black. Because of the poor quality of the gold used for tooling, the decoration has now often oxidised, in some descriptions noted as tooling in silver. The *ex-praemio* is always handwritten. Remarkably, at least for the handful of books that have been documented, contemporary authors predominate and not always with religious texts.[36]

b. The regions under the influence of the Reformation

The Reformation strongly coloured the German educational scene. A new era demanded a new kind of education. Because of the religious troubles the existing schools were in disorder and needed immediate

9. Prize book in red sheepskin, given in the Jesuit school in Emmerich (Nordrhein-Westfalen) in 1630 to Haimo Otten of nearby Calcar. Marcus Antonius Majoragius (i.e. Antonio Maria de Conti), *Orationes et praefationes, una cum dialogo de eloquentia*, Cologne, Johann Gymnich, 1619, 12°. Heverlee, Park Abbey, Pr FII/7.

remedies. The existing grammar schools were reorganised and their number increased. When Maurice of Saxony (1521–1553) founded schools in parallel with the municipal schools which were paid for by the state, he fulfilled a social need. Municipal and state schools developed into the famous German Gymnasium. It was Philipp Melanchthon (1497–1560) who gave German secondary education its true form. He laid the foundations in 1525 with the school regulation of Eisleben and Nuremberg which had a large-scale following.[37]

The school model of Strasbourg, as worked out by Joannes Sturmius (1507–1589), also exerted a great influence. It was Stoic in morality and method. Sturmius had been a pupil of the Brethren of the Common Life, the Hieronymites, at Liège, and when after a professorship at Paris he became head of the new Gymnasium at Strasbourg in 1537, having chosen for the Reformation, he adapted there the model of the *Devotio moderna*.[38]

Sturmius's system inspired Jean Calvin (1509–1564) who taught at the Strasbourg Gymnasium and started his own Gymnasium in Geneva, the *schola privata*, whose rules were written down in the *Leges Academiae Genevensis* (Geneva, 1559). The Geneva model was exported to the Huguenots in France, the Dutch Reformed Church, the Puritans in England and the Presbyterians in Scotland; that is why this model is so important.[39] Alas, none of the prize books from these schools is recorded.

c. Germany and Austria from the end of the eighteenth century

Nevertheless, a first enquiry into prize distributions in German schools provides general confirmation that this kind of event happened widely. In *Das neue Schulsystem*, an address delivered at a prize distribution in Ingolstadt in 1775, Franz Anton Neuhauser (1744–1834), a Jesuit who continued teaching in the Gymnasium after the abolition of the Order, defended the reforms, but also stressed the links with tradition.[40] In a similar address, printed in Magdeburg in 1797, a school director, the antiquary and philologist Johann Gottfried Gurlitt (1754–1827), discoursed on prize givings which 'as is customary are held twice a year' to reward rivalry and exertion, before he said goodbye to the eighteen and nineteen-year old pupils who were moving on to a higher school, the Academy. Then, he continued, 'the time is coming when you, be it as scholar, as business-man or as soldier, will be able to do much good, truly much good, with the knowledge you acquired earlier, the abilities you trained for earlier, the noble principles you imbibed earlier'. Prize books were given which 'are useful and of permanent value and whose aspect

10. German prize book in paper over boards, 1836. Demosthenes, *Opera*, 4 vols, Leipzig, 1829. Munich, BSB, A.gr.b.1140m.

and use will recall to them [the pupils] the school's satisfaction with their hard work and good behaviour and the hope it placed on the progress of their intellectual and moral development'. And he handed them the books with the almost liturgical words: 'Accept this reward herewith with my most deeply felt wishes, my highest expectations'.[41]

In Austria the same tradition seems to have been in vogue. There is a prize binding recorded from 1752 and prize giving was going on in the nineteenth century. The school director in Bruck an der Leitha, Lower Austria, Joseph Bernhard Beichel (1767–1835) wrote a popular novel stating on the title-page, surely as a kind of publicity, that it was suitable as a prize book.[42]

5. Switzerland

In Switzerland it was also the habit to give prizes, ever since the sixteenth century. As stated already, Jean Calvin accepted this model from Joannes Sturmius in Strasbourg. Although the custom is found throughout the whole of the continent, it appears that in Switzerland, both in the Roman Catholic and in the Protestant cantons, mainly medallions and medals were given as prizes, although books were not wanting. This custom remained in vogue until well into the twentieth century.

In the Jesuit college in Lucerne, for example, which was founded between 1574 and 1577, prizes continued to be presented at a solemn ceremony preceded by a dramatic performance, in the same way as had happened in 1579. In 1673 the medals were abolished and only books were given, evidently to the annoyance of pupils and parents, for in 1682 the 'silverlings' were reintroduced. When handing over the prize the head of the school or the form master read a suitable epigram, a habit reminiscent of the written *ex-praemios* in the Southern Netherlands.

This may not have been the same everywhere, but it looks nevertheless as if this was a representative pattern for the whole of Switzerland. In Basle also medals were given, but mainly books, prints and school materials were presented. The school order of 1766 prescribed that they had to be useful but 'not over-expensive books' which could further vary per class and per subject. But it is obvious that also in Switzerland leather-bound books were given, their covers decorated with gold tooling and with gilt edges. The prints that were given could be the portraits of scholars, or maps, etc.[43]

11. Engraved *ex-praemio* of the Metropolitan School in Copenhagen, dated 1930.

6. Scandinavia (Denmark)

No prize books are known from Scandinavia before the nineteenth century. What is certain is that prize books were given during that century and that the *ex-praemios* were handwritten, ready printed or engraved and were sometimes related to a supplying bookshop. Prize bindings as such are not known. The books were supplied by the bookshop and the *ex-praemio* was inserted. This *ex-praemio* could also be a kind of diploma which was not attached to the book and was also larger. A visit to a little antique shop showed that such *ex-praemio* diplomas might at times have been framed.

The girls' school founded in Copenhagen by Ingrid Jespersen (1867–1938) in 1891–92 had a large oak in the middle of the schoolyard and that is why the oak is shown on the *ex-praemio*.[44] The Metropolitanskolen was founded as a Latin (Grammar) school around 1209. A history of it was published in 1916. From that time onward this book was given out as a prize with the formula that after the decease of the former pupil this book should be bequeathed to the Old Boys Association to be given as a prize again, and so on.[45]

7. Great Britain and Ireland (Dublin)

a. Great Britain

In Britain, just as in Germany, the Reformation disrupted the structure of education considerably, but here the school system recovered only with difficulty. In England many grammar schools either disappeared or continued a starved existence with depleted funds, and the state hesitated to intervene in educational affairs as they were regarded entirely as the concern of voluntary or private enterprise. The confusion of social life under George I (1660–1727) and George II (1683–1760) could not lead very easily to any improvement. This was further exacerbated by the slow transition from an agricultural state to a leading position as an industrial nation. At the beginning of the nineteenth century the tide began to turn gradually and government bodies started to organise the educational system.

Against this background it is easy to understand that up to 1800 Britain hardly had any prize books, though the idea of emulation was present in such an influential work as Thomas Elyot's (*c.* 1490–1546) *The Boke named the governour* (1531), that also dealt with rewards of merit in one way or another, an idea emphasised by John Brinsley (1585–1665) in his *Ludus literarius* (1612). With the revival of

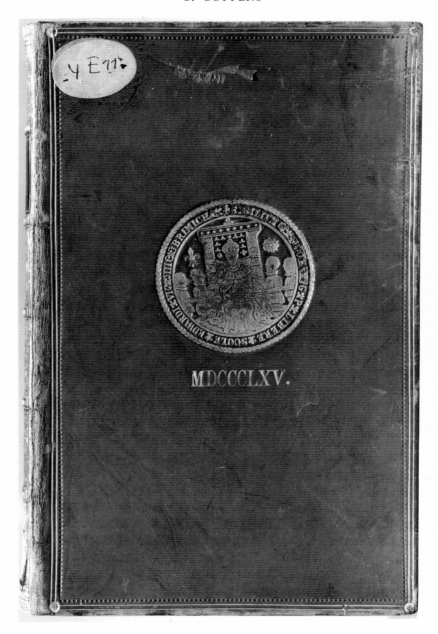

12. Prize book given in the King Edward VI School, Birmingham, to James Crop,
later Vicar of Sturminster Marshall, Dorset, as a prize for mathematics in 1865.
Quintus Horatius Flaccus, *Opera omnia*, London, 1853, 8°.
Leuven, University Library, A1309.

education, the improvement of existing schools and the creation of new ones, and with the Emancipation Act (1829) which helped to bring about greater differentiation and competition and which opened the way to influences from the continent, a new wind blew through the British school system and a phenomenon like the prize book could take firm root and stay vigorous at least until the nineteen-thirties.[46]

The earliest recorded prize book from England dates, as far as is known, from 1785 and was awarded at Trinity College, Cambridge to a Bachelor of Arts. It is a 1783 edition of the New Testament in Greek. This prize is due to a private initiative, a bequest by the Reverend Richard Walker (1679–1764) 'to one or more Scholars of the said College, as shall appear to them (being the Master, Vice-Master, and Senior Dean) best deserving for *regular Behaviour and Proficiency in their Studies*, when they offer in the College for their Grace to proceed Bachelor of Arts. In Trust the said Electors shall dispose of the said Annuity in Money or Books, as they shall judge best for encouraging other Scholars in those Qualifications'.[47]

During the nineteenth century Oxford and Cambridge gave prize books for local examinations to test students who applied for admission. There are surviving prize books from all over Britain right from the beginning of the nineteenth century, until well into the twentieth. The classic British prize book is bound in pale calf, and is decorated with the school coat of arms, a simple border along the edges and with an evenly decorated spine. The arms are quite often lacking and the decoration can now and then be somewhat more elaborate, but it is a type of binding produced both in industrial binderies and in small shops. The *ex-praemio* is often ready printed, but can also be totally handwritten and contains only the basic data of school, year, pupil and prize, but one or more of these data can be absent. The sort of book that was given covered more or less all fields of printed production, but special editions intended for the market in prize books with all kinds of, far too often ideologically motivated, adaptations for the young of historical, popular scientific, or literary works, are completely absent. The classics are of course present, as well as contemporary and older literature, religious and other history, as for example a *History of Latin Christianity* in nine volumes, a book on physics, one about *Notable shipwrecks*, one about *Insects at home* (1887), given in 1896, or *The Life of an elephant* (1901) given as a Latin prize in 1908.[48]

b. Ireland (Dublin)

In the meantime at Trinity College, Dublin a prize distribution system was established in 1732. It was directly derived from the Jesuit system in France and other countries on the continent, as was stressed by the founder, the Reverend Samuel Madden (1684–1765), who himself preferred to give money instead of books. He thought

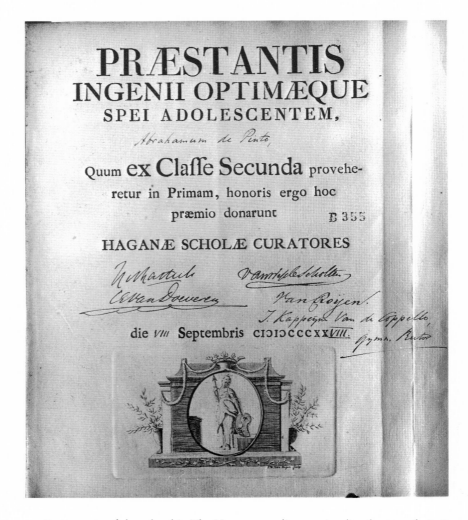

13. *Ex-praemio* of the school in The Hague recording a prize distribution of 1828, on the same pattern as two centuries earlier. Valerius Maximus, *Libri novem factorum dictorumque memorabilium*, Leiden, Samuel Luchtmans, 1726, 4°. Leuven, University Library, B355.

that 'the giving of public testimonials and money would be more beneficial than Presents of books, usual in some Universities, or little honorary marks of Distinction, which are us'd in others'. The prize system was laid down in the statutes. An amount was fixed for the thirteen prizes awarded every term and, Madden's views not withstanding, the Academic Board decided to give 'books of ye most usefull authors and best editions' and to have them lavishly bound for the sons of the 'first Gentlemen' in the Kingdom. This foundation provided well-produced *ex-praemios* and very serious books – no insects or elephants to be found here – dominated by the classics and sometimes printed by the University Press.[49]

8. Holland (The Northern Netherlands)

The best known prize books and the ones most frequently found in the antiquarian booktrade are undoubtedly those from the Northern Netherlands. This profusion is of course not due to chance, but to the large number of prizes that were given and to their uniformity. Like no other prize book, apart perhaps for some French ones, the Dutch prize book has a character all of its own and the organisation of education is responsible for this.

During the fifteenth century many municipal schools in the Northern Netherlands developed into so-called *Grote Scholen* (Great Schools) where Latin was the main subject taught to boys aged seven or eight to about fifteen. The Great Schools enjoyed the protection of the town, in contrast to the private schools, the so-called by-schools. After the Reformation the schools changed their objective. Once the Calvinists had assumed power, the Latin School (grammar school) became an institution preparing its pupils directly for the 'academy' or university.

At the end of the sixteenth century the wish arose in Reformed circles to standardise the educational system. In 1620, after the Synod of Dort, a genuine need was felt to have Calvinist principles embedded in education. In 1623 the States of Holland and West Friesland instructed the Curators of Leiden University to set up a school regulation. The draft was approved and issued by the States on 1 October 1625. The Leiden Curators' expectation that the States of the other Provinces would follow suit did however not materialise. Zeeland for example had already set up its own school regulation in 1583, Friesland had done so in 1588. The Holland school regulation stayed in operation until the time of the French occupation.[50]

14. Typical Dutch prize book, the only one recorded with the coat of arms of Woerden, given between 1762 and *c.* 1780. Eutropius, *Breviarium historiae Romanae*, Leiden, Samuel & Joannes Luchtmans, 1762, 8°. Leuven, University Library, A19040.

Twice yearly prize givings had become the norm in the Latin schools of the Republic from the seventeenth century onwards. For instance, in 1758 fifty-three prizes were allowed according to the regulation at Amsterdam. In the highest class there were three to four ordinary prizes, with on top of these one for diligence, one for Greek and one for Latin verse. These prizes were books in folio format. The next classes received books in quarto and in the lowest class they were octavos. In some schools the population was very limited and classes were rather small by present-day standards. The prize regulation of 1754 for Gouda, for instance, specified that in a class of three pupils two prizes could be awarded. If there were only two pupils in a class, the first of them would still get a prize. Even if the class consisted of only one boy, he deserved a prize as long as he had done his best throughout the six months. That explains why prize books of certain schools are so rare. The pupils had to thank the curators for their prize in Latin with the so-called *Gratiarum actio* or *gratias*. In some places prizes were abolished in the mid-nineteenth century. Although prize giving continued in many schools, and certainly in Catholic ones, the system was past its peak.

Dutch prize bindings are the most characteristic of all. Usually, but not always, they are made of vellum with the slips laced in; the covers are decorated with the municipal arms, as well as with a roll along the edges, and they are usually fitted with linen ties, often in the municipal colours. The binding could also be sewn on cords, and occasionally leather was used as covering material, but this does not change the total aspect.[51]

The yearly turnover of so many prize books was a major focus of the booktrade in Holland, much more so than in other European countries. There was a dedicated production of classical texts intended for this trade. The eighteenth-century Leiden publishers Luchtmans are perhaps the most prominent example. It appears however from a number of copies that German editions on cheap paper were also imported, undoubtedly also in order to reduce the costs of the half-yearly prize distributions. Not only the prize, also the price is of importance here.[52]

EPILOGUE: METHODOLOGICAL PROBLEMS AND POSSIBILITIES

It is clear that the study of prize books opens a very interesting field for bookbinding, as well as for broader book-historical, research. The first difficulty this research encounters is that of finding source material, certainly in a country like Germany where hardly any work has so far been done on prize books. In general it is difficult, if not impossible, to trace examples in libraries where there are no special collections for this material, where provenance indexes are very rare and, if they do exist, cover the collections only very sketchily, and where there is not often a binding index. Moreover the average prize book has attracted only little attention. Even in school museums prize books cannot be found. School textbooks are preserved; few have ever thought of keeping prize books.[53]

Private collections can be of great importance here too. Private collectors have realised that, for instance, for the well-known Dutch prize book a minimum knowledge of educational and school history can teach them much about the rarity and the character of a collectors' item. It is obviously clear that written records and possibly secondary literature are of fundamental importance. Regulations, school histories, theoretical treatises on education, etc. are the best sources for learning how, where and when prize givings took place. A prize book cannot be understood, cannot be 'read', without this background.

Research into prize books offers a particularly interesting angle on the study of bookbinding. In the first place, unless mutilated, they can be dated precisely, as is rarely the case with other bindings. What is more, they are usually not the work of the great and famous binders, but of local craftsmen. Even when these cannot be identified by name this offers a good picture of daily production, from a book-historical point of view often more interesting than the richly decorated bindings of the mighty of this world. Moreover, since the town magistracy generally paid for the books, it is sometimes possible to discover in municipal accounts to whom the work was entrusted. The decoration of the prize bindings, however plain at times, can in turn help with the identification and dating of other bindings from the area.

I have tried to prove that it is obvious that a prize binding is only part of a prize book and that a knowledge of the history of education is needed to understand such an object fully, and I believe that the goal of book history is to widen the field. The prize book offers a wealth of information and is a source of intense enjoyment to many, to the schoolmistress and the historian of education, the genealogist and the bibliophile, the local historian and the antiquarian bookseller, the bibliographer and the book historian, to all those who publicly or privately take pleasure in it. The prize is the proof. But the prize would not be the proof unless it is understood in its wider educational and historical context. The prize books which have come down to us, certainly prove that the system has managed to carry on throughout a tumultuous history of education and has survived quite a few educational revolutions.

Because the intellectual, or rather the intellectualised, culture of the western world represented power, the book could be a point of reference within this society, desirable for the pupil, praiseworthy for the donor. For the pupil the prize book was the proof that he could surpass himself, that he could make the intellectual world his own, that he already had a foot in the door. And if the pupil did not feel this, his parents did. For the school the prize book was the proof of its own prestige in regard to the parents, but also, and no less, in regard to the competition, the other schools. For the donors the prize book was the proof that they contributed to the intellectual culture.

For the educational system based on classical antiquity the prize book was the proof of the justification of the ideal world it created. The prize book throughout the ages has equally been the proof that the child is being brought up to consolidate the existing order and certainly not to think critically. The classical literature contained in the majority of prize books was meant to have little to say, to be rhetorical. The whole intention was to use much rhetoric in order to say nothing, to use much historical show in order not to let anything be seen, and certainly to withhold from the future citizens the frame of reference within which contemporary conditions could be perceived in their true place and therefore critically. Then, as all too often now, education was directed towards reproduction and social conservatism, towards the production of meek followers and not at all of critical minds.

This is the context in which the prize book receives its true interpretation. This is the context which the study of books has to lay bare. The study of books is particularly well placed to undertake this cross-border research precisely because the historical roots of all sciences are confined in books, precisely because books were the vehicles that carried ideas forward or that were, at least, their visible and concrete witnesses.

I will leave open the question exactly what Erasmus meant when he wrote *totum me libris dedo*, but it is really only worth while to dedicate one's life to books if this opens the way to a better understanding of man himself and, as we all know, the study of books can do this exceptionally well.[54] This is moreover the task and the message of every subject of research.

NOTES

1   The basis of this article was Christian Coppens, *De Prijs is het bewijs: vier eeuwen prijsboeken*, Leuven, 1991, but new research has been added. I am very grateful to Dr Anna Simoni for her help with translating this article into English.
2   See e.g. Jean Glénisson, 'Du livre de prix au livre de jeunesse: naissance d'une édition spécialisée' in: Jean Glénisson and Ségolène Le Men (eds), *Le Livre d'enfance et de jeunesse en France*, Bordeaux, 1994, (*Revue française d'histoire du livre*, 63, nos 82–83), pp.13–7.
3   For a general overview of ancient education, see e.g. E. B. Castle, *Ancient education and today*, Harmondsworth, 1961; Stanley F. Bonner, *Education in ancient Rome: from the elder Cato to the younger Pliny*, Berkeley, California, 1977; for Aristotle, see Aristotle, *The 'Art' of rhetoric* (ed. John Henry Freese), Cambridge, Mass./London, 1967, pp. 243–5; for Verrius, see C. Suetonius Tranquillus, *De grammaticis et rhetoribus deperditorum librorum reliquiae* (ed. Karl Ludwig Roth), Leipzig, 1924, pp. 264, (17), 25–30: 'M. Verrius Flaccus libertinus docendi genere maxime claruit. Namque ad exercitanda discentium ingenia aequales inter se committere solebat, proposita non solum materia quam scriberent, sed et praemio quod victor auferret. Id erat liber aliquis antiquus, pulcher aut rarior.'; for Quintilian, see Quintilian, *The Institutio oratoria* (ed. and transl. H. E. Butler), 1, Cambridge, Mass./London, 1989, pp. 30–1 (I, 20).
4   Quintilian, *The Institutio oratoria*, I, 20: '... et rogetur et laudetur et numquam non fecisse se gaudeat, aliquando ipso nolente doceatur alius, cui invideat; contendat interim et saepius vincere se putet ...' (he [the child] must be questioned and praised and taught to rejoice when he has done well; sometimes too, when he refuses instruction, it should be given to some other to excite his envy, at times also he must be engaged in competition and should be allowed to believe himself successful more often than not); see also Erasmus in his *De pueris instituendis* (1529), translated into French (1537), Italian (1545) and English (1551), see J. K. Sowards (ed.), *Collected works of Erasmus: literary and educational writings*, 4. *De pueris instituendis. De recta pronunciatione*, Toronto-Buffalo, New York/London, 1985, p. 340: 'The motives of victory and competition are deeply embedded in our children, and the fear of disgrace and desire for praise are also deeply rooted, especially in children who have outstanding intellectual abilities and energetic personalities. The teacher should exploit these motives to advance their education ... A lazy student should hear his comrades being praised; and a boy who is deaf to his teacher's exhortations will be stirred to action by the desire to emulate his fellows. The palm of victory should not be conferred for good and all, but hope should be held out to the loser that with concentrated effort he may make good his disgrace – this is how commanders exhort their soldiers in war ... In short, by alternating praise and blame, the instructor will awaken in his pupils a useful spirit of rivalry, to use Hesiod's expression' (Hesiod's *Works and days*, pp. 11–2).
5   Francis Bacon, *The Advancement and proficience of learning* ..., Oxford, Leon Lichfield for Robert Young & Edward Forrest, 1640, p. 20, referring to Plutarch in his life of Agesilaus, 'Talis cum sis utinam noster esses'.
6   See Allan P. Farrell, *The Jesuit code of liberal education: development and scope of the ratio studiorum*, Milwaukee, Wisconsin, 1938; Ladislaus Lukacs (ed.), *Ratio atque institutio studiorum Societatis Iesu (1586, 1591, 1599)*, Rome, 1986. See also G. M. Pachtler and Bernhard Duhr, *Ratio studiorum et institutiones scholasticae Societatis Jesu*, 4 vols, Berlin, 1887–1894; Gian Paolo Brizzi, *La 'Ratio studiorum': modelli culturali e practiche educative dei Jesuiti in Italia tra cinque e seicento*, Rome, 1981; C. Labrador, *et al.*, *La 'Ratio studiorum' de los Jesuitas*, Madrid, 1986; *Ratio studiorum: plan raisonné et institution des études dans la Compagnie de Jésus*, édition bilingue latin-français, presented by Adrian Demoustier and Dominique Julia, (transl.

Léone Albrieux and Dolorès Pralon-Julia, ed. Marie-Madeleine Compère), Paris, 1997.

7 Lukacs, *Ratio*, p. 261; see also R. de Scoraille, 'Les Distributions de prix dans les collèges', *Etudes religieuses, philosophiques, historiques et littéraires*, 23 (1879), pp. 269–82, 354–78; J. B. Herman, *La Pédagogie des Jésuites au XVIe siècle: ses sources, ses caractéristiques*, Leuven/Brussels/Paris, 1914, pp. 88–90; François de Dainville, *Les Jésuites et l'éducation de la société française: la naissance de l'humanisme moderne*, 1, Paris, 1940, pp. 148–50.

8 On Jesuit theatre see e.g. William H. McCabe, *An Introduction to the Jesuit theatre* (ed. Louis L. Oldani), Saint Louis, Missouri, 1983, mainly pp. 11–46. On the school theatre in general and the Jesuit theatre in particular, see e.g. L.-V. Gofflot, *Le Théâtre au collège du Moyen Age à nos jours*, Paris, 1907; Raymond van Aerde, *Het Schooldrama bij de Jezuïeten: bijdrage tot de geschiedenis van het toneel te Mechelen*, Mechelen, [1938]; Leonardus van den Boogerd, *Het Jezuïetendrama in de Neder- landen*, Groningen, 1961 (none of the three works mentioned appears in McCabe & Oldani); see also Nigel Griffin, *Jesuit school drama: a checklist of critical literature*, 1 vol. and 1 suppl., London/Wolfeboro, New Hampshire, 1976–1986; Jean-Marie Valentin, *Le Théâtre des Jésuites dans les pays de langue allemande: répertoire chronologique des pièces représentées et des documents conservés (1555–1773)*, 2 vols, Stuttgart, 1983; Louis Desgraves, *Répertoire des programmes des pièces de théâtre jouées dans les collèges en France (1601–1700)*, Geneva, 1986; Jacques R. de Vroomen, *Toneel op school: een historisch en theoretisch onderzoek naar opvattingen over en gebruik van drama in educatie: een wetenschappelijke proeve op het gebied van de letteren*, Nijmegen, 1994. – Prizes were not a free gift but a reward within the educational system, though from the point of view of the donors it was seen as a gift of course, expressed in the formula of the *ex-praemio* 'Ex (liberali) munificentia', 'Ex liberalitate', based on the classics, see Hans Kloft, *Liberalitas principis, Herkunft und Bedeutung: Studien zur Prinzipatsideologie*, Cologne/Vienna, 1970. On gifts see Natalie Zemon Davis, *The Gift in sixteenth-century France*, Madison, Wisconsin, 2000; the author does not deal with prizes but says that 'gifts were used by students to compete with each other, in regard to the amount of food, wine, sweets, and guests' (pp. 47–8).

9 Georges Snyders, *La Pédagogie en France aux XVIIe et XVIIIe siècles*, Paris, 1965, pp. 41–9; Louis Trenard, 'Histoire des sciences de l'éducation (période moderne)', *Revue historique*, 101 (1977), p. 447. See also Michel Foucault, *Surveiller et punir: naissance de la prison*, Paris, 1975, particularly pp. 137–86; Jean de Viguerie, *L'Institution des enfants: l'éducation en France XVIe–XVIIe siècles*, Paris, 1978; Bernard Jolibert, *L'Enfance au XVIIe siècle*, Paris, 1981. On 'ad usum Delphini' see Catherine Volpilhac-Auger et al., *La Collection Ad usum Delphini: l'antiquité au miroir du Grand Siècle*, Grenoble, 2000.

10 Snyders, *La Pédagogie*, p. 81.

11 Gabriel Codina Mir, *Aux sources de la pédagogie des Jésuites: le 'modus parisi- ensis'*, Rome, 1968, pp. 50–3; see also Gian Paolo Brizzi, '"Studia humanitatis" und Organisation des Unterrichts in den ersten italienischen Kollegien der Gesellschaft Jesu' in: Wolfgang Reinhard (ed.), *Humanismus im Bildungswesen des 15. und 16. Jahrhunderts*, Weinheim, 1984, pp. 155–70; Marie-Madeleine Compère, *Du collège au lycée (1500–1850): généalogie de l'enseignement secondaire français*, Paris, 1985, pp. 19–30.

12 Codina Mir, *Aux sources*, pp. 99–109.

13 Codina Mir, *Aux sources*, pp. 109–19, 134–6; on the method of education see also Olga Weijers, *Le Maniement du savoir: pratiques intellectuelles à l'époque des premières universités (XIIIe–XIVe siècles)*, Turnhout, 1996, pp. 39–46 (on the *lectio*), 61–73 (on the *questio*), 77–88 (on the *disputatio*).

14 Codina Mir, *Aux sources*, pp. 151–90.

15 Snyders, *La Pédagogie*, pp. 59–66.

16 Snyders, *La Pédagogie*, pp. 74–83; on Rollin, see Henri Ferté, *Rollin: sa vie, ses œuvres et l'université de son temps*, Paris, 1902; Compère, *Du collège au lycée*, pp. 197–200.

17 *Ratio studiorum*, ed. by Compère, 172 (no. [392]): 'Affigantur carmina scholae parietibus ... additis interdum, non tamen sine rectoris permissu, picturis quae emblemati vel argumento proposito respondeant'.

18 Karel Porteman, *Emblematic exhibitions (affixiones) at the Brussels Jesuit College (1630–1685): a study of the commemorative manuscripts (Royal Library, Brussels)*, Brussels/Turnhout, 1996, in particular pp. 164–7 (and p. 80 for the colour plate); *Idem, Symbolische boekwetenschap of twee vliegen in één klap*, Amsterdam, 1998 (zevende Bert van Selm-lezing); for a comparable emblematic setting, in large gouaches, see Marc van Vaeck and Toon van Houdt, *One in a thousand: ephemeral emblems in the Mechelen Seminarium Archiepiscopale in honour of its president Petrus Dens (1765)*, Leuven, 1996.

19 Jan Spoelder, *Prijsboeken op de Latijnse school: een studie naar het verschijnsel prijsuitreiking en prijsboek op de Latijnse scholen in de Noordelijke Nederlanden, ca. 1585–1876, met een repertorium van wapenstempels*, Amsterdam/Maarssen, 2000, p. 231 and ill. in frontispiece (Delft 1725 and 1728 respectively, engraved by the Leiden engraver Frans van Bleyswyck); see Jean C. Streng, 'The Leiden engraver Frans van Bleyswyck (1671–1746)', *Quaerendo*, 20 (1990), p. 128.

20 Compère, *Du collège au lycée*, ill. 15: on a child's boardgame of *c.* 1800.

21 On French prize books see for instance Charles Hyver, 'Les Agonothètes ou les donateurs de prix à l'Université de Pont-à-Mousson', *Mémoires de la Société Philotechnique de Pont-à-Mousson*, 1 (1874), pp. 103–47; Alfred Hamy, 'Les Prix au collège wallon de Saint-Omer', *Société des Antiquaires de la Morrinie, Bulletin trimestriel*, 10 (1899), pp. 294–306; Frédéric le Guyader, *Catalogue de la bibliothèque de la Ville de Quimper*, 3, Quimper, 1912, pp. 360–1 ('Livres donnés en prix au collège de Quimper par les évêques et autres personnages et reliés aux armes des donateurs'); Jacques Meurgey, 'Quelques livres offerts en prix par le collège de Chalon-sur-Saône au XVIIe siècle: ex-dono Tisserand, Durot, Tapin, Mathieu. L'ex-libris de Jean-François Josse, descendant de Pierre Palliot', *Archives de la Société française des Collectionneurs d'Ex-libris*, 29 (1922), pp. 113–9; Louis Bouland, *Marques de livres anciennes et modernes françaises et étrangères*, Paris, 1925, pp. 10–22 ('Les Agonothètes ou donateurs de prix'); Jacques Meurgey and L. Armand-Calliat, 'Essai d'un catalogue des livres offerts en prix par le collège de Chalon-sur-Saône au XVIIe siècle', *Mémoires de la Société d'Histoire et d'Archéologie de Chalon-sur-Saône*, 24 (1930–1931), pp. 41–82; Fritz Juntke, 'Französische Prämienbände des 17. Jahrhunderts', *Gutenberg-Jahrbuch*, 1959, pp. 291–5; Albert Labarre, 'Anciens livres de prix à la Bibliothèque Municipale d'Amiens', *Gutenberg-Jahrbuch*, 1965, pp. 377–87; *Idem*, 'Livres de prix des collèges parisiens au XVIIe et au XVIIIe siècles', *Gutenberg-Jahrbuch*, 1972, pp. 257–66; Fritz Juntke, 'Über einen französischen Prämienband des 17. Jahrhunderts', *Gutenberg-Jahrbuch*, 1975, pp. 320–2; Albert Labarre, 'Les reliures des anciens livres de prix', *Revue française d'histoire du livre*, 37 (1982), pp. 477–88; Jean Jenny, 'Deux livres de prix de Bourdaloue', *Bulletin du bibliophile*, 1988, pp. 304–15; Dominique Julia, 'Livres de classe et usages pédagogiques' (with 'Annexe. Le livre de prix'), in: Roger Chartier and Henri-Jean Martin (eds), *Histoire de l'édition française*, 2. *Le livre triomphant, 1660–1830*, Paris, 1990, pp. 615–56; Christian Coppens, 'Wanneer een band een andere verbergt: een prijsband uit Arras', *Ex officina: bulletin van de vrienden van de Leuvense Universiteitsbibliotheek*, 6 (1989), pp. 30–46; *Idem, De Prijs is het bewijs: vier eeuwen prijsboeken*, Leuven, 1991, pp. 27–60; Giles Barber, 'Iure ac merito: French prize books of the seventeenth century', *The Bodleian Library record*, 15 (1996), pp. 383–407.

22   The author's translation. On this matter, see Roger Chartier, Marie-Madeleine Compère and Dominique Julia, *L'Éducation en France du XVIe au XVIIIe siècle*, Paris, 1976, pp. 207–8; Compère, *Du collège au lycée*, pp. 169–80.

23   See Snyders, *La Pédagogie*, pp. 345–80; François Lebrun, Marc Venard and Jean Queniart, *Histoire générale de l'enseignement et de l'éducation en France, 2. De Gutenberg aux Lumières*, Paris, 1981, pp. 532–8.

24   See e.g. Maurice Gontard, *L'Enseignement secondaire en France de la fin de l'Ancien Régime à la Loi Falloux (1750–1850)*, La Calade, 1984; on the teaching of history, geography and exact sciences of the Jesuits, see François de Dainville, *L'Éducation des Jésuites (XVIe–XVIIIe siècles)* (ed. Marie-Madeleine Compère), Paris, 1978, pp. 311–533; see also Pierre Costabel (ed.), *L'Enseignement classique au XVIIIe siècle: collèges et universités*, Paris, 1986.

25   Gontard, *L'Enseignement secondaire en France*, pp. 35–60; on the school during the revolutionary period in particular see Dominique Julia, *Les Trois couleurs du tableau noir: la Révolution*, Paris, 1981.

26   On Mame, see Alfred [II] Mame (ed.), *Mame: Angers-Paris-Tours: deux siècles du livre*, Tours/Paris, 1989, with many bindings and prize books reproduced; Sophie Malavieille, *Reliures et cartonnages d'éditeur en France au XIXe siècle (1815–1865)*, Paris, 1985; Jean Glénisson, 'Le Livre pour la jeunesse' in: Roger Chartier and Henri-Jean Martin (eds), *Histoire de l'édition française, 3. Le temps des éditeurs: du Romantisme à la Belle Epoque*, Paris, 1990, pp. 461–89; on the use and ideologisation of history see, for example, Christian Amalvi, 'Les Personnages exemplaires du passé proposés à l'admiration de la jeunesse dans les livres de lecture et de prix de 1814 à 1914', *Revue française d'histoire du livre*, 63, nos 84–85 (1994), pp. 241–58.

27   Christian Coppens, 'Prijsboeken aan de universiteit: de rechtsfaculteit te Caen', *Ex officina: bulletin van de vrienden van de Leuvense Universiteitsbibliotheek*, 9 (1992), pp. 143–51.

28   Francesco Malaguzzi, *Preziosi in biblioteca: mostra di legature in raccolte private piemontesi*, Turin, 1994, pp. 149–53, 156–7, 159–62, 166–8, the Bellarmino (Torino, 1843) mentioned on p. 153, was given as a prize in Carmagnola (Piedmont) (date not mentioned); Idem, *De libris compactis: legature di pregio in Piemonte, 1. Il Canavese*, Turin, 1995, pl. 104 (three prize books issued during the French occupation, 1800–1815, not further identified, but 'Frequenti nelle biblioteche pubbliche piemontesi esemplari di premio risalenti al periodo francese', p. 135); Idem, *De libris compactis: legature di pregio in Piemonte, 2. Il Biellese*, Turin, 1996, pl. 90 (an edition of 1810 also given during the French occupation) and 116 (six prize books from the Seminario de Giuniori in Biella, as before, with the *ex-praemio* tooled on the paper covers of the half leather bindings, dated between 1873 and 1880).

29   Manfred von Arnim, *Europäische Einbandkunst aus sechs Jahrhunderten: Beispiele aus der Bibliothek Otto Schäfer*, Schweinfurt, 1992, pp. 75–6, the magnificently tooled binding contains Livy, *Libri omnes* (ed. Franciscus Modius), Frankfurt, 1588, fol., given as a prize in the Brussels Jesuit college in 1605 by the governors; Luc Duerlo and Werner Thomas (eds), *Albert et Isabella 1598–1621*, Turnhout, 1998, no. 305; see for the earlier provenance of this binding Martin Breslauer, Inc. (Bernard H. Breslauer), *Catalogue 110*, New York, 1992, no. 71; Sotheby & Co, *Catalogue of valuable printed books and fine bindings from the celebrated collection the property of Major J. R. Abbey*, [part I], London, 21–3 June 1965, lot 450 (the Charles Butler copy, sale Sotheby London, 19 March 1912, lot 2592). In general, the 'better binding' in the Southern Netherlands seems to be decorated more often than not with centre- and corner-pieces on a semé, not necessarily of high quality tooling, nor made of very good leather.

30   Coppens, *De Prijs*, pp. 133–96, for prizes in the Southern Netherlands in general, and pp.161–3, for the book given by Barthélémy Louant (d. 1753), Abbot of the Abbey of Aulne in Hainault, which possessed a college in town from 1629 onwards.

The book is: Florent de Cocq, *De jure, justitia et annexis, tractatus quatuor, theologo – canonice expositi*, Brussels, Eugène-Henri Fricx, 1708, 4°. It was given in Trinity College, Leuven, in 1734. See also Paul Culot and Claude Sorgeloos, *Quatre siècles de reliure en Belgique 1500–1900*, 3 vols, Brussels, 1988–1998 (vol. 1, nos. 22–3, 38–9, 96–8; vol. 2, nos. 12–9, 37, 44, 51, 120–1, 133, 158–62; vol. 3, nos. 15–6, 19, 40, 43, 151–7, 159–61).

31   See e.g. Alfred Poncelet, *Histoire de la Compagnie de Jésus dans les anciens Pays-Bas*, 2, Brussels, 1928, pp. 71–3; Ch. van der Vorst, 'Instructions pédagogiques de 1625 et 1647 pour les collèges de la province flandro-belge', *Archivum historicum Societatis Jesu*, 19 (1950), pp. 181–236; on the prescriptions for the augustinian schools, see L. Lamy, 'Les grandes écoles à Bruxelles depuis les origines jusqu'à l'établissement des Jésuites et des Augustins', *Revue de l'Université de Bruxelles*, 30 (1924–1925), pp. 48–64; Norbertus Teeuwen, 'Programma van het Augustijnen-college te Gent in 1643–1645', *Augustiniana*, 2 (1952), pp. 168–80; Amand Vermeulen, 'Zeventiende-eeuws augustijns humaniora-onderwijs in de Zuidelijke Nederlanden', *Annalen van het Thijmgenootschap*, 45 (1957), pp. 94–117; *Zeven eeuwen Augustijnen: een kloostergemeenschap schrijft geschiedenis*, Gent, 1996, pp. 93–100; Goran Proot, 'Het toneel van de Antwerpse Augustijnen (1671–1783)', *De Gulden passer*, 76–77 (1998–1999), pp. 184–294; on the punning on the name see Thomas Delforge, 'Sur trois douzaines de vieux prix', *Les Études classiques*, 31 (1963), pp. 311–7; when the name was not immediately appropriate to pun on, the master made an anagram, as for instance for Joannes Baptista van Bouchautte, 'Bouccautte anagramma tuba vocet' and the verses start with 'Quam tuba pro meriti dederit bene signa triumphi' (1724) (Coppens, *De Prijs*, p. 156); for a Petrus Franciscus Vandermeersch in 1744 there is an 'allusio ad nomen Petri, Latine petra' (*Ibid.*, p. 173).

32   Giovanni Pierio Valeriano, *Pro sacerdotum barbis ... declamatio*, Lyon, for Paul Frelon, 1621, fol.; Idem, *Hieroglyphicorum collectanea*, Lyon, for Paul Frelon, 1626, fol.; Louis de Caseneuve, *Hieroglyphicorum et medicorum emblematum dodeka-krounos*, Lyon, for Paul Frelon, 1626, fol. – Joannes Wiggers (1571–1639), *Commentaria in primam partem Divi Thomae De Deo trino & uno ...*, Leuven, Gulielmus Stryckwant and Brussels, Franciscus 't Serstevens (*in fine* Hieronymus Nempaeus, Leuven, 1676), 1702, fol. and Idem, *Commentaria in primam secundae Divi Thomae Aquinatis*, Leuven, Gulielmus Stryckwant, 1701, fol., given in 1731. François de Salignac de La Mothe Fénelon, *Œuvres complètes*, 11. *Lettres spirituelles*, Toulouse, Jean-Joseph Benichet senior, 1810, 12°, given in 1840. – *Bibliothèque instructive pour les curez et pasteurs chargez du salut des âmes*, Lyon, Société des Libraires, 1725, 4°, given in 1744. Albert, Abbot of Salzburg, *Catalogus: cum historiae compendio abbatum monasterii S. Petri Salisburgi, ex antiquis chronicis ... extractus ab Alberto eiusdem monasterii, anno à Virgine Matre M.DC.XLVII*, Salzburg, Christophorus Katzenberger, 1646, 4°; *Copia instrumenti publici, concernentis resignationem sepulchri, & susceptionem reliquiarum S. Ruperti, factam Anno 1627. 22. Junij (& 9 Julij)*, [Salzburg, 1627?]; *Brevis historia de origine, consecratione, et reparatione speluncae seu Eremitorij, ejusque capellae, in monte prope coemeterium Monasterij S. Petri in civitate Salisburgensi*, Salzburg, Joannes Baptista Mayr, 1661, 4°; *Historia de corpore S. Amandi ... ex antiquis monumentis Monasterii S. Petri collecta*, Salzburg, Joannes Baptista Mayr, 1669, 4°; *Disquisitiones in vitam et miracula Sanctissimi Vitalis ... Episcopi secundi Salisburgensis*, Salzburg, Joannes Baptista Mayr, 1663, 4°; *Relatio historica, de venerando corpore S. Martini Episcopi Turonensis ... Ex antiquis monumentis & scripturis Monasterij S. Petri Salisburgi*, Salzburg, Joannes Baptista Mayr, 1664, 4°. – Valère Regnault, *Praxis fori poenitentialis ad directionem confessarii*, Lyon, Jacques du Creux, alias Molliard for Horace Cardon, 1616, fol. – All books mentioned are described in Coppens, *De Prijs*.

33   Coppens, *De Prijs*, pp. 166–9 (with a book given in 1791, after the Revolution in Liège (1790), when the city took over the college; the whole is in the traditional style with verses alluding to the revolution). The Hieronymite school passed to the Jesuits in 1581. After the abolition of the Jesuits in 1773 the enlighted prince-bishop, Franciscus-Carolus Velbruck (1719–1784) founded his *Grand Collège*. The prince-bishop had to flee with the Revolution in 1790. On the history of Liège during the 16th century, see Paul Harsin, *Etudes critiques sur l'histoire de la Principauté de Liège 1477–1795*, 3 vols, Liège, 1957–1959. On the schools see Léon Halkin, 'Les origines du collège des Jésuites et du séminaire de Liège', *Bulletin de l'Institut Archéologique liégeois*, 51 (1926), pp. 83–190; *Idem*, 'Le collège liégeois des Frères de la Vie Commune' in: Joseph Balon (ed.), *Fédération archéologique et historique de Belgique: XXXIme session: congrès de Namur 1938: annales*, 1, Namur, 1938, pp. 299–311; *Idem*, 'Les Frères de la Vie Commune de la maison Saint-Jérôme de Liège (1495–1595)', *Bulletin de l'Institut Archéologique liégeois*, 65 (1945), pp. 5–70; *Idem*, 'Jean Sturm et le Collège Saint-Jérôme de Liège', *Bulletin de l'Institut Archéologique liégeois*, 67 (1949–1950), pp. 103–10; Marie Delcourt and Jean Hoyoux, 'Documents inédits sur le collège liégeois des Jéronimites (1524–1526)', *Annuaire d'histoire liégeoise*, 25 (1957), pp. 933–79; René Hoven, 'Cicéron, Pline le Jeune et l'enseignement liégeois au début du XVIe siècle', *Leodium*, 53 (1966), pp. 33–41; *Idem*, 'Programmes d'écoles latines dans les Pays-Bas et la Principauté de Liège au XVIe siècle' in: *Acta conventus neo-latini Amstelodamensis: proceedings of the second international congress of neo-Latin studies, Amsterdam 19–24 August 1973*, Munich, 1979, pp. 546–59; *Idem*, *L'Enseignement des humanités au Pays de Liège, de la Renaissance à la Révolution*, Liège, 1983; on prize books see Joseph Brassinne, *La Reliure mosane*, 1, Liège, 1912, nos XL (1613), XLI (c. 1630), XLVbis (1607), XLVter (1608), LVI (1782); Raf van Laere and Andries Welkenhuysen, 'Een Prijsboek van een Hasselts student te Luik (1790)', *Limburg*, 68 (1989), pp. 23–6; *La Reliure parure du livre, du XVe au XXe siècle*, Liège, 1991, no. 14 (the same as Brassine XLVter; an edition of Ingolstadt 1606). – The prize book offered by the German antiquarian bookseller Konrad Meuschel in his catalogue 87 (April 2000), item 4, as a 'Belgian prize book' might rather be German (Cologne(?) or further away, Dillingen(?), the book being an Augustin edition printed in Dillingen by Sebald Mayer in 1571), though I am not sure. It is in any case an exceptional prize book. Dated 1577 on the binding, it is by far the earliest recorded book that, not only was certainly given as a prize, but that has a proper prize binding. The first association of course is a Jesuit connection, and the central block might point to the Bavarian area, though it is maybe too common to be sure. It would be extremely exceptional of course if it did originate in Liège, in 1577 the school still being under the rule of the Brethren. The basic decorative pattern with the ex-praemio tooled on the covers was in use later on in Liège, and books printed in, for example, Ingolstadt were given there. See figure 8.

34   Coppens, *De Prijs*, pp. 134–81 passim, pp. 181–90 on catholic prizes in particular, pp. 190–6 on books given by the government. At least from the beginning of the twentieth century the 'Ligue de l'Enseignement. Union Nationale pour la Défense de l'Enseignement Public', founded around 1865, published a list with 'books for prize distributions and school libraries', ordered by publisher, with some bibliographical information and with the price. Still in 1981 a 'ministerial catalogue of schoolbooks, prize books' etc. was published.

35   Bernard Duhr, *Geschichte der Jesuiten in den Ländern deutscher Zunge*, 6 vols, Freiburg i.B., 1907–1928; Josef Kuchhoff, *Die Geschichte des Gymnasium Tricoronatum: ein Querschnitt durch die Geschichte der Jugenderziehung in Köln vom 15. bis zum 18. Jahrhundert*, Cologne, 1931; Klemens Honselmann (ed.), *Von der Domschule zum Gymnasium Theodorianum in Paderborn*, Paderborn, 1962; Thomas Specht, *Geschichte der ehemaligen Universität Dillingen (1549–1804) und der mit ihr verbundenen Lehr- und Erziehungsanstalten*, Freiburg i.B., 1902.

36   See Max Joseph Husung, 'Über Preis- oder Prämienbände und deren Einband', *Archiv für Buchbinderei*, 27 (1927), pp. 25–6; Ernst Kyriss, 'Bücher als Schulprämien', *Imprimatur*, 12 (1964–1965), pp. 226–8; *Idem*, 'Deutsche Schulprämienbände des 17. und 18. Jahrhunderts', *Archiv für Geschichte des Buchwesens*, 4 (1963), pp. 1581–6.

37   See Wilhelm Roessler, *Die Entstehung des modernen Erziehungswesen in Deutschland*, Stuttgart, 1961; Karl Hartfelder, *Philipp Melanchthon als Praeceptor Germaniae*, Berlin, 1889; Hermann-Adolf Stempel, *Melanchthons pedagogisches Wirken*, Bielefeld, 1979; Jürgen Leonhardt (ed.), *Melanchthon und das Lehrbuch des 16. Jahrhunderts*, Rostock, 1997.

38   See Charles Schmidt, *La Vie et les travaux de Jean Sturm, premier recteur de l'Académie de Strasbourg*, Strasbourg, 1855; Walter Sohm, *Die Schule Johann Sturms und die Kirche Strassburgs in ihrem gegenseitigen Verhältnis 1530–1581: ein Beitrag zur Geschichte deutscher Renaissance*, Munich/Berlin, 1912; Pierre Schang and Georges Livet (eds), *Histoire du Gymnase Jean Sturm: berceau de l'Université de Strasbourg*, Strasbourg, 1988; Lewis William Spitz and Barbara Sher Tinsley, *Johann Sturm on education: the Reformation and humanist learning*, Saint Louis, Missouri, 1995; see also n. 33 and in general also Miriam Usher Chrisman, *Lay culture, learned culture: books and social change in Strasbourg, 1480–1559*, New Haven/London, 1982, especially on Sturm's educational work, see pp. 192–201.

39   *Ratio* (ed. Compere), p. 15; Hermann Paasch, *J. Sturms und Calvins Schulwesen: ein Vergleich*, Diesdorf/Gäbersdorf, 1915.

40   Franz Anton Neuhauser, *Das neue Schulsystem gegen Unwissenheit, Vorurtheile und Stolz bey der feyerlichen Austheilung der Prämien vertheidigt*, Munich, Johann Nepomuk Fritz, 1775, p. 29.

41   Johann Gottfried Gurlitt, *Biographische und literarische Notiz von Johann Winckelmann: bei Gelegenheit des öffentlichen mit einigen Redeübungen verbundenen Examens auf der Schule des Klosters Bergen, dem 28. und 29. September um 2 Uhr*, Magdeburg, Pansaische Buchdruckerey, 1797, in the Bayerische Staatsbibliothek in Munich (4 Diss. 3237.10) bound together with: *Rede von den Pflichten, Freuden und Leiden des Lehrers der Jugend bei Erteilung der Schulprämien und bei Entlassung der zur Academie afgehenden Jünglinge gehalten im Kloster Bergen am 29. September 1797 vom Professor und Director Gurlitt*, Magdeburg, Georg Christian Keil, [1797]:

> So ist es für Lehrer der Jugend Pflicht der Gerechtigkeit das Gute an den Zöglingen willig und mit Freuden anzuerkennen, und diese Anerkennung zuweilen auch öffentlich an der Tag zu legen. Wir thun diess gewöhnlich halb-jährig, durch Ertheilung brauchbarer Bücher von bleibenden Werthe, deren Anblick und Gebrauch Sie, meine theuersten Jünglinge, lebenslang, an unsere Zufriedenheit mit Ihrem Fleisse und Wohlverhalten, und an die Hofnung, die wir auf Ihr Fortschreiten in gelehrter und sittlicher Ausbildung fetzten, erinnern, und zugleich das Bestreben in Ihnen rege erhalten solle, diese unsere angenehme Hoffnung, diesem unserem sehnlichsten Wunsch mit möglichster Kraft-Anstrengung zu erfüllen (pp. 9–10)

He continues to say that because of the good results for drawing, prints will be given as prizes for this subject. He concludes that 'dann die Zeit komme, wo Sie, sei es als Gelehrte, als Geschäftsmänner oder als Krieger [!], mit den früher erworbenen Kentnissen, mit den früher geübten Kräften, mit den früher eingesogenen edlen Grundsätzen und grossen Gesinnungen, des Guten viel, recht viel Stiften können' (p. 11). From 1778 onwards Gurlitt was a teacher and, from the following year, also the director of the convent school of Bergen close to Magdeburg.

42   Ernst Kyriss, 'Oesterreichischer Schulprämienband von 1752', *Gutenberg-Jahrbuch*, 1973, pp. 436–8, a prize given at the school of the Benedictine Abbey of

Kremsmünster, being Franciscus Wagner, *Historia Josephi I Caesaris*, Vienna, 1746, fol., in a richly tooled binding with the arms of the Abbot; Joseph Bernhard Beichel, *Georg Treumuth, der österreichische Robinson: ein Volksbuch zur nützlichen Unterhaltung und zur Erweckung guter Gesinnungen, auch zu Prämien für die fleissige und wohlgesittete Jugend* ... Zweyte umgearbeitete Auflage, Vienna, Im Verlage der Aloys Doll'schen Buchhandlung, 1827 (not in Reinhard Stach and Jutta Schmidt, *Robinson und Robinsonaden in der deutsprachigen Literatur: eine Bibliographie*, Würzburg, 1991); see also Ulrich G. Herrmann, *Sozialgeschichte des Bildungswesen als Regionalanalyse: die höheren Schulen Westfalens im 19. Jahrhunderts*, Cologne/Weimar/Vienna, 1991.

43   See Albert Meier and Gottfried Häusler, *Die Schulprämien der Schweiz*, Hilterfingen, 1991, particularly p. 9:

> Lange bevor Medaillen abgegeben wurden, verlieh man an den meisten Orten Bücher als Schulprämien. In Solothurn handelte es sich um Unterrichtsbücher, kleine Andachtsschriften, lateinische Lehr- und Übungsbücher, ganz oben in der Schule um Werke griechischer und römischer Klassiker in Leder gebunden, mit geschmackvoller Deckpressung und Goldschnitt versehen. Wir gehen sicher nicht fehl, wenn wir annehmen, dass es an den meisten Schulen so gehalten wurden.
>
> In der Regel waren die Bücher seitens des Spenders, der Behörde zum Beispiel, gekennzeichnet und trugen auf der vordern Deckelinnenseite ein eingeklebtes Blatt, das auch den Namen des Preisträgers enthielt. In einer Sammlung fanden wir ein in Halbleder gebundenes schmuckes Büchlein "Schweizerischer Ehrenspiegel", gedruckt zu Bern 1828, das als eingeklebte Widmung unter dem Bernerwappen die Worte trägt: "Geschenk des Kirchen- und Schulrathes der Stadt und Republik Bern an Elisabeth Hostettler als Belohnung für seinen Fleiss und Wohlverhalten".
>
> Nach Abschaffung der Medaillenauszeichnung kehrte man vielerorts wieder zur Bücherabgabe zurück, bis man, meist, noch im letzten Jahrhundert, auf jegliche Preise verzichtete und allen Schülern einen kleinen Geldbetrag, – im Kanton Bern Examenbatzen genannt, – ausrichtete, wobei für die Höhe des Betrages nicht die Leistungen massgebend waren, sondern die Zahl der zurückgelegten Schuljahre.

See also pp. 93–4 for books as prizes. For a prize given in the primary school of Geneva in 1922 (Alphonse Daudet, *Le Petit Chose: histoire d'un enfant*, Paris, n.d.), see Malaguzzi, *Preziosi*, p. 169, a publisher's binding with gold-blocking with a floral motif and the word 'PRIX'. On prize medals in general, see Herbert J. Erlanger, *Origin and development of the European prize medal to the XVIIIth century*, Haarlem, 1975.

44   On Jespersen, see Vagn Skovgaard-Petersen, 'Jespersen, Ingrid', in: *Dansk biografisk leksikon*, 7, Copenhagen, 1981, pp. 370–1, her father was a book-dealer.

45   C. A. S. Dalberg and P. M. Plum, together with Axel Sørensen, J. Østrup, H. U. Ramsing and N. P. Plum, *Metropolitan skolen gennem 700 aar*, Copenhagen, 1916. I am grateful to Mr Christian Glenstrup of the Dansk Skolemuseum, Copenhagen for this information.

46   See e.g. H. C. Barnard, *A short history of English education from 1760 to 1944*, London, 1947; S. J. Curtis, *History of education in Great Britain*, London, 1950; M. L. Clarke, *Classical education in Britain 1500–1900*, Cambridge, 1959; Patience Hunkin, *Enseignement et politique en France et en Angleterre: étude historique et comparée des législations relatives à l'enseignement en France et en Angleterre, depuis 1789*, Paris, 1962; W. H. G. Armytage, *Four hundred years of English education*, Cambridge, 1965; Nicholas Hans, *New trends in education in the eighteenth century*, London, 1966; R. J. W. Selleck, *The New education: the English background 1870–1914*, Melbourne, 1968; Michalina Vaughan, *Social conflict and educational change*

in England and France 1789–1848, Cambridge, 1971; Malcolm Seaborne, *The English school: its architecture and organisation 1370–1870*, London, 1971; Brian Gardner, *The Public schools: an historical survey*, London, 1973; Rosemary O'Day, *Education and society, 1500–1800: the social foundations of education in early modern Britain*, London/New York, 1982.

47 William B. Todd, *Prize books: awards granted to scholars 1671–1935 in the schools and colleges of England, Scotland, Wales, Ireland, France, Holland, Luxemburg*, Austin, Texas, 1961, no. 98 (an exhibition based mainly on Todd's collection).

48 Todd, *Prize books*, nos 36, 29, 51, 90 and 60 respectively: Henry Hart Milman, *History of Latin Christianity*, 9 vols, London, 1872, given in Rugby School, Warwickshire (no date given); Adolphe Ganot, *Elementary treatise on physics*, London, 1893, given at Christ's Hospital, Sussex, in 1893; Uncle Hardy (i.e. William Senior), *Notable shipwrecks*, London, 1873, given in the grammar school of Monmouth in 1877, as a gift of the Haberdashers' Company; J. G. Wood, *Insects at home*, London, 1887, given at Eton in 1896 to Leopold Reginald ('Rex') Hargreaves (1883–1916), son of Alice Pleasance Liddell (1852–1934), the Alice of *Alice in Wonderland*; *The Life of an elephant*, 'by the author of "The Life of a Bear"' (translated from the French?), London, 1901, given in Colwall Grammar School, Herefordshire, in 1908 as a prize for Latin. See also Coppens, *De Prijs*, pp. 70–7. An obviously remarkable prize book was offered for sale in 2001, see Andrew Stewart, *Catalogue 58*, Helpringham, Lincolnshire, 2001, no. 68: Demosthenes and Aeschines, *Opera*, Frankfurt, Claude de Marne & heirs of Johann I Aubry, 1604, fol., 'c19th crushed morocco prize binding of Saint Paul's School, London (prize awarded to Edward Howes), details of prize lettered on upper cover surrounded by elaborate gilt and floral rules, lower cover with the bust of John Colet surrounded by elaborate gilt and floral rules'. – It might be noted here that prize giving has a tradition in the United States as well, brought there by emigrants from the British Isles and Ireland, such as the Puritans, see Patricia Fenn and Alfred P. Malpa, *Rewards of merit: tokens of a child's progress and a teacher's esteem as an enduring aspect of American religious and secular education*, Charlottesville, Virginia, 1994, mostly ephemera (published by the Ephemera Society of America) and medals, but also some books.

49 Joseph McDonnell and Patrick Healy, *Gold-tooled bookbindings commissioned by Trinity College Dublin in the eighteenth century*, Leixlip, Co. Kildare, 1987, for Madden, see pp. 14–23. See also pp. 227–9 below.

50 Petrus Nicolaas Maria Bot, *Humanisme en onderwijs in Nederland*, Utrecht/Antwerpen, 1955; H. W. Fortgens, *Schola Latina: uit het verleden van ons voorbereidend hoger onderwijs*, Zwolle, 1958; Ernst Jan Kuiper, *De Hollandse 'schoolorde' van 1625: een studie over het onderwijs op de Latijnse scholen in Nederland in de 17de en 18de eeuw*, Groningen, 1958; J. G. C. A. Briels, 'Enkele dokumenten betreffende het onderwijs in Noord-Nederland uit het laatste kwartaal der 16de eeuw', *Pedagogische studiën*, 49 (1972), pp. 389–411; Engelina Petronella de Booy, *De Weldaet der scholen: het plattelandsonderwijs in de provincie Utrecht van 1580 tot het begin van de 19de eeuw*, Utrecht, 1977; *Idem, Kweekhoven der wijsheid: basis- en vervolgonderwijs in de steden van de provincie Utrecht van 1580 tot het begin der 19de eeuw*, Zutphen, 1980; H. Q. Röling, 'Onderwijs in Nederland' in: Bernard Kruithof, Jan Noordman and Piet de Rooy (eds), *Geschiedenis van opvoeding en onderwijs: inleiding, bronnen, onderzoek*, Nijmegen, 1982, pp. 66–86; Willem Frijhoff, 'Van onderwijs naar opvoedend onderwijs: ontwikkelingslijnen van opvoeding en onderwijs in Noord-Nederland in de achttiende eeuw' in: *Onderwijs & opvoeding in de achttiende eeuw: verslag van het symposium, Doesburg 1982*, Amsterdam/Maarssen, 1983, pp. 3–39; R. Bastiaanse, H. Bots and M. Evers (eds), *'Tot meesten nut ende dienst van de jeught': een onderzoek naar zeventien Gelderse Latijnse scholen ca. 1580–1815*, Zutphen, 1985; Jan Lenders, *De Burger en de volksschool: culturele en mentale achtergronden van de onderwijshervorming, Nederland 1780–1850*, Nijmegen, 1988.

51   Isak Collijn, 'Hollandsche prijsboeken uit de 17de en de 18de eeuw', *Tijdschrift voor boek- en bibliotheekwezen*, 5 (1907), pp. 220–4; J. P. W. A. Smit, *Prijsbanden: een toelichting op een onderdeel van de tentoonstelling van werken uit de Fabri-bibliotheek gehouden van 13 februari tot 20 maart 1964 in het Museum van het Boek te 's-Gravenhage*, 's-Gravenhage, 1964; Jan Spoelder, 'Prijsboeken op de Latijnse scholen', *Spiegel historiael*, 16 (1981), pp. 386–91; David Pearson and Richard Ovenden, 'Dutch prize bindings in Durham libraries', *Quaerendo*, 17 (1987), pp. 148–56; A. R. A. Croiset van Uchelen, 'Over een gegraveerde prijs' in: *Het oude en het nieuwe boek, de oude en de nieuwe bibliotheek* (Festschrift H. D. L. Vervliet), Kapellen, 1988, pp. 225–33; Jan Spoelder, 'Trotse trofeeën, een collectie prijsboeken in Teylers Museum', *Teylers Museum: magazijn*, 22 (1989), pp. 7–12; Jan Storm van Leeuwen, 'Some very early Dutch Prize Bindings', *Quaerendo*, 28 (1998), pp. 128–40; Jan Spoelder, *Prijsboeken op de Latijnse school: een studie naar het verschijnsel prijsuit-reiking en prijsboek op de Latijnse scholen in de Noordelijke Nederlanden, ca. 1585–1876, met een repertorium van wapenstempels*, Amsterdam/Maarssen, 2000, the definitive work on Dutch prize books. It is striking that the author in a general chapter about the phenomenon denies that it is based on the *modus parisiensis* which is based in turn on the education of the Brethren of the Common Life, without giving a serious reason for his denial. It is the more unbelievable as all the literature concerned explains the phenomenon of prize books in this way.

52   On Luchtmans, see *Luchtmans & Brill: driehonderd jaar uitgevers en drukkers in Leiden 1683–1983*, Leiden, 1983.

53   There is the collection of William Burton Todd (b. 1919) in Texas, already mentioned; there are the collection of the educationist Franz Pöggeler (b. 1926) at the Rheinisch-Westfälische Technische Hochschule, Aachen, and that in the Bavarian School museum in Ichenhausen. There are some smaller collections, and for Dutch prize books, for example, there are many private collections. On the Todd collection, consisting of some 900 items, see William B. Todd, 'Academic prize books', *The Book Collector*, 49 (2000), pp. 442–4.

54   Erasmus in a letter from Paris to James Batt (*c.* 1466–1502) near Bergen op Zoom, Zeeland, The Netherlands, 2 May 1499, P. S. Allen (ed.), *Opus epistolarum Des. Erasmi Roterodami*, 1, Oxford, 1906, p. 234 (Ep. 95).

1

2

3

4

1. Four examples showing the centre-piece style at various levels of sophistication:
1) *Orationes clarorum hominum*, Venice, 1559, bound in Oxford (Balliol College,
Oxford, 650.b.1); 2) R. Hospinianus, *Concordia discors*, Zurich, 1607, bound in
Oxford (Balliol College, 540.b.10); 3) J. White, *The Way to the true church*,
London, 1612, bound in London (author's collection); 4) *Biblia Sacra*, Antwerp,
1599, bound in London (Emmanuel College, Cambridge, S.1.4.36).

ENGLISH CENTRE-PIECE BOOKBINDINGS

1560–1640

David Pearson

AT THE END of the sixteenth century and the beginning of the seventeenth, the most popular style for decorating English bookbindings made use of large single stamps placed at the centres of the boards, commonly described as centre-pieces.

A centre-piece binding may be defined as one whose principal decorative feature is a single stamp, of abstract design, placed in the centres of the covers. The stamps employed were usually oval or lozenge shaped, or a cross between the two, and they incorporated elaborate designs of interlacing strapwork. The designs were always symmetrical – if sliced in half either vertically or horizontally, the resulting halves are mirror images – although the engraved tools themselves rarely achieved such mathematical perfection in practice. Most of the stamps used in England varied in size from about one inch to about five inches from top to bottom, although a few were even larger. Centre-pieces are found on both leather and vellum bindings, tooled either in blind or in gold, and additional decoration may or may not be present. The simplest centre-piece bindings have a blind-tooled centre-piece, blind fillets round the perimeters of the covers, and correspondingly basic spine decoration. The most elaborate may have a gilt centre-piece and corner-pieces – large ornaments placed at the four corners of the frame, with a design often allied to that of the centre-piece – as well as all-over gilt decoration on boards and spine, using small tools and rolls. In between these extremes, a common decorative pattern makes use of two or three rectangular frames of fillets on the covers, with a centre-piece in the middle and small fleurons or similar tools at the corners of the inner frame or frames. Fig. 1 illustrates these standard possibilities and the progression from the simple to the elaborate. The centre-piece style was applied across a wide spectrum of binding work, from school books to presentation copies for the nobility. Individual tools are found on bindings of varying degrees of sophistication, and it is not unusual to find a particular tool applied sometimes in blind and sometimes in gold.

This style of decoration originated in medieval Islamic culture in the middle east, and it can be found there as early as the thirteenth century.[1] It has long been recognised that European Renaissance bookbinding was influenced in both style and technique by Islamic practice, and that the centre-piece style spread to Europe through Venice and the Italian trading ports in the second half of the fifteenth century.[2] Its popularity in Europe took off in the middle of the sixteenth century, and it came to England around 1560, after which it became the most common decorative style for the remainder of the century. Older catalogues sometimes refer to centre-piece bindings as the 'Lyon' or 'Lyonese' style of binding, reflecting the notion that it was developed in Lyon, but this is erroneous and misleading, and the term should be dropped from the vocabulary of binding literature.[3] The centre-piece style was used all over Europe in the late sixteenth century and examples can be found from many countries.[4]

Other styles, using smaller tools, began coming into vogue in English binding early in the seventeenth century, but centre-pieces continued in common use well into the 1620s, gradually declining thereafter through the 1630s. By 1640 centre-pieces had effectively fallen out of use, and their employment by English binders is extremely uncommon thereafter, until the nineteenth century. The basic idea of dominating the decoration of boards with a large central pattern is of course a feature of many seventeenth- and eighteenth-century bindings, made after centre-pieces ceased to be fashionable, but the central decoration came to be made up of many small tools rather than one large one, without the arabesque flavour which dominates the centre-pieces of the Elizabethan and Jacobean periods.[5] A noteworthy phenomenon, outside the scope of this essay but deserving further study, is the use of large centre-piece designs on nineteenth-century bindings, which are exact replicas of sixteenth-century stamps. The vellum bindings on William Pickering's facsimiles of early prayer books have bindings like this, but there are many examples of nineteenth-century gold-blocked cloth bindings, on books with no apparent sixteenth-century connection, which make use of centre-piece designs.[6]

Despite the importance of the centre-piece style in English bookbinding history, it has never received the systematic study devoted to the preceding generations of bindings. The rolls, panels and stamps of the earlier sixteenth century have been thoroughly documented by Oldham and others, but the literature on centre-pieces is scanty. The most extensive survey is that begun by Neil Ker as part of his work on manuscript fragments used as paste-downs in Oxford bindings, and the recently published supplement to his 1954 *Pastedowns* illustrates sixty centre-pieces used there, but this deals only with Oxford.[7] Cambridge has been less thoroughly surveyed, with nineteen centre-pieces used there reproduced in a brief overview of late sixteenth-century Cambridge binding published in 2000.[8] London, where more centre-piece tools were used than anywhere else, remains largely uncharted territory. Howard Nixon published a short lecture in 1963 which covers the centre-piece style in a very summary way, and his article on Elizabethan gold-tooled bindings in the 1970 Scholderer festschrift is relevant, but deals only with the top end of the market.[9] A number of centre-piece bindings are included in the Henry Davis Gift, as documented by Mirjam Foot, and some information will be found in the numerous published studies and exhibition catalogues which cover English binding over a wide time span, but all this represents a scattered body of work and there is always a tendency to concentrate on the output of a few leading workshops.

Although the use of centre-pieces became the dominant decorative fashion in English bookbinding in the last quarter of the sixteenth century, it is important to stress that it was never the only style in use. Roll-decorated bindings, which began to be produced in England around 1500, continued to be made throughout the sixteenth century, and well into the seventeenth.[10] Rolls and centre-pieces were sometimes used together, with the centre-piece placed at the focus of a rectangular frame made with a roll, but this was never a common practice. Throughout this period there was a growing call for armorial bindings, incorporating the arms of the owner, but in terms of decorative style these are closely related to centre-piece bindings, with an armorial stamp taking the place of the centre-piece.[11] Centre-pieces were used on many cheap and utilitarian bindings, including school books and university text books. Completely plain leather bindings, decorated only with fillets round the borders, were uncommon before about 1600, but became very common during the first half of the seventeenth century. It must also be remembered that many books circulated during this period in more temporary bindings, merely stab-stitched, without boards, or bound in undecorated limp vellum, although such bindings survive today in unrepresentatively small quantities. J. J. Hall has pointed out that Peterborough Cathedral Library, rich in STC material gathered by White Kennett in the early eighteenth century and relatively untouched by rebinding since, offers great potential for studying the simpler English binding styles of the sixteenth and seventeenth centuries.[12] In the course of working through 400 books from that collection with imprints between 1560 and 1640 it was found that 155 – over a third – have contemporary plain limp vellum covers.

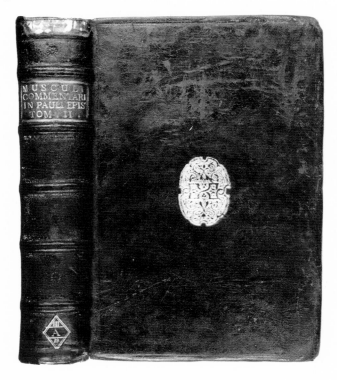

2. A Cambridge centre-piece binding, *c.* 1570–75. W. Musculus, *In epistolas ... Pauli ad Galatos et Ephesios*, Basle, 1569, fol. Durham University Library, Bamburgh A.III.19.

Fig. 2 shows an example of a simple and straightforward centre-piece binding, typical of many thousands which were produced at the time, on a folio biblical commentary by Musculus, printed in Basle in 1569 and bound in Cambridge *c.* 1570–75.[13] The title label and the label at the foot of the spine are not contemporary, but are later additions. The book is bound using coarse grey pasteboards covered in dark brown calf, and the covers are decorated only with a gilt oval centre-piece and a three-line blind fillet round the perimeter. The spine has five raised bands and is decorated with blind fillets above and below the bands, and a small flower-head tool applied in each of the compartments, originally in gold which has now rubbed off.

There are no paste-downs, but two separate flyleaves, cut from leaves of an earlier sixteenth-century printed legal text, sewn in by folding them together at one side leaving two small paper stubs on one side of the fold. The structure is strengthened by wrapping a parchment stub round the flyleaves and their stubs, in this case a small fragment from a thirteenth-century manuscript biblical commentary. The endleaf construction clearly invites the pasting down of the outer flyleaf at each end, to give a paste-down and a single flyleaf rather than two flyleaves, but this was often not done in bindings like this.

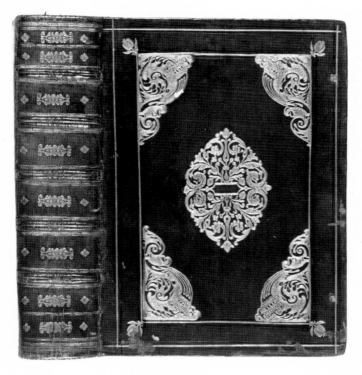

3. A London centre- and corner-piece binding, *c.* 1605. J. Mariana,
Historiae de rebus Hispaniae libri XXX, Mainz, 1605, 4to.
John Rylands University Library, 10921.

Fig. 3 is an illustration of a slightly later centre-piece binding, and also a more elaborate one, from the first decade of the seventeenth century, on a quarto book printed in Mainz in 1605 and bound in London shortly thereafter. Here the book is bound in pasteboards covered in mid-brown calf, and the covers are decorated not only with a gilt centre-piece, but also with gilt corner-pieces and small pomegranate ornaments placed at the inner of two frames of three fillets (blind-gold-blind). The cornucopia design of the corner-pieces was a popular one, in use throughout the centre-piece period, and many variants are known. The spine has five raised bands, decorated with gold-tooled ornaments in the compartments, gilt fillets across the bands, and a narrow roll at either side of the bands, and at the head and tail. A gold-tooled roll (of continuous diamonds) is run round the edges of the boards, and the edges of the leaves are gilt and gauffered. The remains of pink cloth ties survive. The endleaf construction is similar to that of the 1569 Musculus, but here the outer leaf is pasted down, plain white paper is used, and there are no parchment strengthening stubs.

The observations and generalisations about centre-piece bindings made here are based on evidence which has been gathered by working round college, cathedral, university and other libraries, with a view to recording systematically all the English centre-piece bindings they contain. Beside taking rubbings, standard practice has been to note the colour and nature of the leather used, the decoration of covers, spine and edges, the endbands, the nature and construction of the endleaves, and other physical characteristics. I currently have details of this kind of well over 3000 centre-piece bindings although many thousands more survive in libraries and private collections all over the world.

Most of the centre-piece bindings produced in England were constructed of leather over pasteboards, which were usually made from layers of coarse grey-brown paper pasted together. Boards made up from printers' waste or dismembered books are very rarely encountered. Wooden boards were still occasionally used for large books, but they are very much the exception rather than the rule after the middle of the sixteenth century. Centre-pieces were sometimes used to decorate vellum bindings, usually vellum over boards or more rarely limp vellum, but these account for only about 3% of the 3000 or so I have examined. Turkey leather (i.e. tanned goatskin) was used for some of the finest bindings at the top end of the market, but the great majority of centre-piece bindings made in England used tanned calfskin. Occasionally, books bound in sheep were decorated with centre-pieces, but survivals today are few and far between. The use of sheep at this time was subject to Stationers' Company regulations, as it was cheaper than calf but poorer in quality, and there are references in the Court Books to tradesmen being fined for binding large books in sheep, contrary to order.[14] Very dark brown calf is a characteristic feature of books bound in the latter half of the sixteenth century, and, looking across the whole period 1560–1640, a tendency towards lighter brown or sprinkled leathers is a noticeable trend after the turn of the seventeenth century. This is not to suggest that dark brown calf was not used in the 1620s or that light brown is not found in the 1570s, rather that there was a discernible shift in taste or popularity.

Books were normally sewn on supports of tanned or tawed leather, and spines usually had raised bands, although the use of recessed thongs or canvas padding to produce smooth spines is also found throughout the centre-piece period, often on finer bindings. End-bands were commonly, but not invariably, made with thread of two colours, sewn round a narrow strip of leather and tied down into the gatherings. The simplest bindings have no decoration on the spine save for blind fillets around the bands, and possibly strips of blind hatching at head and tail; more elaborate bindings have the spine compartments decorated with varying degrees of sophistication in blind or, more commonly, in gold. The earliest known English binding to have the title tooled directly on the spine in gold-tooled letters dates from the 1560s, but this is an isolated example and the next recorded case is a centre-piece binding of 1604 by Williamson of Eton.[15] Integral gold-tooled titles of this kind are very uncommon on English bindings of the centre-piece period. During the sixteenth century the edges of the boards were almost invariably decorated with a single blind fillet, although the use of a gilt fillet, or a narrow gold-tooled roll, often showing diamonds or continuous dots, became common in the first and second decades of the seventeenth century.[16] Hatching on the top and tail edges of the boards, adjacent to the spine – usually a short series of diagonal lines, in blind – is commonly found on books the board-edges of which are otherwise decorated with a blind fillet. This feature was commented on by Strickland Gibson and by Oldham, with particular reference to the Oxford practice of hatching the edges of the boards with a series of diagonal lines, terminated by one or more horizontal lines drawn at right angles to the length of the boards. Oldham surmised that 'Cambridge hatching on the edges was most commonly a number of diagonal lines running in the same direction, sometimes terminated with a single line drawn straight across, and the termination of the diagonals by *two or more* lines drawn straight across the edge was probably peculiar to Oxford'.[17] Further observations confirm that there is something to be said for this as a rule of thumb – Oxford bindings often do have two or more horizontal lines terminating the diagonal ones – but that the conventions of the time were less clear cut than later bibliographers would like.[18]

The practice of colouring the edges of the leaves of books is very ancient, possibly as old as the codex itself.[19] In the late sixteenth and early seventeenth centuries the most popular colour used on English bindings was yellow, and rather more than a third of the leaves of centre-piece bindings in my sample of 3000 plus recorded to date have yellow edges. Another third have no colouring at all, but a variety of other colouring patterns can be found, most notably green or red. Red and red sprinkled edges are commoner in the seventeenth century than in the sixteenth. On fine bindings the edges of the leaves were often gilt, or gilt and gauffered.[20] Clasps, which are common on early sixteenth-century bindings, are not often found on centre-piece bindings, but ties, almost invariably of green cloth, are much commoner, and at least 35% of the books I have noted originally had green cloth ties.

There are a number of common patterns for endleaf construction in late sixteenth- and early seventeenth-century bindings, and the most frequently encountered ones are described and illustrated by Bernard Middleton in his *History of English craft bookbinding technique*.[21] As a general rule, the finer bindings have a paste-down and one or more flyleaves of plain white paper at each end, but more run-of-the-mill bindings often have flyleaves but no paste-downs, or a double flyleaf construction which invites the pasting down of the outer flyleaf, without this ever having been done. Book structures were commonly strengthened by incorporating strips of parchment around the endleaves. The use of printed and manuscript fragments in the making of endleaves was very common until well into the seventeenth century; Neil Ker pointed out that the use of medieval manuscript fragments as paste-downs was not practised outside Oxford after 1570, but binders in London, Cambridge and elsewhere regularly used strips from manuscripts to strengthen their hinges throughout the centre-piece period. Binders of the late sixteenth and early seventeenth centuries made extensive use of printed waste in constructing endleaves, although overall the use of plain white paper was always commoner, and it became more prevalent as time progressed. The material came from unbound waste sheets of contemporary publications, or from earlier books which were surplus to requirements. Obsolete law books were regularly used, but a wide variety of other material is found. Sometimes, marginal annotation on printed endleaves, which predate the book being bound, make it clear that the fragments themselves were once bound up as books, and were not printers' waste. Very occasionally coarse brown paper was used for endleaves, but this was never a common practice.

My observations to date suggest that the kinds of physical features described here may often be helpful in dating a binding, but more rarely in localising it to a particular place or workshop. To put it the other way round, groups of bindings which presumably are from the same workshop, because they share the same tools but are more or less contemporary in date, do not always display uniformity in other aspects of construction or finishing. This must be partly due to the bespoke element in binding in the hand-press period, and the wishes of individual customers – one notes, for example, that Andrew Perne's books normally have uncoloured edges, that those of Richard Bancroft's books are usually coloured (often brightly, and sometimes elaborately decorated), and that William Branthwaite felt so strongly about edge colouring that he left directions in his will, concerning the books he bequeathed to Gonville and Caius College, that 'the leaves of all the said books shall be cast into one convenient colour'.[22] This is understandable in an age when books were shelved fore-edge outwards, but should we expect customers to be similarly interested in endleaf construction? The Musculus illustrated in fig. 2 is one of about a hundred bindings I have seen which share that same centre-piece, all bound in a workshop associated with John Sheres in Cambridge *c.* 1570–80. Although many of them have identical endleaf construction, many do not; there is variety in the materials used, and in the way they are put together. There are several possible reasons for this, such as customer wishes, the varying availability of materials, the technical requirements of books of differing shapes and sizes, and the consistency of approach (or otherwise) of individual binders. No doubt all these factors play a part, and we should be wary of making simplistic assumptions about the ways in which sixteenth-century binders worked.

The centre-pieces themselves are always based on elaborate arabesque patterns, difficult to describe in words, and are either oval-shaped, lozenge-shaped, or a sort of cross between the two. There is no consistent established terminology which can be applied to them as patterns. The proliferation of lozenge-shaped designs belongs to the second half of the centre-piece period, while ovals are very common up to about 1600, but much less used thereafter. Although it is generally assumed that tools were unique, designs were not, and it

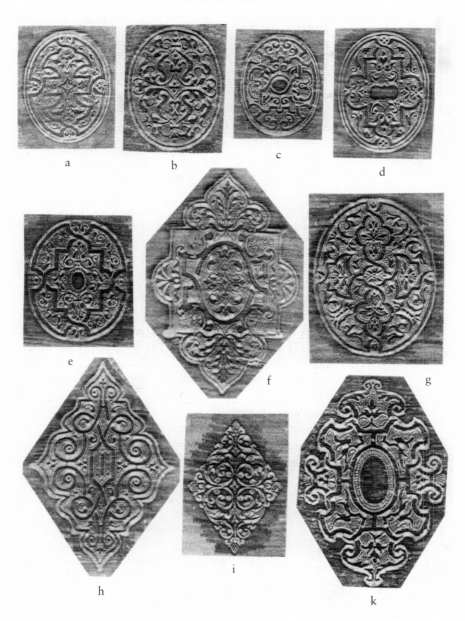

4. Examples of common designs for centre-piece tools.

is common to find a number of different tools based on the same design in use independently, in different workshops or places, over a period of time. They can often be distinguished not only because they are slightly different in shape or size, but also because they have different patterns of hatching or dots in their backgrounds and it is very important, when recording centre-pieces, to note such details carefully. Fig. 4 shows a range of centre-piece designs which were all popular in England, and spawned many individual variants; fig. 5 shows eight different tools based on one particular design. Although they are reduced from full size (each tool is about 70–80 cm high), it should be possible to see that they are all based on the same pattern, but that no two are identical. Number 5 is one of the earliest centre-pieces to be used in England, used in London in the early 1560s by the craftsman who was christened the 'Morocco binder' by Howard Nixon.[23] Numbers 1 and 2 were used in Oxford from about 1570 onwards, and numbers 3, 4 and 8 were used in Cambridge around the same time.[24] Number 7 was probably a London tool, while number 6 was used in Edinburgh around the turn of the seventeenth century, and at least as late as 1615.[25] This is not a complete list of the tools based on this design which were used in Britain.

The systematic classification of bookbinding tools by design is not a subject which has ever received much consideration among British binding historians, although more interest has been shown in the Netherlands.[26] Centre-pieces clearly invite a scientific approach which brings together tools which look similar, along the lines devised by Oldham for sixteenth-century rolls. I have found that a hierarchical classification system for centre-pieces, based first on separation into outline shapes and then on particular characteristics within those shapes can help to make sense of the many hundreds of tools which were in circulation, and that it is possible to identify a little over 150 basic patterns to which most tools can be related.[27]

The study of these bindings provokes a wide series of questions beyond the obvious ones about who bound the books, and when and where. The binders were one element in a network of artisans involved in the booktrade, along with printers and booksellers, but they also constituted links in other trading networks, such as those involved in the production of leather and metalwork. Who designed the bookbinders' tools, and who cut them? Who was responsible for producing the patterns, and where did they come from? We know that the general stylistic concept came first from the Arab world, but the tools which were used to decorate English bindings were not by

5. Rubbings of eight centre-piece tools in use between *c.* 1560 and *c.* 1615.

any means direct imitations of the Islamic originals; they were the fruit of European interpretation and reworking of the artistic idea. In this context it is important to consider bookbindings within the general framework of Renaissance ornament, and not to look at them in isolation. Many continental designers and engravers were busy during the sixteenth century producing arabesque patterns with an Islamic flavour for many branches of the decorative arts – woodwork, ironwork, jewellery and embroidery, for example – and bookbindings form one part of the overall picture.[28] The collections of Moresque designs engraved and published by Balthasar Sylvius in Antwerp in the middle of the sixteenth century, for example, contain a number of circular designs, and one oval one, which are very close in character to centre-pieces.[29] The publication and circulation of material like this clearly helped to create a common currency of design ideas which could be drawn on by individual artists all over Europe. It is well known that pattern books were published from the early sixteenth century onwards, containing designs for executing various types of handiwork, although the survival rate for such material is understandably low. The only English pattern books of the STC period which are still extant are concerned with needlework, although others may have existed.[30] There may once have been pattern books for centre-piece bookbinding tools, although the relatively limited market for binders' tools may have meant that the designs were never engraved to be printed. They must however have been drawn on paper before being executed in metal, and it is highly unlikely that the binders themselves were the designers. The existence of numerous centre-pieces which are variants of the same pattern suggests that tools were sometimes copied from other tools, and many of the designs used in England are also found on the continent, where they will have originated. There does however appear to have been a fertile native industry for creating new designs and amending existing ones, suggesting that most of the tools used in Britain were also made there.[31] The fact that some designs were popular, and copied into numerous different centre-piece tools of varying sizes, while others which are apparently just as aesthetically appealing generated very few variants or none at all, is just one among a series of puzzles that surrounds the production of these tools.

As regards the tools themselves, it is generally believed that they were engraved in brass, and were the work of professional seal-cutters or goldsmiths; the trade in bookbinding tools can never have been more than a sideline among a wider range of trading concerns.

In 1990, Staffan Fogelmark published his stimulating book on Flemish panel-stamped bindings of the fifteenth and early sixteenth centuries, in which he marshalled a great deal of evidence to argue that these panel-stamp tools were more often cast than engraved, suggesting that multiple identical stamps from the same die may have circulated widely in Europe, perhaps being traded at fairs or via other established commercial routes.[32] He has rightly pointed out that, if this is the case, much of the work on bindings of this type published over the last century must be revisited, as the basic assumption that every individual tool is unique and usable only in one place at any one time is overturned. His work does not touch on centre-piece bindings, or on any other bindings of the late sixteenth century, but there are obvious parallels: centre-pieces, like panels, tend to be large tools, widely used across Europe, and if panels can be cast, there seems to be no reason not to suggest that centre-pieces might be cast also.

Fogelmark's arguments regarding panel stamps rest on a number of different categories of evidence, which may be briefly summarised under the headings of nailmarks (apparently identical panel stamps have nailmarks in different places), press-work and alignment (remarkable evenness and accuracy were often achieved when producing bindings with repeated panels side by side), and design (some panels appear to have been produced by stamping smaller hand-tools into a mould). Although these observations are all relevant to panel-stamps, it seems fair to say that they do not apply to centre-pieces, which do not exhibit nailmarks, were always used singly (that is, one per cover), and whose designs do not incorporate smaller tools. The existence of multiple variants of particular centre-piece designs, which can be distinguished because they have different patterns of dots or fine hatching in their backgrounds, suggests that these tools were normally engraved, in line with Fogelmark's observation that 'engraving [of tools] seems to invite background design ... the background is often dotted'.[33] The obvious halfway house would be the production of multiple, variant centre-piece tools by casting from a basic design and then using engraving to finish off the background hatching patterns, but repeated examination of families of tools has hitherto failed to find a set which could be explained like this; the evidence invariably points the other way. This is an area in which we should keep an open mind, particularly as we know so little about the actual routines of the metalworking trades at this time.

The assessment of this question would be greatly helped if surviving centre-piece tools could be examined, but they are not to be found.

The only bookbinding tools of this period which I have been able to trace are one or two armorial stamps, which are at least comparable in shape and size. A stamp showing the royal arms, used as a centre-piece in Oxford in the 1580s, survives today in Oriel College Library and is described and reproduced in *Oxford bookbinding 1500–1640*.[34] One of the armorial stamps of Christopher Hatton, first Baron Hatton (1605?–1670) is preserved in the British Museum. It was probably made sometime between 1626, when Hatton was made a Knight of the Bath, and 1643, when he was raised to the peerage.[35] It is made of brass, is about 120 mm long, 55 mm wide and 9 mm thick, and has the marks of four sawn-off prongs on the back, with which it was presumably attached to a wooden block to give it stability in a press. On close examination it is clear that the design is wholly engraved, although the basic brass block may have been cast and then filed down round the edge.[36] Many centre-piece tools must once have been similar to this. The disappearance of so many sizeable and non-biodegradable objects – there must have been thousands of bookbinders' tools in use during the centre-piece period – is presumably testimony to the efficiency of previous generations in recycling obsolete metalware. Although the word shruff, meaning old brass, has now dropped out of the language, it was a valuable traded commodity in the sixteenth and seventeenth centuries, and it seems reasonable to suppose that most centre-piece tools were melted down for reuse of the brass in some other form once their period of usefulness at the binder's workbench was over.[37]

To turn more particularly to the booktrade, our ability to tie in particular tools with individual binders or their workshops is at present very poor, especially for London, where vast amounts of binding work went on. A number of factors conspire to create difficulties even in learning the names of the men and women who were involved in bookbinding, let alone identifying their work. Throughout the hand-press period, binders were at the bottom of the booktrade structure, socially and financially, and the obscurity in which many of them passed their lives is now difficult to penetrate. The principal reference works on the booktrade personnel of the period, Plomer's biographical dictionaries and more recently the third volume of STC, are chiefly based on imprints in books, and therefore give information on only a selective upper stratum of the trade. To illustrate this point with just one example, we could look at the man appointed bookbinder to King James I in 1604, John Bateman, who held that office for the next thirty years or so. Although he might sound anything but an obscure member of the booktrade, he is not mentioned in Plomer or STC III. In fact his career has been rescued from obscurity and documented by Mirjam Foot in the first volume of *The Henry Davis Gift*, but what about the people who learnt from him?[38] During his career Bateman had fifteen apprentices, five of whom appear never to have been freed, and one of whom was his son Abraham, who shared his father's royal apppointment.[39] One of those who was freed was Francis Ash, who later became a bookseller and binder in Worcester, and who is one of the few seventeenth-century bookbinders (the only one?) whose skills are immortalised in printed verse. In the words of Clement Barksdale, first published in 1651:

> None can compare to you, so finely well
> You bind, that your books for the outside sell.[40]

Of the other eight Bateman apprentices, the William Brooks who was freed in 1616 is probably the Brooks whom Plomer records as a bookseller in London in the late 1630s, and Simon Pawley who was freed in 1602 has a shadowy entry in Plomer, where he is described as a 'bookseller (?)'.[41] The remaining six – Luke Bayard, William Best, John Bolton, Thomas Harrison, Leonard Needham and William Teton – have vanished completely from view. One wonders what they learnt from Bateman, and how their careers were spent.

Arber's transcript of the registers of the Stationers' Company includes lists of all the men freed by the Company over the period 1555–1640. Only about half these names are found in Plomer. There is no reason to suppose that the other half were binders, but some of them may well have been, or may have combined bookselling with bookbinding. Many people at this time must have fluctuated between the two, working as journeymen bookbinders while aspiring to the more lucrative profession of bookselling, or dealing in stationery. Booktrade directories have a tendency to categorise people firmly in our minds as booksellers or bookbinders in a way which oversimplifies a situation in which the dividing lines were less firmly drawn. Contemporary terminology was much more fluid, and it is not uncommon to find the same man referred to several times in early parish records, sometimes as a stationer or bookseller, sometimes as a bookbinder.[42] By working through such sources as parish registers, indexes to wills and probate documents, and the reports of the Royal Commission on Historical Manuscripts, it is easy to double the number of bookbinders who can be identified from Plomer, but we are still a long way from being able to assemble a comprehensive list of binding personnel in the period 1560–1640. Although there was considerable overlap between booksellers and bookbinders, it is evident from the numerous petitions which were presented to various authorities by the book-binders of London that there was a sizeable body of men who derived their income primarily from bookbinding.[43] As these petitions regu-larly refer to problems of competition from denizated aliens and others who were not freemen of the Stationers' Company, but were sometimes involved in other trades, it is clear that the bookbinding industry in London was a complicated network.

At the end of his *magnum opus* on *English blind-stamped bindings*, Basil Oldham wrote of the increasing bewilderment which bedevilled his 'attempts to disentangle the individuals who produced our earlier English bindings', and spoke of 'a maze of paths leading in different directions and ending nowhere'.[44] The frustrations attendant upon those who study the worlds of the Dragon binder and the Half-Stamp binder are equally familiar to those who direct their attention to the centre-piece era of a century later. Although many bindings from this time are still extant, vast numbers have disappeared over the years, by destruction or total rebinding, and many of the survivors are now walking wounded as a result of repair or other interference with the original structure. Books which contain conclusive written evidence as to the origin of their binding are extremely rare, and disappointingly large numbers have no clue as to who first owned them. Documentary evidence allowing direct links between particular books and surviving vouchers or accounts is almost non-existent. The thrust of binding studies is moving away from the kind of obsession with attributions which has perhaps been too strong a theme in the past; we are, rightly, more interested in the contribution which binding history can make to the wider history of the book than with the tool sets of individual workshops or with a complete list of the output of a particular binder. We are also coming to understand that traditional assumptions about discrete workshops and uniquely identifiable tools may need to be revised; close observation suggests that the trade did not work as neatly as this. Solid knowledge, however, remains as important as ever: if we are to understand the historical messages of bindings, we need to be able to locate and date them and we need to be able to assess the place of a particular binding within the hierarchy of choices which customers faced. The centre-piece period arguably represents the last generation of English bookbinding for which it is possible to attempt a comprehensive tool-based census of the Oldham variety and this body of work was begun with an aim of that kind in view. That goal has yet to be achieved but I continue to believe that it is one which would be worth having.

NOTES

1   See, for example, R. Ettinghausen, 'Near Eastern book covers and their influence on European bindings', *Ars Orientalis*, 3 (1959), pp. 113–31, figs 12 and 13.

2   Documented most recently by A. R. A. Hobson in *Humanists and bookbinders: the origins and diffusion of the humanistic bookbinding 1459–1559*, Cambridge, 1989, in particular chapter 3, 'The Humanistic binding: Islamic sources'. See also Ettinghausen, 'Near Eastern book covers'.

3   See, for example, *A Catalogue of English and foreign bookbindings offered for sale by Bernard Quaritch Ltd*, London, 1921, nos 21–29; and Howard Nixon's reference to the term in 'Elizabethan gold-tooled bindings' in: D. E. Rhodes (ed.), *Essays in honour of Victor Scholderer*, Mainz, 1970, pp. 219–70, p. 224.

4   A Russo-Polish centre-piece binding of *c.* 1580 is reproduced in G. D. Hobson, *Bindings in Cambridge libraries*, Cambridge, 1929, pl. XXXVI; Dutch and German examples are illustrated in M. M. Foot, *The Henry Davis Gift*, vol. II, London, 1983, nos 305, 306, 341.

5   See, for example, Foot, *Henry Davis Gift*, II, nos 83, 115, 161, 165, 172; or F. Bearman *et al.* (eds), *Fine and historic bindings from the Folger Shakespeare Library*, Washington, 1992, no. 5:9.

6   To take an example at random, see the publisher's binding on E. J. Thackwell, *Narrative of the Second Seikh War*, London, 1851.

7   D. Pearson, *Oxford bookbinding 1500–1640: including a supplement to Neil Ker's Fragments of medieval manuscripts used as pastedowns in Oxford bindings*, Oxford, 2000.

8   D. Pearson, 'Bookbinding in Cambridge in the second half of the sixteenth century' in: D. Pearson (ed.), *'For the love of the binding': studies in bookbinding history presented to Mirjam Foot*, London, 2000, pp. 169–96.

9   H. M. Nixon, *The Development of certain styles of bookbinding*, London, 1963; *Idem.*, 'Elizabethan gold-tooled bindings'.

10   The standard authority is J. B. Oldham, *English blind-stamped bindings*, Cambridge, 1952; see especially pp.13–4.

11   See D. Pearson, *Provenance research in book history*, London, 1994, chapter 4, 'Armorials, binding stamps, and other external features'.

12   J. J. Hall (ed.), *Peterborough Cathedral Library: a catalogue of books printed before 1800*, Cambridge, 1986, p. viii.

13   Centre-piece C1 in Pearson, 'Bookbinding in Cambridge', p. 179.

14   E. Arber, *A Transcript of the registers of the Stationers' Company, 1554–1640*, London, 1875–94, I, p. 100; W. A. Jackson, *Records of the Court of the Stationers' Company 1602–1640*, London, 1957, p. 176.

15   H. M. Nixon and M. M. Foot, *The History of decorated bookbinding in England*, Oxford, 1992, p. 52; G. Pollard, 'Changes in the style of bookbinding 1550–1830', *The Library*, 5th series, 11 (1956), pp. 71–94, p. 84.

16   The popularity of a gold-tooled roll comprising a row of diamonds in the period 1610–20 was noted by W. Oakeshott, 'Carew Ralegh's copy of Spenser', *The Library*, 5th series, 26 (1971), pp. 1–21, pp. 2–3; his fig. II shows some examples of common patterns.

17   J. B. Oldham, *Shrewsbury School Library bindings*, Oxford, 1943, pp. 20–1.

18   See Pearson, *Oxford bookbinding*, pp. 37–8, for more details of practices and patterns in Oxford.

19   B. Middleton, *A History of English craft bookbinding technique*, 4th ed., New Castle and London, 1996, p. 88.

20   A number of examples of gilt and gauffered edges on bindings of this period are described and illustrated by A. Derolez, 'La Tranche dorée et ciselée d'après les collections de la Bibliothèque de l'Université de Gand' in: G. Colin (ed.), *De libris compactis miscellanea*, Brussels, 1984, pp. 251–72, although none of the examples is English.

21   Middleton, *English craft bookbinding technique*, pp. 39–41.

22   John Caius, *The Annals of Gonville and Caius College* (ed. J. Venn), Cambridge, 1904, p. 285. Branthwaite's directions were carried out and the books from his bequest in Caius Library all have red edges; there are examples where it can clearly be seen that the red colouring was added on top of an earlier dye, usually yellow, e.g. Gonville and Caius, F.11.13, F.34.1, M.12.10, M.14.10.

23   H. M. Nixon, *Five centuries of English bookbinding*, London, 1978, no. 18.

24   Pearson, *Oxford bookbinding*, centre-pieces ix, xxviii; 'Bookbinding in Cambridge', centre-pieces C8, C9, C10.

25   By the Andro Hart bindery; see W. S. Mitchell, *A History of Scottish bookbinding 1432 to 1650*, Edinburgh, 1955, pp. 71 ff. and plate 27.

26   See E. Cockx-Indestege *et al*, 'Boekbandstempels: systeem voor het ordenen van wrijfsels', *Archives et bibliothèques de Belgique*, 62 (1991), pp. 1–98.

27   The only other attempt at a classification system like this for centre-pieces I have seen is W. Hohl, 'Ornamentplatten', *Gutenberg-Jahrbuch* 1989, pp. 324–9. This also relies on grouping by inner and outer shapes.

28   A useful book which brings together contemporary designs from various branches of the decorative arts is J. S. Byrne, *Renaissance ornament: prints and drawings*, New York, 1981 (the catalogue of an exhibition at the Metropolitan Museum of Art). See also the opening chapters of P. Thornton, *Form and decoration: innovation in the decorative arts 1470–1870*, London, 1998.

29   Reprinted in B. Sylvius, *Quatres suites d'ornaments*, The Hague, 1893.

30   See STC 21826 ff., 23775.5 ff., 24765 ff.

31   I have written further on this theme in *Oxford bookbinding*, p. 54 ff.

32   S. Fogelmark, *Flemish and related panel-stamped bindings: evidence and principles*, New York, 1990.

33   Fogelmark, *op. cit.*, p. 123.

34   Pearson, *Oxford bookbinding*, p. 57.

35   British Museum, Dept. of Medieval and Later Antiquities, 1913, 7–10, 7. A book on which the stamp was used is described and illustrated in Foot, *Henry Davis Gift*, II, no. 97.

36   I am indebted to Dr M. Jones, previously Keeper of Coins and Medals at the British Museum, for advice and observations here.

37   See D. Woodward, 'Swords into ploughshares: recycling in pre-industrial England', *Economic history review*, 2nd series, 38 (1985), pp. 175–91, especially pp. 184–5. I am glad to be able to renew my thanks to Robert Laurie for pointing this reference out to me.

38   M. M. Foot, *The Henry Davis Gift*, vol. I, London, 1978, pp. 35–49.

39   Arber, *Transcript*, II, pp. 116, 124, 151, 177, 198, 258, 291; D. F. McKenzie, *Stationers' Company apprentices 1605–1640*, Charlottesville, 1961, pp. 39–40.

40   C. Barksdale, *Nympha libethris, or the Cotswold muse*, London, 1651, p. 96. Ash's career is further documented in H. R. Plomer, *A Dictionary of the booksellers and printers ... 1641 to 1667*, London, 1907, p. 7, and in G. Henderson, 'Bible illustration in the age of Laud', *Transactions of the Cambridge Bibliographical Society*, 8 (1982), pp. 173–216, pp. 184–5. Examples of Ash's binding work are yet to be identified.

41   H. G. Aldis *et al.*, *A Dictionary of printers and booksellers ... 1557–1640*, London, 1910, pp. 50, 211. Brooks is included in the index of printers and publishers in STC vol. III, but not Pawley.

42   To take some examples from the registers of St Giles, Cripplegate, London: Jeremy Jackson (d. 1625) is described once as a bookbinder and six times as a stationer; Robert Lawe (fl. 1604–10) is described twice as a bookbinder and six times as a stationer; Thomas Newton (fl. 1579–1613) is described once as a bookbinder and five times as a stationer.

43   For example, the petition of 1597, presented to the Lord Mayor and Aldermen of London by 46 bookbinders, printed in Arber, *Transcript*, III, pp. 40–2; the petition of 1621, presented to Parliament by the bookbinders of London, against the monopoly of the goldbeaters, STC 16768.8; the petition of 1635, presented to the Court of the Stationers' Company by the bookbinders, printed in Jackson, *Records ... 1602–1640*, p. 273.

44   Oldham, *English blind-stamped bindings*, p. 40.

THE INTERPRETATION OF BOOKBINDING STRUCTURE

An Examination of Sixteenth-Century Bindings in the Ramey Collection in the Pierpont Morgan Library

Nicholas Pickwoad

IT IS PROBABLY TRUE to say of all manufactured objects that the more closely they are observed, the less similar they will appear, and this is most certainly true of the seemingly endless variety of ways in which binders have put books together. Whilst there may be a limited number of basic structures – books bound in boards,[1] limp bindings,[2] long stitch bindings,[3] stitched bindings[4] and so on – when it comes to the details of the individual components, the variations seem infinite. The are two obvious explanations for this variety, one being the process of development over time, particularly as the trade adjusted to the increasing flow of books from the printing presses and attempted to increase output and lower costs, and the other the way in which different countries and centres of book production arrived at different solutions in response to their varied traditions and locally available materials. In addition, individual workshops or craftsmen may also have had their own special techniques. As the binders of everyday books have a habit of remaining stubbornly anonymous, and have left little or nothing in the way of written evidence of the manner in which they worked, in most cases only the bindings themselves are left as witness of their work. It has been my assumption that if it was possible to put together detailed information about the structure and materials of surviving early or original bindings in sufficient quantity, the variations found between them would tend, given the probability that most books will have been bound within, let us say, a decade of printing, to fall into clearly defined date-patterns which would identify their appearance, popularity and disappearance. Given a collection of books with a known history and produced within a reasonably limited period, an analysis of that information should begin to show patterns and connections more quickly and reliably. These patterns in turn would cast light on the organization and economics of the bookselling trade, since the binders' work gives tangible evidence of the link between bookseller and reader, indicating economic status, the movement of books within and between countries and to some extent the expectations of the readers.

An opportunity to put this theory to the test came in 1989 with the Ramey collection, which the Pierpont Morgan Library was then in the process of buying, and which appeared to offer a suitable collection to start on.[5] The basic research involved working through the 359 volumes (containing 456 titles) which make up the collection, examining and recording the structures of the bindings and entering the information so gathered onto a spreadsheet[6] to allow a more rapid analysis of the information – a process which still continues. The entries, which described, after basic bibliographical information and measurements, the binding process in the order followed by the binder, consisted of a maximum of 222 pieces of information for each binding in boards and 135 for each limp binding. The element of overkill implicit in such figures was not accidental, in that part of the exercise was to identify those areas where variation seemed to offer the most significant results. However, before discussing some of the more interesting conclusions which can be drawn from the analytical work, it is necessary to say something about the collection and the family which put it together.

The Ramey family lived in St-Just-en-Chevalet, some fifty miles to the west of Lyon, close to Montbrison and in the centre of an important papermaking area. They were closely involved in the law from at least 1485, when a Claude Ramey was described as 'notaire'.[7] The two members of the family who concern us most are Jehan Ramey 'greffier et juge d'Ogerolles' in 1582 and in particular his son Jean Ramey, born on the 25th of August 1558, also active in the law and given the soubriquet 'Le Juge'. He was 'licencié ès lois, avocat au baillage de Forez' and 'juge général du comté d'Urfé, St-Just-en-Chevalet, et de toutes les terres da la maison d'Urfé en Fourest'. He died on 1 October 1631.[8] The books that they bought and others added by subsequent generations, remained untouched in the possession of the family until the recent decision to sell all the books printed before 1601, and it is these books that the Morgan Library was able to buy. A number of books remained in the house in St-Just which I was able to examine in 1997. These included sixteen editions printed before 1600 and a further thirteen printed before 1631 (the date given for the death of Jean Ramey, see note 8). These are not included in my analysis of the books now owned by the

Pierpont Morgan Library unless otherwise stated, nor did I include the single sixteenth-century edition in a seventeenth-century binding, now in the Morgan Library.

Given the professional interests of the family, it is not surprising that books about law, concerned with both Roman Law and French law and customs, form the largest single group within the collection (almost 40%), followed by classical and humanistic texts in Latin, as well as some Greek philosophy (including five volumes of Aristotle), both in Latin and in French translation (though none in Greek), together with histories of the ancient world in French, which take up in all a further 25%. Theology forms almost as large a group, at just over 21%. The family was Catholic, and although the works of Erasmus and other Catholic humanists such as Jacques Lefèvre d'Etaples and Cuthbert Tunstall are represented, refutations of Protestantism are prominent. Literature is primarily represented by Italian authors, particularly Tasso (five separate works), and Petrarch, and works in Italian include a translation of the New Testament into Tuscan.[9] We cannot know what books may have been lost.[10]

Since the books bought by the Morgan Library were confined to pre-1601 imprints, and Jean Ramey (who seems usually to have signed his name Joannes Ramey) did not die until 1631,[11] the Morgan books do not represent his collection in full. The range of date of imprints represented in the collection, however, indicates that the purchase of books dropped off significantly in the last decade of the sixteenth century, showing a tightly defined grouping of imprints between 1525 and 1590 (graph 1). However, a large proportion of the books contains indications of previous ownership, having been bought second-hand, and some of these earlier inscriptions can be dated at least as late as 1589.[12] This may indicate that a significant proportion of the collection came into the possession of the Ramey family only late in the century, perhaps corresponding to the peak on the right of graph 1. One possible reason for this is that Jean Ramey's interest in books might have been a comparatively youthful phenomenon, and that once he was established in his career and certainly after his marriage in 1601 at the late age of forty-three, the accumulation of a library was not a high priority. It is also, of course, possible that some books printed before 1600 were brought into the family after that date.[13]

The presence of so many second-hand books also suggests one of the reasons why the collection is so special. The Ramey family did not collect books for show, and were clearly keen to accumulate the

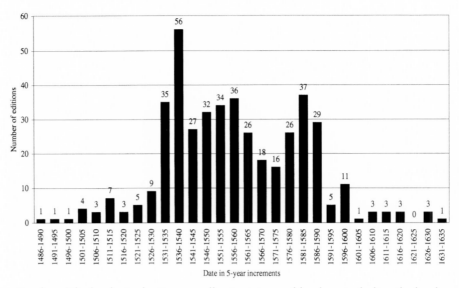

Graph 1. The books in the Ramey collection arranged by date, including the books still kept in St-Just-en-Chevalet. Volumes with multiple texts count as single volumes, dated by their latest imprint.

texts they wanted to read as economically as possible. There are no fine gold-tooled bindings, the nearest to a 'fine' binding being a Lyon imprint of 1552 in heavily worn black silk with silk ties,[14] and the great majority have little gold or silver tooling, if they are tooled at all. The large number of cheap limp parchment bindings,[15] the presence of one uncut sewn textblock which never had a binding (fig. 1)[16] and another bound in boards which never received a covering (fig. 2)[17] are clear signs that the Rameys were not concerned with making their books pretty – not even with making them durable. While they were surely not unique in this, the collection is unusual in having survived intact and largely untouched, though a small number of books were already in their second bindings before they came into the collection. One book which 'escaped' temporarily before the Morgan bought the collection was promptly rebound by its new owner,[18] and serves as a warning of the precarious survival of such modest looking books. Now safe from that risk, the Ramey collection offers the unusual chance to study in detail bindings which were never thought of as being permanent or even worthy of note.

Given the limited geographical ambit of the Ramey family (there is apparently no evidence that any member of the family at this date lived anywhere else than in or close to St-Just), it seemed reasonable

1. Eguinarius Baro, *Institutionum civilium ab Iustiniano Caesare editarum libri IIII*, Bourges, 1546. The uncut tail edge of this sewn but otherwise unbound textblock is visible to the right.The book is sewn on double tanned supports, now somewhat brittle, and the slips have broken off. Pierpont Morgan Library, 125300.

2. Io. Baptista Folengius, *Commentaria in primam D. Joannis Epistolam*, Antwerp, ex officina Ioannis Loei, 1547. Bound in boards with cut edges, but never having had either endbands or covering material. Fragments of a seventeenth-century paper title label, of a type found on most of the Ramey books, can be seen on the spine. PML 125286.

to expect that a survey would identify groups of bindings by a limited number of different shops, possibly with some indication of where the work had been done. What appeared instead was a near bewildering array of different structural variants. I have so far found only three sets of bindings which are even nearly identical in terms of structure – one group of three books printed in Paris in the

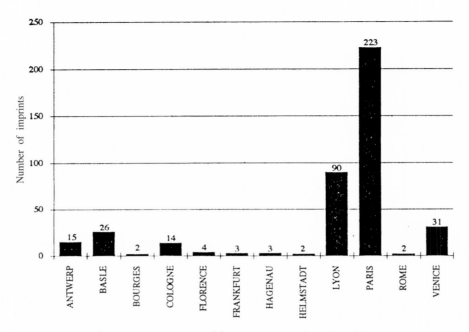

Graph 2. Cities represented by two or more imprints (Pierpont
Morgan Library books only).

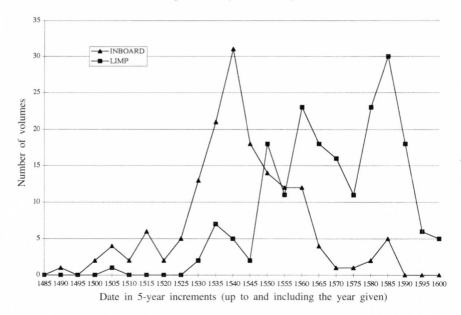

Date in 5-year increments (up to and including the year given)

Graph 3. The date distribution of limp bindings and bindings in boards
(Pierpont Morgan Library books only).

1580s bound in boards and covered in leather,[19] one of two volumes in boards and covered in leather printed in Lyon in the 1550s,[20] and one also of two books bound only in limp parchment, printed in Paris in the 1580s.[21] Two volumes, each of the first two sets, those bound in boards, bear the name of the publishers, Gilles Gorbin and the successors of Giunta, but this falls far short even of suggesting a 'house style' in binding.

I had assumed that the majority of the books would have been bound in or near Lyon, but the presence of a book printed in Lyon in a binding bearing the stamp of the Paris publishers Les Angeliers (which has within it the initials CL for Charles L'Angelier),[22] and of another Lyon-printed book in a parchment binding which is clearly German in technique,[23] to say nothing of the books printed outside France which are in bindings from those countries, rapidly destroyed that assumption.

There was also the possibility of finding a correlation between groups of bindings and individual publishers, and thus some indication of what might be described as publishers' retail bindings, but given the small number of identical structures, no pattern of this sort emerged. Given also that there are in the collection books issued by upwards of 120 publishers, of whom only one is responsible for more than six books – Sebastianus Gryphius with twenty-five (and none in identical bindings) – the scope for such groups was in any case limited. Of the forty-one volumes containing multiple editions, only fourteen consist of the works of a single publisher, and none of the publishers is represented in more than one of these tract volumes, so that no comparisons between them are possible. Seven such multiple-text volumes contain works printed in more than one town. Twenty-seven different towns are represented in the collection as a whole, but here at least some pattern begins to emerge. Only twelve printing towns offer two or more editions, and of these twelve, only six are represented by more than ten titles – four of them, Antwerp, Basle, Cologne and Venice, in only a modest way.[24] Editions printed in Paris and Lyon dominate the collection, the former having more than twice the number of editions as the latter, at 223 to ninety (graph 2).

The date distribution of limp bindings and bindings in boards (graph 3) begins to show the potential of the analytical method. The economic distinction between bindings in boards and limp bindings is simple, in that the latter, in this collection of parchment only, is essentially quicker and cheaper to make than the former. It is immediately clear from the graph that the bindings in boards (all covered in leather apart from one in silk, one in parchment and another without covering) form the bulk of the earlier part of the collection and that the limp parchment bindings form the bulk of the latter part. The change over occurred in the 1550s, probably in response to a Europe-wide worsening of economic conditions and a general rise in prices. It is also interesting to note that there is a consistent decline in the proportion of Lyon imprints to those of Paris after the 1550s.[25] During that decade they briefly outnumber Paris imprints, having shadowed them at a more or less constant 50% of the Paris total until then, and declining to less than 7% of the Paris total in the last twenty years of the century.

Although the coincidence of economic trouble and the introduction of a less complex binding structure suggests a move towards cheaper book production, other evidence is required to prove this. In the absence of archival evidence, it is again to the books that we have to turn, using at first one simple structural feature – the number of supports on which the books are sewn (between two and seven in this collection). The calculation is based on some very straightforward facts: the more supports a book is sewn on, the longer it takes to sew it, and therefore the more expensive it will be to make. Equally, the larger the book, the more supports it is likely to be sewn on, so it is no surprise that in this collection there are no octavos on seven supports and no folios on two. If a comparison is made, however, between the number of supports used within each format for both bindings in boards and limp bindings, an interesting difference becomes evident. In the limp bindings, 101 books, approximately 200 mm in height or smaller and mostly octavos with a few duodecimos and the occasional smaller quarto, are sewn on three supports, whereas only nineteen within the same height range are sewn on four. Forty-one books of more than 200 mm, out of a total of fifty-one (all quartos and folios), are sewn on four supports. The one book under 200 mm high sewn on five supports is an octavo printed in Troyes in 1578,[26] and the contrast between its elaborate structure and simple sheep parchment wrapper raises the question whether it might not be an example of a temporary wrapper added to a book intended for something more expensive. The remaining eight books on five supports and the two on six supports are all either quartos or folios.

The distribution of numbers of sewing supports among the bindings in boards is entirely different. Firstly, only twelve octavos of 200 mm or less are sewn on three supports, whereas ninety-five books in the same size range (all octavos except for a single duodecimo) are sewn on either four or five supports (forty-eight and forty-seven respectively). The spread of quartos and folios, taken together, between four- and five-support structures is again nearly equal (ten to fourteen). What such simple analyses show us is not only that a much higher proportion of the limp parchment bindings has the less elaborate three-support structure, which indicates that a cheaper binding structure typically went with the cheaper covering technique, but that within the bindings in boards, where three-support structures are found on less than 10% of the books, not only the bulk (over 75%) of the books are sewn on four or five supports, but also that the distribution of octavos, quartos and folios between them is almost equal. The question then arises as to what distinction there may be between books with four- and five-support structures. That this again reflects economic priorities within the group of bindings in boards is borne out by another simple economic indicator: the choice of covering material.

The skins of three animals are used for covering these books: sheep, calf and goat, in rising order of cost.[27] Of the books bound in boards and sewn on four supports, the numbers in calf and sheep are almost the same (twenty-eight to twenty-nine), whereas on the more expensive five-support structures, calf is clearly the preferred material, with fifty-seven volumes as against eight in sheep.

One calfskin binding on a Paris edition of 1535, and bound very soon after that date, gives unexpected evidence of this process (fig. 3).[28] It is the only book covered in calf sewn on three supports, and would therefore appear to contradict the covering material/structure equation just put forward. However, it has been made to look as if it has five supports by the addition of two false ones, that is to say it has five raised bands on the spine, but only three of them are sewn around. This suggests that there was by then an expectation on the part of the buyer that a well-made book should have five sewing supports, and that here the binder has given the outward appearance of the structure deemed suitable for calf binding while economising on the actual structure. It is the earliest instance of this phenomenon that I have seen, although it was common in England in the 1670s and 1680s.[29] How many more French bindings of the sixteenth century might also show this or similar deceptive practices will only be revealed by detailed examination of a large number of books.

The 195 limp parchment bindings are almost universally made of sheepskin, or the skins of hair-sheep, a cross-breed between goat and sheep, with only twenty-five in true goat, and twelve in calves

3. Joannes Copus, *De fructibus libri quatuor*, Paris, Christian Wechel, 1535.
A contemporary French binding sewn on three supports, with two
additional, false, supports. PML 125028.

vellum. There are only two vellum bindings with any gold-tooling. Again, the covering material goes hand in hand with other indications of status.

The goatskin bindings in boards, which account for over half the bindings in boards sewn on three supports, are typically found on books of the first quarter of the century, and mostly on a group of sixteen bindings that share both French and some Italian structural and decorative features.[30] This supports the argument that these bindings in goatskin, of which there are nine, including two Lyon and two Venice imprints, are influenced also in their covering material by Italian practice. Given the strong links between Lyon and Italy at this date, it would be no surprise to find that they were all Lyonnais bindings. It is probably significant that there are no goatskin bindings of the 1540s or later in the collection, which suggests that the presence of these early goatskin bindings in the Ramey collection is as much due to their purchase second-hand as to any Italian influence on the Lyon booktrade. By the 1540s goatskin was associated almost exclusively with the luxury market.

These earlier bindings have another characteristic which may at first sight seem to contradict the significance of the number of sewing supports which I have just described: they tend to be sewn on rather widely spaced sewing supports, which results in both octavos and quartos being sewn on three supports only, and in the folios being sewn on four instead of five, six or even seven supports as in the rest of the collection. Although this too might be seen as reflecting Italian influence, since it would appear that three-support structures are much more commonly found on books bound in boards and covered with leather in Italy than in France at this period, it is as much a matter of chronology. Comparatively large books are found sewn on three supports in northern as well as southern European countries from the late fourteenth to the early sixteenth century, and it is only later in the latter century that the Italian examples really stand out. These larger bindings sewn on three supports are not found in the Ramey collection on books printed after 1532. The choice of the number of supports on which to sew a book, however, was only the first stage of the sewing process; the binder had then to choose how to sew the gatherings to the supports, a process which was likewise influenced by economic pressure.

For books with little or no decoration, sewing would usually constitute the single longest process undergone in the course of binding, and it is not surprising that binders under pressure to reduce

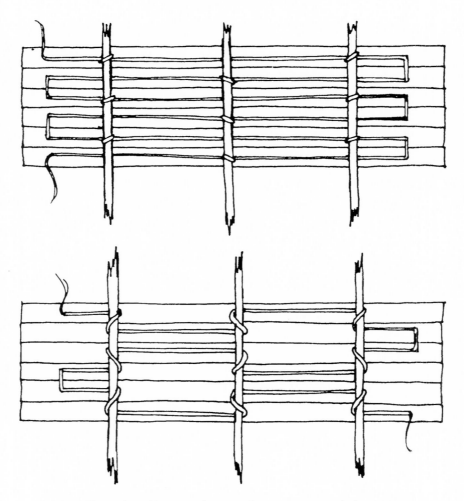

4. Examples of bypass (above) and two-on sewing (below) on
three supports. The kettle stitches are not shown.

costs would attempt to speed it up. The reduction of the number of
supports for cheaper books is one simple way of doing that. However,
it was clearly not enough, and this collection bears witness to the
introduction of two techniques intended to produce further savings
(fig. 4). Throughout the collection, but exclusively only until the
1540s, the books are sewn all-along. In this technique, used almost
throughout the earlier history of European bookbinding, the sewing
thread was taken from head to tail of each gathering, fastening the
gatherings to each of the sewing supports in turn. The first of the

sewing short-cuts economised by omitting to sew around one or more of the sewing supports in each gathering, alternating the supports missed out from gathering to gathering, so that the structure will remain viable, even though weakened. This technique is known as bypass sewing. Its appearance in the books bound in boards is clearly marked by 1540 and in fact overtakes all-along sewing in the later 1550s, as the number of books bound in boards declines.[31] It appears at much the same time in the limp bindings, but is there joined in the 1550s by another still faster technique, two-on sewing, in which each length of thread between head and tail is used to secure two gatherings to the supports, alternating between them, and almost doubling the speed of sewing. Significantly, this technique is not found at all in the books bound in boards, but is used increasingly, along with bypass sewing, in the limp bindings, reinforcing the identification of the lowly economic status of these bindings, as does the rapid abandonment of the more time-consuming all-along sewing in the 1560s. The presence, therefore, of all-along sewing in just six out of fifty-two books from the 1580s and one out of eleven from the 1590s, does not come as a surprise, but does raise questions about the type of binder who still uses such a technique on cheaper books at such a late date.

There is one more form of sewing economy to look at: the substitution of single for double supports, which again accelerates the sewing process. Double supports, the typical choice for fifteenth-century and earlier bindings, remain far and away the preferred support-type for bindings in boards, though, not surprisingly, single supports are found on a larger proportion of books from the mid-century onwards as binding in boards fell in popularity and the pressure to reduce costs increased. With limp bindings, we find that single supports are in use from the start in just over a third of the books so bound and in half of them by the 1580s. In the next century they will take over almost completely, with economy as the driving force.

The ultimate structural economy is not to sew the textblock at all, but to stitch it with thread through the inner margins. In England this was clearly a recent introduction in 1586, when it was referred to as a technique which was replacing sewing on a sewing press, 'as heretofore has been the custom',[32] and the presence of only seven examples in the Ramey collection would seem to suggest that it was not widely used in France before 1600. It is otherwise hard to understand why a family so little concerned with the presentation of

5. *Brevis augustissimi ac summe venerandi sacrosanctae missae sacrificii ex
sanctis patrib. contra impium Francisci Stancari Mantuani scriptum, assertio,*
Cologne, Haeredes Arnoldi Birckmanni, 1577. Elaborate stitching through
five holes. The parchment cover was originally secured only by the outer
flyleaf used as a paste-down at front and back. PML 125222.

its books – they were also buying damaged books – would not have
taken advantage of the economies offered by stitching. It could
be that stitched pamphlets were not retained in what became the
family library, and it is perhaps significant that the extensive pamphlet
material produced in France during the religious wars of the second
half of the sixteenth century (the period during which the collection
was formed) is not represented either in the Morgan Library or
among the books remaining in St-Just. However, even with such
basic structures there is ample room for variety, and no two are the
same. They range from elaborate stitching through five holes (fig. 5)
to the most basic loop through two holes, and come from Cologne
(the wrapper of manuscript waste bears the name Sigismund suggesting that this elaborate stitching is likely to be German),[33] from
Antwerp (where the economy of stitching is disguised with endbands,
a most unusual combination and again suggestive of deceptive practices),[34] Florence (the most basic, with textblock edges hacked away
with what could almost have been a saw),[35] Lyon[36] and Paris. Three
are on Paris imprints,[37] and one dated 1562 now contains a stiff note
from a cataloguer to the effect that the binder 'has failed to separate
G4 from G3 and insert it in the right place'. It would seem more likely
that a binder has never seen this book, and that it was stitched as it
came from the press or by a retail bookseller at a later date, and it
was the binder who was next to deal with it who would have carried

out the necessary re-arrangement of the leaves – a formality which the Ramey family felt able to forego. The fact that the leaves have not been re-arranged would further suggest that this is a book that the Rameys bought new rather than second-hand. It has no marks of ownership or other inscriptions.

Given that the use of plain limp parchment bindings, at least in the early period, was seen as a temporary expedient, the question inevitably arises what became of the discarded wrappers, if their destination was not the glue pot. The Ramey collection contains seven books wrapped in re-used covers, some with folio covers cut in half for octavos,[38] and others with octavo covers transferred to another octavo (fig. 6). The presence of one such cover on a stitched book confirms their lowly status, though the cover was reversed (to expose the flesh-side of the skin) to present a cleaner face to the world.[39] Reversing the skin on a limp parchment binding is typically an Italian habit (represented in this collection by a 1550 Florentine imprint in a contemporary Italian limp binding)[40] – presumably to show off the white flesh-side of the skin in preference to the toned hair-side – and it is interesting to note that whereas Paris imprints account for more than four times the Lyon total of hair-side-outside covers (eighty-nine to twenty, compared with a total of 169 volumes with Paris imprints and seventy-five with Lyon imprints), Lyon offers more than twice the Paris total of reversed skins (ten to four). Is this another instance of Italian influence, or perhaps simply a southern as opposed to a northern habit? It should be added that fourteen of the sixteen Venetian imprints in the collection also have covers with the hair side outwards, but only six of them are in Italian bindings; the rest are recognisably French.

There is also a group of thirteen bindings in boards covered in reversed skins, but here the skins are reversed tawed sheepskin, stained a shade of olive green on the flesh-side. Although the imprints range in date from 1535 to 1577 (the 1506 Parma imprint must be in a later, and certainly not Italian, binding),[41] the fact that this material is found elsewhere on books printed as late as the mid-seventeenth century means that the cut-off date for the collection of 1600 prevents this selection from identifying the end of the date range. Reversed tawed skin was often used on fifteenth-century manuscript bindings both in France and England, and its use on printed books in France can be traced back at least to the late fifteenth century. Its appearance in the Ramey collection only on books dating from the later 1530s cannot therefore indicate the period at which it was introduced, and

6. Wilhelmus Damasus Lindanus, *Paraphraseων in psalmos Davidicos tomus*, Antwerp, Christophe Plantin, 1574. The parchment cover from a slightly larger book reversed and re-used. The directions from which the earlier set of holes were pushed through the parchment show that it was first used hair side outwards. PML 125128.

is most probably a consequence of the large increase in the number of editions from that decade onwards (see graph 1). In terms of economy, it seems that here too there is little to be learnt, since most of the books lack other signs of markedly economical treatment (eight sewn all-along, five bypass).[42] The absence of any decorative tooling on these volumes is more likely to be due to the difficulty of gold-tooling on reversed skins. In fact with their brightly coloured edges they must when new have presented a rather gawdy appearance.[43] The geographical evidence is inconclusive, with only four Paris imprints (and one from Rennes) as against three from Lyon, two from Basle and one each from Parma, Toulouse and Tübingen. Evidence from the Bouhéreau collection in Marsh's Library in Dublin, which has thirty-six books bound in this type of skin, and examples in other collections indicate a specifically, and I believe uniquely, French preference for this material in the sixteenth century.

Another very accessible economic indicator on bindings is the presence or absence of endbands, an originally structural but increasingly decorative feature. Until the last quarter of the fifteenth century, the endband was an important part of the structure of a book, tied down in most if not all the gatherings and with its slips laced into the boards to reinforce the board attachment at its most vulnerable point. By the end of the first quarter of the sixteenth century, however, the structural purpose of the endband begins to disappear, particularly in the cheaper books, and the Ramey collection charts this process. Of the nine books which have endband slips laced into boards, six are on texts printed in or before 1513.[44] Thereafter the vast majority of books bound in boards have endbands with the slips cut at the joints, if they have endbands at all. Of the bindings in boards, in fact, only a small proportion lack them (seventeen out of 158), and they keep the company we should expect: fourteen of the seventeen are in sheepskin, just three in calf. Of those with endbands, ninety-three are in calf against thirty-five in sheep. There is no geographical or chronological pattern to this, only an economic one. There is however a chronological pattern to the absence of endbands amongst the limp parchment bindings, except that it works in the opposite direction to what might be expected. In the interest of cheapness, it would seem logical to expect to find more books in limp parchment bindings without endbands as the century progresses, but that is not what happens. In fact, the increase in the use of endbands in limp bindings is the direct result of the introduction of a new binding technique which necessitated endbands.

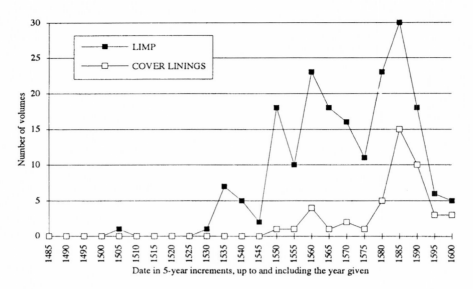

Graph 4. The date distribution of limp bindings with cover linings
together with the total number of limp bindings.

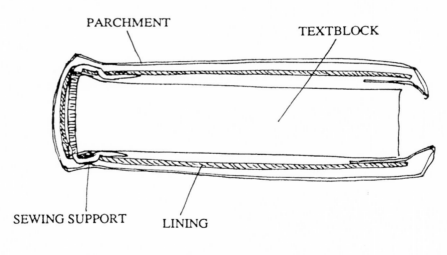

PARCHMENT

TEXTBLOCK

SEWING SUPPORT

LINING

3-HOLE VARIANT LACING

7. Cross-section of a limp parchment binding with a cover lining, showing
the sewing support slips laced through the lining only. The endband slips
are laced through both cover and lining.

This new structure, which appears on a small group of imprints around 1560, but not in larger numbers until the early 1580s (graph 4) – making it likely that the first group comprises old texts bound later – is distinguished by having a double cover. First a lining, usually of cartonnage or laminated paper, is wrapped around the sewn text block, and the main sewing support slips are laced through it. The parchment cover is then folded around the lining, and the endband slips are laced through both, a feature which makes them easily recognisable as the main sewing support slips do not appear on the outside of the binding (fig. 7).[45] It appears to be an especially French structure, and a date for its introduction in the late 1570s accords with examples in other collections. The name often used to describe this structure is 'semi-limp' parchment, but this can be confused with bindings which have thin, separate, flexible boards inserted into them, and thus form an entirely different structure. In the absence of any historical name, it is most reliably referred to as a limp, laced-case parchment binding with a cover lining.

Given that the necessary use of an endband seems to have been more of an elaboration of structure than a simplification, the reason for the introduction of these bindings is not immediately apparent. However, the lining – often of waste material, but occasionally (and twice in the Ramey collection) of parchment[46] – allowed a thinner, weaker and therefore cheaper covering skin to be used. It should also be noted in this connection that a high proportion of parchment covers in the Ramey collection consist of pieces of skin that are in some way damaged by clumsy flaying, leaving knife marks or flay-holes, or come from the less desirable areas around the periphery of the animal's skin, close to the belly or legs, where the fibre structure is looser and the skin therefore weaker. They often show flanky and horny areas, the areas generally avoided for better quality work. The skins over cover linings are more likely to be grain splits, that is, the outer layer of the skin of a sheep split through its thickness to give two pieces of parchment. The inner, or flesh split, was typically used for writing on. It may also be that their comparatively clean external appearance, with only the endband slips laced in, contributed to their popularity, which continued well into the seventeenth century.[47]

In common with every other structure which appears more than once in this collection, there are no two identical examples: the bindings are found with linings made of cartonnage, sheets of toned, plain, printed[48] and manuscript paper and parchment. The sewing support slips may also be laced into the cover lining through one, two or three holes, providing yet another opportunity for variation. Usually the lining is cut to the height of the turned-in cover, but one rather unusual example in the collection not only has the sewing support slips laced through both lining and cover, which effectively puts it in a different structural category, but also has the lining cut to the size of the unturned-in cover, and turned in with it.[49] There is no evidence in this collection to suggest any one location where they were made, and it seems that they are as likely to have been made in Lyon as Paris (nine against seventeen, though whether the five Venice and six Basle imprints might alter that picture it is hard to say). Many more examples need to be recorded before a clearer picture can be established. The significance or otherwise of the higher proportion of Lyon parchment bindings (over 50%) without endbands compared with less than 20% for Paris can also only be tested with a much wider sample.

The use of endbands in a limp binding almost invariably means that the slips will be laced through the cover and used to hold the cover to the textblock. With the books bound in boards, as noted before, this is not necessarily so, and in addition to the presence of endbands, their being laced in or not can also therefore serve as an economic indicator – simply cutting the slips at the joints rather than attaching them to the boards saved time and therefore money. The majority of French fine bindings of the sixteenth century seem to have had some form of endband/board attachment, but given the nature of the Ramey books it is not surprising that of the 137 books bound in boards which have endbands, 121 have endbands without slips – that is the core is cut at the joint and there is no board attachment (nineteen were bound without endbands). In only sixteen volumes, therefore, are the endband slips used to reinforce the board attachment, nine of them with tawed thongs laced through holes in the boards (the traditional method inherited from the fifteenth-century and earlier)[50] and seven using what seems to be a uniquely French technique. This consists of using cord endband cores, fraying out the slips and pasting them to the outside of the boards before the book was covered.[51] German binders used this attachment technique for sewing support slips (on one of the Basle imprints in the collection this form of board attachment has been used),[52] but do not appear to have used it for endbands. As an endband attachment, it is however used in some of the highest quality bindings made in Paris from at least the 1530s right through to the beginning of the seventeenth century (for instance, this technique is used in books belonging to both Grolier and de Thou). Its association with quality is shown not only by such elevated collectors' bindings as those and the sparse numbers in the Ramey collection (seven to 121), but again in the company they keep in the books in which they appear – the silk binding, for instance, has them and is also the only book in the collection with recessed supports.[53] This feature, at this date, is a sign not of poor binding, but high fashion, quality and cost (which is why there is only one of them in the Ramey collection).[54]

Spine linings also show differences in quality, though the number of different types is limited to only four, or five, if the twenty-five bindings which have no linings at all are included.[55] The most popular type of lining, the panel lining, consists simply of a piece of paper – either clean or printed or manuscript waste – pasted onto each panel of the spine but not extending across the joints. Approximately 80% of bindings with linings, both limp and those in boards, have this type of lining, the three other types being represented in only a tiny proportion of the collection. Just seven books have transverse linings – that is, linings which extend across the spine onto the boards, which were common in the sixteenth century in both Italy and Germany. It is therefore no surprise to find that of the three limp bindings with transverse linings, two are Italian and one German. Of the four bindings in boards with the same type of linings, two are very early and in contemporary or near contemporary bindings,[56] and the other two show other unusual features.[57] One book, with the binding in black silk, has as a lining a large piece of parchment which runs across the spine and onto the inside of the boards, with holes punched through it to allow the sewing support slips to be laced through the boards from the outside.[58] As this is the only book in the collection with recessed sewing supports, which make such a lining practicable, its unique appearance is perhaps not surprising. The more typical 'expensive' lining (in terms of French binding at least) is the parchment comb lining, apparently borrowed from either German or Italian practice at the beginning of the sixteenth century and destined to become by the beginning of the seventeenth century the classic French lining.[59]

There are eleven examples of comb linings, three on Italian bindings and one on a German binding, leaving seven French examples. Of these, all but one also have endleaves of a particular format which is typically associated with high quality French bindings of the sixteenth century. It is a simple four-leaf construction (one fold of plain paper inside another with the outside leaf at each end used as a paste-down, or not, as required), but which is without the guard so often found next to or around the endleaves on less expensive French bindings, since the comb lining also performs the function of joint reinforcement. Paradoxically, therefore, this simple endleaf format, at least on French bindings, is frequently a sign of quality, though its comparatively lavish use of paper is conspicuous at a time when binders were content even on calf-covered bindings to save on paper when the textblock provided blank leaves at the end, and allowed them to reduce the number of leaves they felt it necessary to add. There are fourteen instances of this phenomenon in the collection.[60] The double-fold format also appears on the unusual parchment-bound octavo from Troyes sewn on five double supports,[61] reinforcing the impression of high quality that makes it likely that the plain sheep parchment cover was only ever intended to be temporary.

A limp binding on a Paris imprint of 1542 also has the double fold endleaf and comb lining combination.[62] This is found together with a cover which makes an extraordinarily expensive use of calves vellum, in which the head and tail turn-ins overlap each other, creating a double thickness cover. The twelve sewing support slips (the book is sewn on six supports), have been taken from the inside through both thicknesses of the cover along the joint and return only through the outer layer, thus leaving the ends of the slips sandwiched between the turn-ins and the cover, and therefore invisible from both the inside and the outside of the cover (fig. 8). Only the endband slips are brought back through both thicknesses and show on the inside of the turn-ins; all four of which have been neatly trimmed. It is unusually sophisticated work, especially for the Ramey collection, and in structural terms represents the apogee of French limp parchment binding of the sixteenth century. I have seen six other limp bindings with such extra wide turn-ins which use a similar lacing technique, including a superbly executed example for Jacques-Auguste de Thou, all but one of which have the same double fold endleaf construction and all have parchment comb linings. Two of these are on Paris imprints, a third was presumably bound in Paris (the de Thou volume), a fourth was printed in Lyon, and the other two, although the texts were printed in Italy, were undoubtedly bound in France.[63]

Identifying such indicators of quality can place comparatively plain volumes at a much higher level than their plain exteriors might suggest, and shows that quality is not always associated with elaborate decoration. Such qualities come together in the Ramey collection in a single binding on a 1530 Paris imprint, which apart from a single

8. Aristotle, *Politica, ab Iacobo Lodoico Strebaeo nomine Joannis Bertrandi Senatoris Judicisque sapientissime conversa*, Paris, Michel de Vascosan, 1542. Overlapping head and tail turn-ins inside the back cover; comb lining of medieval parchment manuscript; and sewing support slips laced through a single hole on the inside of the cover. PML 125102.

gilt fillet running around the edge of the covers and a small flower tool in each spine panel, is completely undecorated and reveals its pedigree only in the list of high class techniques to be found in it.[64] It is a folio sewn all-along on six double supports, it has the double-fold endleaf format with comb linings in parchment, the sewing support slips are recessed into knife-cut triangular recesses on the inside of the boards, the endbands are worked over cord in a plain thread primary sewing with five tie-downs on a comparatively slim volume, and secondary, decorative sewing in yellow and green silk with a crowning core (the only example of silk secondary sewing in this collection), the slips are frayed out and pasted to the outside of the boards (fig. 9), and the book is covered with clean, unblemished dark-brown calf skin with neatly trimmed turn-ins. Without even coloured let alone gilt edges, it stands for quality. It is certainly unusual among the Ramey bindings.

With an example like this, it becomes apparent that one of the uses of the sort of information obtained by this structural survey lies in establishing the factors which could be used, almost like a scoring system, to compile an economic hierarchy for the bindings. In some

9. Thucydides, *L'Hystoire de Thucydide Athenien de la guerre qui fut entre les Peloponesiens et Atheniens* (transl. Claude de Seyssel), Paris, Gilles Gormont, 1530. The headband, showing the tie-downs of the primary sewing in plain thread, worked through the parchment comb linings, the secondary sewing in coloured silk, incorporating a smaller diameter crowning core of thin cord, and the main core of thicker cord taken across the back joint, frayed out and pasted onto the board under the leather. PML 125273.

cases this depends on external knowledge, such as knowing that sheep is cheaper than calf, and that goat is more expensive than calf, and that some techniques take longer than others. But other features show their place only by repeated association, such as double-fold endleaves, comb linings, etc. The accumulation of such information also offers the potential to identify the date and place of execution of otherwise anonymous bindings, though here the firm conclusions can only be drawn from a much wider sample. This will eliminate the risk that any one collection presents a deceptive picture, but even within the 359 books of the Ramey collection, dates begin to emerge, such as that for the change-over from bindings in boards to limp bindings. The arrival of a new technique or material is marked on a graph by a scattering of early dates representing old unbound sheets getting their first bindings or books being rebound. When the imprints contemporary with the new technique appear, the numbers will rise rapidly and establish the approximate date of introduction. Additional examples should serve only to define the date range more precisely.

This account of the bindings in the Ramey collection has so far concentrated on a small sample of techniques which reveal some of

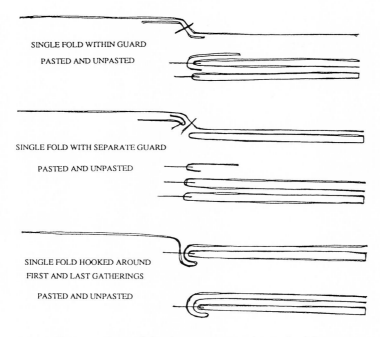

SINGLE FOLD WITHIN GUARD
PASTED AND UNPASTED

SINGLE FOLD WITH SEPARATE GUARD
PASTED AND UNPASTED

SINGLE FOLD HOOKED AROUND
FIRST AND LAST GATHERINGS
PASTED AND UNPASTED

10. Cross-sections of the three most popular endleaf formats
found on books bound in boards.

the more generally significant trends, but there is a much greater
range of technique to be found than this selection suggests. One
expensive endleaf format has been discussed, but there are other
much more typical endleaf formats, as well as a whole range of much
less commonly found types. To take first the endleaves found on
books bound in boards (fig. 10), it is immediately apparent that the
choice is dominated by the format consisting of a single fold of paper
with a parchment guard folded round it, with smaller contributions
from the types consisting of a single fold of paper with a separate
guard sewn outside it and a single fold of paper hooked around first
and last gatherings. An analysis of the date-distribution of these three
different types suggests that the separate-guard-and-fold variety
slowly takes over from the more popular fold-within-a-guard type in
the second half of the century. Around these three formats lies a mass
of variations, none appearing in more than four examples each. The
situation is even more complex in the limp bindings, where five
different formats are most commonly found (including the three
found on the bindings in boards) with the same surrounding mass
of variants. In all, forty distinctly different ways of constructing

endleaves are to be found within the 359 pre-1601 books in this collection, rising to sixty-eight if the pasted-down and unpasted-down versions of the same format are distinguished. It is difficult to extract a sense of geographical preference from this wide variety within such a small collection, but there does appear to be a distinct bias in favour of Lyon imprints in limp bindings with paste-downs and Paris imprints without them.[65]

The same is true of bypass sewing, where there are five different patterns each on three- and four-support sewing, and a further three each on five and six supports. With the single two-support type (there is only one option with two supports), this gives seventeen different patterns in all. The varieties of two-on sewing offers a further eight variants. Add to that all-along sewing, and the collection offers twenty-six different ways of sewing a textblock. Some of these variants may have been short-lived, some may even be mistakes, but some must be the preferred technique of individual binders or shops and could help to identify the work of these shops. Two examples of an unusual endleaf format, for instance, identified the only parchment bindings to share virtually all their technical features so far discovered in the collection. This profusion of techniques is suggestive of two possibilities. One is that the binding trade, particularly towards its lower levels, was full of small, one-man (or woman) businesses, improvising, cutting corners, and generally grubbing for a living; or alternatively, that larger shops took on and laid off workers according to need and therefore had a shifting population with their own work habits. Whether either or both of these possibilities obtained, the picture created is of a trade which was in a period of rapid evolution and experimentation, coping with both increasing costs and output.

Analysis of the attachment of the boards to the sewing supports by lacing the support slips through holes in the boards gives a similar result, with sixteen variants in all, though the variant given the name 'Perpendicular 1' is far and away the most popular (eighty-five instances, or slightly over half the total number of bindings in boards: see fig. 11). Similar board-lacing variations are to be found in English books of the seventeenth and eighteenth centuries, and surely indicate different shops. Nowhere in this collection is there an example of three-hole lacing-in into boards, which was to become quintessentially French in the next century. During this period, however, it seems to have been still restricted to the more exotic books, and is perhaps not much found outside high-class Parisian work. It is particularly

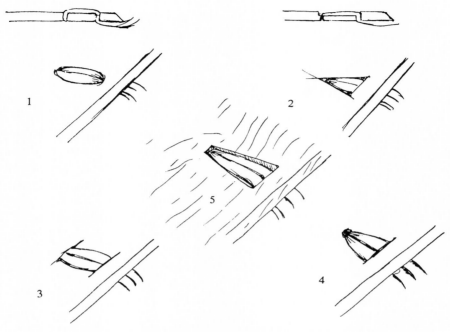

11. Lacing-in patterns, with the holes arranged perpendicularly to the back edge of the board. Type 5 is found only with thick wooden boards.

associated with books sewn on thin recessed double cord supports, which would have easily pulled out of two-hole lacing-in.[66]

Different ways of lacing ties, typically of alum-tawed skin, into the parchment covers of limp bindings seem also to offer a distinction between Paris and Lyon, at least so far as the two most common types (1 and 2) of the thirteen found in the collection are concerned (fig. 12). The simplest of them all, type 1, in which a tapered tie is simply pulled through a single hole in the cover until it is jammed tight, is found in almost equal numbers between Paris and Lyon (fifteen to fourteen), which, given the heavy preponderance of Paris imprints overall, implies a definite bias towards Lyon. Type 2, however, is found on fifty-one Paris imprints and only ten Lyon imprints. Add to this ten examples of type 1 on Venetian imprints, which are perhaps more likely to have arrived in Lyon direct from Venice and not via Paris, and only one Venetian imprint with type 2, and the tally for type 1 becomes twenty-five Lyon to fifteen Paris. Although the numbers are small, it is interesting also to note that the Antwerp imprints have only two of type 1 to five of type 2, perhaps

TYPE 1

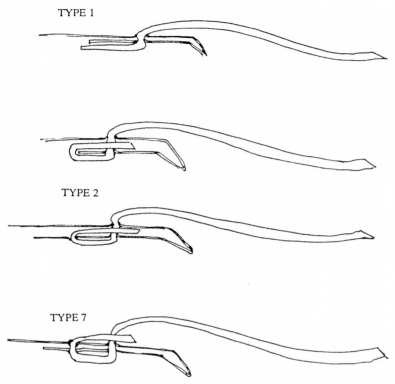

TYPE 2

TYPE 7

12. Tie attachment types 1, 2 and 7. Type 2 appears in two slightly different forms, depending on the width of the turn-ins where they are found. If the turn-in is narrow enough, the tie is taken around its back edge, if wide enough, it is punched through it before passing to the outside of the cover through both thicknesses of parchment.

indicating that they got to St-Just-en-Chevalet through Paris. This would make geographical sense, and since four of the group of five books with type 2 tie-lacing were printed by Plantin (who maintained a branch in Paris until 1577, sold it in that year, but continued to deal with the bookseller to whom he sold it),[67] it would make commercial sense too. Perhaps the fact that one Plantin imprint has type 1 lacing[68] indicates that it came to Lyon in sheets or by a different route. Lacing type 7, of which only seven examples are found, appears on six Paris imprints and one from Dillingen: again, highly suggestive of a Parisian origin. All share some other structural features, but none share all of them, which, as they span imprint dates covering almost forty years, is perhaps not surprising. There are in all thirteen different kinds of tie-attachment.

The different ways in which binders worked their endbands, even though not all the bindings reveal this very easily, are particularly bewildering. Some of the differences relate to expense, and simply counting the number of tie-downs relative to the thickness of the textblock gives some notion of status, in that the greater the number of tie-downs, the longer will have been the time spent on this element of the structure. The Ramey collection shows evidence of a tendency I have observed elsewhere for Italian binders to use the well-worked endband with multiple tie-downs and laced-in slips for longer than other European countries. But the significance of why some binders of the 179 limp bindings in the Ramey collection with endbands chose to take the outermost tie-downs down through the endleaf sections (129 including nine who do it at one end only), while others tied-down two or three gatherings in from each end (eighty-six in all), or why in just over a quarter of the limp bindings the endbands start and finish with a stab-stitch through the joint and the rest do not, is much harder to work out. The figures suggest that the stab-stitch tie-downs become more common only in the 1580s and 1590s, at which period they are about half as numerous as those without such tie-downs. Lyon imprints show almost equal numbers of first and last tie-downs in endleaf sections and text gatherings, while the endleaf variety in Paris imprints is more than three times as common as the text gathering type. Once again, the figures are hard to interpret in a definitive manner without a larger sample. There is just one binding in this collection where the endbands are worked from right to left instead of left to right like every other one, but the significance of this is obscure.[69]

Only twenty-one bindings (three of them limp) are sewn on tanned leather sewing supports, whereas 212 are sewn on tawed supports, but there appears to be no chronological or geographical pattern to this. However, the use of tawed supports is so typically French during the sixteenth century, that the use of tanned leather stands out and needs explaining. Among the limp bindings, the ways in which the cover was made and attached to the textblock disclose another wide range of variations, including sixteen different methods of folding the corners. There is also a small group of five very cheap bindings where the sewing supports are placed outside parchment wrappers which have no turn-ins (fig. 13).[70] This seems to be a specifically French technique and is found at least as late as 1613.[71] Four of the five examples are on Paris imprints, the fifth on a Lyon imprint, which offers no real clue as to where they come from. There is, in any case, in the Houghton Library at Harvard a 1551 Lyon edition in a rather elaborate version of the same structure, though this has an early inscription on the front flyleaf from Sens, which leaves open the question of where it might have been bound.[72] The Ramey collection also has four limp bindings which have yapp edges at head, tail and fore-edge, linked at the corners by a tongue of parchment inserted from the head- and tail-edge yapps into the folded fore-edge yapp (fig. 14). Two are on Paris editions and two on Lyon editions, but the date range of the imprints is quite narrow, all

13. *Upper:* Fr. Balduinus, *Ad leges maiestatis sive perduellionis commentarius*, Paris, Claude Fremy, 1563. Sewn on two external supports of rolled parchment, with a sheep parchment wrapper without turn-ins. PML 125345.

Lower: Philo, Episcop. Carpathius, *In Canticum Canticorum interpretatio ad Eustathium Praesbyterum et Eusebium Diaconum, Stephano Salutato Pisciense interprete*, Paris, Christian Wechel, 1537. Sewn on three external double supports of rolled alum-tawed skin, also with a sheepskin parchment wrapper without turn-ins. PML 125263.

falling between 1546 and 1552. Examples found elsewhere, however, expand this range from 1541 to 1568.[73] Although on the four Ramey examples the linked yapp edges are formed using three different corner-folding techniques, other structural features, as well as their appearance in the collection, suggest that it is a French style of binding, and it is not apparently recorded elsewhere.[74]

Even where the basic structural techniques used on the limp bindings are very similar, it is clear that some of them are much more neatly finished off than others. There are those which have their turn-ins and the ends of the sewing support slips trimmed neat and straight, and others where the turn-in edges are left uneven, as they were found on the skins as they came from the parchment makers; the sewing support slips are left dangling half way across the inside of the front and back covers, the pointed ends used to get them through the holes punched in the cover left intact. The question is whether this indicates different shops or craftsmen or different levels

14. Masuerius, *Practica forensis, castigatius quam antehac edita*, Paris, Galiot du Pré, 1546. Limp parchment binding with linked yapp edges. Note also the ties at head and tail as well as on the fore-edge. PML 125150.

of cost within the same shops – a question which applies to many other differences in the care with which books are put together. Cost may be the reason that some bindings have wide turn-ins and others have very narrow ones, or it may be simply the result of the size of the pieces of skin available on the day the binding was completed. Yet where economy measures are often so marked, the unnecessary use of skin does seem worthy of note. Economy certainly influenced the twelve books which have no turn-ins at all, as well as the five which have fore-edge turn-ins only.

With the exception of the sewn but otherwise unbound textblock from Bourges,[75] all the books in the collection have cut edges, ranging from a small number of mostly older books with gilt and gauffered edges[76] to books whose edges have been cut crudely with an

15. Crude knife-cut tail edge on: Fr. Balduinus, *Ad leges maiestatis sive perduellionis commentarius*, Paris, Claude Fremy, 1563. PML 125345.

instrument like a carpenters' draw knife (fig. 15) which has left diagonal marks on the edges.[77] The great majority of the books, 310 in all, show little or no sign of how the edges were cut, and were probably therefore cut with a binders' plough, as illustrated by Jost Amman in his well known woodcut of the bookbinder of 1568.[78] It is quite clear that the knife-cut edges appear largely in the first half of the century, since no imprint date later than 1547 is found with such edges among the bindings in boards, and only seven among the limp parchment bindings (with a date range of 1534–1582). This suggests that once the plough was introduced, the draw knife was used only on cheaper books, as was the case in Germany in the eighteenth century.[79]

One hundred and four imprints came to the collection from outside France,[80] but there are comparatively few bindings that can readily be identified as non-French. There are seven apparently Italian limp parchment bindings, but there is some question as to whether in fact they are all wholly Italian. A 1580 Venice imprint with a reversed cover of fine goatskin parchment and endband cores of tanned goatskin is almost certainly Italian, although its linked, 'herringbone' sewing on double tawed supports and paper panel linings are more typically French.[81] The comb linings cut from a fifteenth-century Italian manuscript offer convincing evidence that the binding on a 1549 Florentine imprint is also Italian, but the cover has type 2 tie lacing, which might indicate that a sewn textblock was all that arrived in France, to be put into its cover in Paris or by a binder

16. Pliny the Elder, *Naturalis historiae libri XXXVII*, Paris, François Regnault, 1511. Sewn all-along on four tanned and tawed double supports, endbands with primary and secondary sewing and slips laced into wooden boards, covered with polished tan goatskin, with a rectangular frame composed of repeated impressions of a tool bearing the initials IAP. PML 125275.

17. Pietro Bembo, *Epistolarum Leonis Decimi Pont. Max. nomine scriptarum libri XVI*, Lyon, Haeredes Simonis Vincent, 1538 (detail of lower cover). PML 125047.

trained in Paris.[82] Since there is a sewn textblock from Bourges in the collection still waiting for its cover, such speculation is not entirely idle, and underlines the importance of being able to identify at least the broader national structural characteristics. There are still questions, of course, even when these are identified. Although the stuck-on endbands, transverse linings, sewn single-fold endleaves, solid red-painted edges and a Strasbourg watermark (one of the very few identifiable ones) in the endleaves identify one limp parchment binding as undeniably German, the fact that it is found on a Lyon imprint of 1565 which ended up in a French-owned collection some fifty miles to the west of Lyon still needs explanation.[83] It is possible of course that a German binder might have joined his compatriots in the Lyon booktrade, but once again, more evidence is required to draw firm conclusions. A more widely based and well defined 'geography' of structural types will almost certainly identify other examples of the movement of books back and forth (such as the book with the Angeliers block)[84] within comparatively few years of publication.

This study of the Ramey collection shows the potential for drawing such conclusions from a study of the structure and materials of the bindings, with scarcely a sideways glance at tooling, which has as yet offered little potential help in localising and dating bindings in this particular collection. To date, only four bindings share any of the tools published by Denise Gid,[85] though one of these matches raises the interesting proposition of a 1499 Basle edition gathering a Norman binding on its way to St-Just-en-Chevalet.[86] One binding only, a splendid example from the shop of Claude Chevallon with the roll

18. Headband of the 1538 Bembo, showing the end of the length of wood which serves as an endband core. PML 125047.

containing his rebus,[87] can be attached to a name, though on another early binding, each cover has a rectangular frame made up from repeated impressions of a tool bearing the initials IAP (fig. 16).[88] Every bit as recognisable is the delightful cat (or is it a dog?) bearing another small animal on its back (fig. 17),[89] which would appear to be taken from the device of the Parisian bookseller Poncet le Preux, where it is found on the shield supported by two winged dragons. Described by Davies as a wolf,[90] it is presumably another example of a bookseller's retail binding, this time from the shop of Le Preux on a book printed in Lyon. If the block was used by a single binder who worked for (or was employed by) Le Preux, the shop might be as easily distinguished by its eccentric use of a length of wood as an endband core (fig. 18).

Finally, the Ramey collection has a Lyon imprint of 1535 in a structure which is, apparently, unique.[91] Each gathering is sewn separately to three tanned leather straps with lengths of thread knotted at head and tail of the individual gatherings, with no thread link between the gatherings (fig. 19). A piece of manuscript waste written on thin flesh-split sheep parchment is secured to the structure with tackets of thread around the three leather supports along each joint. As no similar bindings are available for comparison, it is impossible to place or even accurately date this structure, beyond saying that there is no apparent reason for it not to be contemporary. The assumption that a Lyon imprint in this particular library is likely

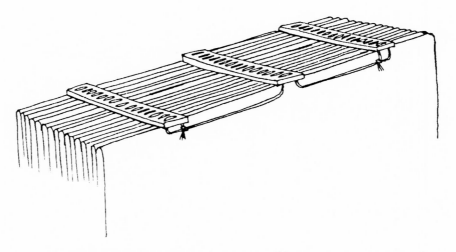

19. M. T. Cicero, *Rhetoricorum ad Herennium libri IIII*, Lyon, Vincentius de
Portonariis, 1535. Sewing structure, showing how each gathering is secured
to the tanned leather supports with separate lengths of thread. PML 125182.

to be in a Lyon binding, is, as has been shown, not necessarily safe,
but should we, confronted by such eccentric work, look for a binder
even closer to the Ramey family home – a cobbler in Montbrison
perhaps? It is impossible to know unless other examples turn up, and
we can never know the answers to many such questions until more of
this information is recorded from such books as remain intact for our
exploration. Small as it is, this collection alone has much more yet to
offer, and the analysis of the structural information recorded continues. It does show that there is much to be learnt from structure,
even if the sample is too limited to offer definitive answers to more
than a hand-full of the questions it raises. However, identifying the
potentially useful questions allows the many thousands of examples
of such bindings scattered across the libraries of the world to play a
more coherent part in finding the answers. It should also show that
even small details of the meanest and plainest of bindings can contribute to our understanding of the economics of the booktrade and
the movement of books across Europe.

NOTES

1 Defined as books in which the uncovered boards of the book are attached to the sewn textblock, either by the sewing support slips or by some part of the endleaves, before the book is covered. This is the structure found on almost all leather- and textile-bound books within the era of the hand press and many parchment-covered books also.

2 Defined as books whose covering material, typically parchment but also paper and occasionally leather, is not wrapped around stiff boards, but forms the sole component of the cover. Such covers, which can be prepared off the book, are usually secured to the sewn textblock by the sewing supports and/or the endband slips at the final stage of the binding process.

3 In long stitch bindings, the book is sewn through both the gatherings and the covering material (typically parchment or thick paper) at the same time, and results in lengths of thread showing in one or more rows across the spine. It was a rapid and economical way to hold books together, and was often used for temporary, retail bindings and cheaper blank books from the late fifteenth-century onwards.

4 Usefully defined in the decree of the Lord Mayor and Court of Aldermen of 25 March 1586 as 'any booke in any volume whatsoever which is or shalbe bored or prycked thoroughe [the inner margin] with bodkyn, alle, needle or other instrument, and stitched with thryd, slyp of leather, or other suche devise, (but suche onelie, and none other, as shalbe sowed upon a sowing presse as heretofore hathe bene accustomed)'. See David Foxon, 'Stitched books', *The Book Collector*, 24, no. 1 (Spring 1975), pp. 111–24, and Giles Barber, 'Continental paper wrappers and publishers' bindings in the 18th century', *ibid.*, pp. 37–49.

5 I am grateful to Paul Needham, then at the Pierpont Morgan library, for introducing me to the Ramey collection, which he had successfully secured for that library, and to George Fletcher, his successor, for his continuing help and encouragement. I should also like to thank the staff in the reading room under Inge Dupont for unfailing courtesy and help while handling the large quantities of material which I needed to see.

6 Lotus 1-2-3 was first used, and subsequently Excel 4.0. I am grateful to Sid Kemp of the Columbia University School of Library Science for his advice and patient help in mastering the necessary computer skills.

7 I am grateful to Professor Dennis L. Bark of Stanford University and his wife, a descendant of the Ramey family, not only for the information given here about the family, but also for their interest in and encouragement of my research into the library. The information comes from an unpublished history of the family which makes extensive use of family and parochial archives as well as the departmental archives of the Loire and Rhone. It is tempting to speculate on the influence that proximity to the famous library of the d'Urfé family, patrons of the Rameys, might have had on the Ramey collection. Honoré d'Urfé, author of *L'Astrée*, was an almost exact contemporary of Jean Ramey.

8 This date is given in the family papers, but the signature generally assumed to be that of Jean Ramey is to be found in a book printed in 1633, still in the family house in St-Just: Jean Dauxiron, *Lyderic, premier forestier de Flandre, ou philosophie morale de la victoire de nos passions, sur le fonds d'une noble histoire*, Lyon, Claude Larjot, 1633. Clearly, either the date of Jean Ramey's death has been wrongly recorded, or the signature found throughout the collection is that of another Jean Ramey.

9 *Il Nuovo Testamento tradotto in lingua Toscana corretto dal R. Padre Fra Zaccharia da Firenze*, Venice, Lucantonio Giunta, 1536 (PML 125288).

10 Professor Bark, in a letter dated 11 November, 1993, informed me that there is no family record of any sales of books from the library, though a division of the estate into

three parts in 1804 may have seen the distribution of 'the large and finely bound books' – though whether this would have affected the 16th-century collection is open to doubt.

11   See note 8 above.

12   A copy of Jean de Marconville, *Traicté enseignant d'ou procède la diversité des opinions des hommes*, Paris, Jean Dallier, 1563 (PML 125158).

13   The copy of Petrus Marcellus, *De vitis principum et gestis Venetorum liber*, Venice, 1554 (PML 125357), for instance, bears the name of 'Claudius Ramey subdiaconus' dated 1679. It is impossible to know whether this was one of Jehan or Jean Ramey's books subsequently used by this Claude Ramey, or a book bought by the latter which ended up in the family library. The copy of Herodian, *Libri octo ab Angelo Politiano latinate donati*, Paris, Simon Colines, 1529 (PML 125308) bears the inscription on an inserted blank bifolium 'ex libris Antonii de Renusson humanistae' dated 1642, which must, presumably, be a seventeenth-century or later addition to the library.

14   Joannes Crozetius, *In sextum decalogi praeceptum, non moechaberis*, Lyon, Jean de Tournes, 1552 (PML 125012).

15   I use the term 'parchment' as the generic, and define it when necessary (and possible) by the animal whose skin is used to make it (e.g. sheep parchment). I use the term 'vellum' only of parchment made from calf skins. [As it is as a rule very difficult to distinguish between the various animal skins used for making parchment or vellum, the other authors in this volume have followed the normal convention of using 'vellum' for the binding material and 'parchment' for the writing material. (Ed.)]

16   Eguinarius Baro, *Institutionum civilium ab Iustiniano Caesare editarum libri IIII*, Bourges, 1546 (PML 125300). Figs 1–3, 5–6, 8–9, 13–18 have been reproduced by kind permission of the Pierpont Morgan Library.

17   Io. Baptista Folengius, *Commentaria in primam D. Joannis Epistolam*, Antwerp, ex officina Joannis Loei, 1547 (PML125286).

18   Edmond du Boullay, *La Vie et trespas des deux Princes de Paix, le bon Duc Anthoine & saige Duc Françoys premiers de leurs noms*, Metz, Jehan Pallier, 1547 (PML 125017).

19   Franciscus Patricius, *De regno et regis institutione libri IX*, Paris, Gilles Gorbin, 1582 (PML 125046); Franciscus Patricius, *De institutione reipublicae libri novem*, Paris, Gilles Gorbin, 1585 (PML125336); Nonius Marcellus, *De proprietate sermonis et Fulgentius Planciades, De prisco sermone*, Paris, Gilles Beys, 1583 (PML125056).

20   Pausanias, *Veteris Graeciae descriptio Romulo Amaseo interprete*, Lyon, Haeredus Giuntae & Iacobus Forus, 1558 (PML 125316), and *Dictionarium poeticum*, Lyon, Haeredes Jacobi Giuntae, 1556 (PML 125346).

21   Philibert Boyer, *Le Style de la cour de parlement*, Paris, Galiot Corrozet, 1584 (PML 125161), and Nicolas Vignier, *De la noblesse, ancienneté, remarques et merites d'honneur de la troisiesme maison de France*, Paris, Abel L'Angelier, 1587 (PML 125145).

22   Johannes Ferrarius Montanus, *Ad titulum pandectarum, de regulis iuris, integer commentarius*, Lyon, Sebastianus Gryphius, 1537 (PML 125072). For a discussion of other books bearing the same stamp see E. Ph. Goldschmidt, *Gothic & Renaissance bookbindings*, London, 1928, pp. 33–42, 264, and Martin Breslauer, Inc., Cat. 104, pt 2, *Fine books in fine bindings*, pp. 242–3, which illustrates a binding apparently identical to that on the Ramey Montanus.

23   Lilius Gregorius Gyraldus, *De deis gentium libri sive syntagmata XVII*, Lyon, Haeredes Iacobi Iunctae, 1565 (PML 125008).

24   The totals are: Venice 31, Basle 27, Antwerp 15 and Cologne 14.

25   See Lucien Febvre and Henri-Jean Martin, *The Coming of the book* (transl. David Gerard), London, 1984, p. 193.

26 Jean du Tillet, *Les Memoires et les recherches de Jean du Tillet Greffier de la cour de Parlement a Paris*, Troyes, Philippe de Chams, 1578 (PML 125152). The preparation of the textblock in this instance displays a number of expensive techniques in addition to the five sewing supports. It is sewn all-along, it has two complete folds of clean paper to make up the endleaves at each end, and uses comb-type spine linings made from medieval manuscript waste. The cover, by contrast, is of a yellowish sheep parchment, without ties and with only three of the five supports laced through the cover. It seems likely that the cover was intended as a temporary expedient.

27 Some of the 'goatskin' used is not true goat, but the skin of the hair-sheep.

28 Joannes Copus, *De fructibus libri quatuor*, Paris, Christian Wechel, 1535 (PML 125028). The book is neatly finished, and although it uses the cheapest endleaf format (single folds of paper hooked around first and last gatherings), there would be no reason to suspect that the false bands were not functional, as they are both laced into the boards, without a close examination of the sewing. It is possible that the book was first bought in a temporary binding, either in uncovered boards or with a parchment cover (or without cover at all), and that either the binder or an early owner decided to dress it up without going to the expense of resewing it, possibly to match other books. The existence of temporary bindings suggests that such hybrids cannot be uncommon – the problem is to identify them.

29 I have described some of these English bindings in 'Cutting corners: some deceptive practices in seventeenth-century English bookbinding' in: J. L. Sharpe (ed.), *Roger Powell: the compleat binder. Bibliologia*, 14, Turnhout, 1996, pp. 272–9.

30 PML 125020, 125030, 125033, 125034, 125039, 125040, 125050, 125210, 125239, 125265, 125266, 125275, 125301, 125328, 125333, 125351. Such features at this date as ties at head and tail as well as on the foredge, flat or near flat spines, endbands without front beads, and transverse spine linings, while by no means exclusively Italian, are more typical of Italian binding, especially in combination. The use of goatskin could also reflect southern animal husbandry as much as Italian influence.

31 The earliest example now known to me of intentional bypass sewing is found in a near contemporary binding in boards, covered in blind-tooled tanned goatskin, on a copy of Franciscus Patricius, *De institutione reipublicae libri novem … hactenus nunquam impraessi, cum Joannis Savignei annotationibus marineis*, Paris, Pierre Vidoue for Galiot du Pré, 1518 (Bibliotheca Ecclesiastica Narni, B 24 VG 1339). I know of no other example of this early date.

32 This extract from a decree dated 25 March 1586 is quoted in full in a number of places, but most usefully in David Foxon, 'Stitched books', pp. 111.

33 *Brevis augustissimi ac summe venerandi sacrosanctae missae sacrificii ex sanctis patribus contra impium Francisci Stancari Mantuani scriptum, assertio*, Cologne, Haeredes Arnoldi Birckmanni, 1577 (PML 125222).

34 Wilhelmus Damasus Lindanus, *Paraphraseωn in psalmos Davidicos tomus*, Antwerp, Christophe Plantin, 1574 (PML 125128).

35 Joannes Franciscus Sardis, *Tractatus de essentia infantis, proximi infanti et proximi pubertati*, Florence, Giunta, 1568 (PML 125227).

36 Justus Lipsius, *De constantia libri duo. Editio sexta*, Lyon, Hug. à Porta, 1596 (PML 125178).

37 Franciscus Hotomanus, *De gradibus cognationis et affinitatis libri duo*, Paris, Joannes Bogardus, 1547 (PML 125122); Saint Ignatius, *Les Epistres*, Paris, Guillaume Morel, 1562 (PML 125170); C. le Bret, *Recueil d'aucuns plaidoyez faict en la cour des Aides*, Paris, Iamet Mettayer & Pierre L'Huillier, 1597 (PML 125166).

38 Joannes Oldendorp, *Enchiridion exceptionum forensium*, Lyon, Sebastianus Gryphius, 1556 [bound with] *Idem, Topicorum legalium traditio*, Lyon, Sebastianus Gryphius, 1556, (PML 125154). The cover is illustrated in Nicholas Pickwoad,

'Onward and downward: how binders coped with the printing press before 1800' in: R. Myers and M. Harris (eds), *A Millenium of the book: production, design and illustration in manuscript and print (900–1900)*, Winchester, 1994, p. 87.

39 See note 34.

40 Eustathius, *Gli amori d'Ismenio composti per Eustathio philosopho et di Greco tradotti per Lelio Cassani*, Florence, Lorenzo Torentino, 1550 (PML125143). Apart from the reversed skin, the broad transverse linings cut from a fragment of medieval manuscript and the primary endband sewing with eleven tie-downs mark this binding as Italian. Very unusually, however, for any European country at this date, it has unsewn single fold endleaves.

41 Franciscus Maria Grapaldi, *De partibus aedium*, Parma, Franciscus Ugoletus, 1506 (PML 125014). A Paris-printed post-incunable, *Epistole et orationes Gaguini*, Paris, Durand Gerlier, [*c.* 1505] (Houghton Library, *FC.G1234.D505E, Goff G-17) also has an early binding covered in a reversed tawed skin, though of a different colour, a shade of purply-brown, and an incunable, Robertus Caracciolus, *Sermones quadragesimales de peccatis*, Venice, Andreas Torresanus, 1488 (*Incunabula from the court library at Donaueschingen*, London, Sotheby's, 1 July 1994, p. 88, no. 85) also has a reversed, tawed sheepskin covering, but this was probably added to the original Italian cartonnage long stitch binding by the Franciscans of Villingen in South Germany, who owned the book in the sixteenth century and stamped their initials on it.

42 The 1506 Parma edition (see note 41) is in a markedly cheaper binding, without endbands and with very crudely cut edges. One other example lacks endbands, Gregory IX, *Decretales epistolae supremi ortodoxe ecclesie principis Gregorii noni ab infinitis mendis de novo expurgate*, Paris, Johannes Kerbriand, 1537 (PML 125016), but is in other respects a well-made book.

43 The thirteen examples in the collection have between them the following edge colours: three mauve, two red, one pink, and one purple. The five brown edges were most probably originally yellow (several of the brown edges in the collection show traces of yellow in protected areas). The only uncoloured edge in the group is on the Parma imprint, whose crudely cut edges would not have lent themselves to colouring.

44 PML 125019 (Paris, 1489), PML 125328 (Venice, 1504), PML 125351 (Venice, 1505), PML 125275 (Paris, 1511), PML 125020 (Paris, 1512), and PML 125039 (Lyon, 1513).

45 There is also an unlined kind of limp parchment binding in which these slips are not laced in, also found towards the end of the sixteenth century, but these seem to be mostly Italian. I have so far seen only one French example, which is both comparatively late (1602) and small (167 mm high). It is on a copy of *Recueil de quelques vers amoureux*, Paris, par la veuve Mamert Patisson, 1602 (Houghton Library, *FC5.B4614.602r). In any case, a careful examination may be needed to determine which structure is which.

46 Petrus Gregorius, *Praeludia optimi iurisconsulti, probique magistrates*, Lyon, Antonius Gryphius, 1583 (PML 125202) and Lodovico Paterno, *Le Nuove fiamme*, Lyon, Gulielmus Rovillius, 1568 (PML 125211).

47 There are numerous elegant versions of the cover lining binding, typically tooled in gold on calf vellum with gilt edges. Their appearance clearly appealed to de Thou, amongst others, and his library had several examples. The question of which type, the elegant or the cheap version, came first and influenced the other will only be resolved by the identification of many more examples, but it should be remembered that in the history of bookbinding, structural developments do not always work 'top down'.

48 A copy of R. Constantinus (ed.), *Thesaurus linguae Latinae seu promptuarium dictionum et loquendi formularum omnium ad Latini sermonis perfectuam notitiam assequendam pertinentium: ex optimis auctoribus concinnatum*, Lyon, 1573, remaining in the family collection at St-Just, makes use of three copies of the first sheet of an

early sixteenth-century edition of Jason de Maino, *Lectura ... super nodos titulo de actionibus institutionum.*

49   Rochus Curtius, *Enarrationes in celeberrimum iuris cap. 'cum tanto'*, Lyon, Haeredes Jacobi Giuntae, 1551 (PML 125132). The covering technique (lacing the sewing support slips through cover and lining) found on this book appears to be more commonly found on German imprints, but all the other structural features of this binding are specifically French.

50   For the earlier editions, see note 44. Of the bindings on later imprints, one is on a volume containing a Basle and a Cologne imprint of 1530 and is German (PML 125329), the second contains a Tübingen imprint of 1530, together with two Cologne imprints of 1538 and 1534 (PML 125229, a French binding in reversed tawed sheep), and the third covers a Paris imprint of 1531.

51   Of these seven volumes, five have Paris imprints dating from between 1505 and 1533 (PML 125037, 125050, 125224, 125293 and 125301), one has a Florentine imprint of 1531 in a French binding (PML 125311) and the remaining one is bound in black silk (Lyon, 1552, PML 125012).

52   A single volume containing two works by Erasmus: *Declarationes ad censuras Lutetiae vulgatas sub nomine Facultatis Theologicae Parisiensis*, Basle, Froben, 1532 and *Dilutio eorumque Iodocus Clithoueus scripsit adversus declamationem suasoriam matrimonii*, Basle, Froben, 1532 (PML125237).

53   See note 14.

54   Recessed supports were introduced into French bookbinding in response to the demand to imitate Greek-style bindings with smooth spines following François I's decision in the late 1530s to create a Greek library in France (see Anthony Hobson, *Humanists and bookbinders,* Cambridge, 1989, p. 179, and Nicholas Pickwood, 'Italian and French sixteenth-century bookbindings', *Gazette of the Grolier Club,* NS 43, 1991, pp. 66–74). That there is a direct connection between what was then a new structure and traditional Greek-style binding is indicated by the use of the French word 'grequer' for sawing-in, and in referring to the sawn-in recess itself as 'un grec' (see, for example, Jean-Vincent Capronnier de Gauffecourt, *Traité de la relieure des livres* (transl. Claude Benaiteau with an introduction by John P. Chalmers), Austin, Texas, 1987, p. 93).

55   Eight bindings in boards and twenty-five limp bindings have no linings, and in a further twenty-six bindings it was impossible to tell whether or not there were linings.

56   Jean Gerson, *Operum pars prima,* [Nuremberg, Georg Stuchs], 1489 (PML 125019) and Cassiodorus, *Hystoria tripartita Cassiodori senatoris ... de regimine ecclesie,* Paris, François Regnault, [after 1500] (PML 125239, Goff C-242).

57   The copy of Valerius Maximus, *Dictorum ac factorum memorabilium tam Romanorum, quam extremorum collecteana, cum Oliveri Arzignanensis commentario, et Iodoci Badii Ascensii familiarissima ac plane dilucida expositione,* Paris, Poncet Le Preux, 1535 (PML 125224), has the ends of the transverse linings pasted onto the outside of the wooden boards, a technique more common in fifteenth- and early sixteenth-century German and Italian bindings, and the copy of *In P. Cornelium Tacitum annotationes Beati Rhenani, Alciati ac Beroaldi,* Lyon, Sebastianus Gryphius, 1542 (PML125015), bound in reversed tawed sheepskin, has ties on the fore-edge and the tail only, for which I know of no precedent. In addition it has transverse linings in only the odd numbered panels of the spine (one, three and five, numbering from the head), together with slips recessed in small triangular cut-out recesses on the inside of the boards, a technique normally associated with much more expensive bindings than this.

58   PML 125012, see note 14. Such linings are probably unusual, but I have seen one on an extremely elaborate binding by Jean de Planche for Sir Nicholas Bacon on a copy of Conrad Lycosthenes, *Theatrum vitae humanae,* Basle, 1565, in the library of

Kingston Lacey, now the property of the National Trust (see G. Jackson-Stops (ed.), *The Treasure houses of Britain*, London and New Haven, 1985, pp. 404–5).

59   The comb lining is illustrated in M. Dudin, *The Art of the bookbinder and gilder*, 1772 (transl. R. M. Atkinson), Leeds, 1977, plate 9, and is clearly described in Ephraim Chambers' *Cyclopaedia* of 1728: 'After this in the French binding, a book is put into Parchment, i.e. a slip of parchment the length of the book, is apply'd on the inside of each Pasteboard; so, however, as that being cut or indented in the Places against the Bands, it comes out between the Edge of the Pasteboard and the Leaves of the Book to cover the Back: This Preparation, call'd Indorsing, seems peculiar to the French Binders; who are enjoyn'd by Ordonnance to back their Books with Parchment, on Penalty of 300 Livres, and the Rebinding of the Book.' (E. Chambers, *Cyclopaedia; or, an universal dictionary of arts and sciences,* London, 1728, vol. I, pp. 116–7, which is largely translated from Jacques Savary des Bruslons, *Dictionnaire universel de commerce*, Paris, 1723).

60   Only two of these are found on bindings in boards, PML 125054 (Paris, 1545 and with an inscription on the front flyleaf dated 1548) and PML125341 (Lyon, 1546, in a contemporary binding). The other twelve are all on limp bindings, ranging in date from 1553 to 1595.

61   See note 26.

62   Aristotle, *Politica, ab Iacobo Lodoico Strebaeo nomine Joannis Bertrandi Senatoris Judicisque sapientissime conversa*, Paris, Michel de Vascosan, 1542 (PML 125102).

63   The books are: Plautus, *Comoediae XX*, Venice, Lazarus Soardus, 1511 (Butler Library, Columbia University, Butler Folio 1511 P698); Jacopo Silvestro, *Opus novum*, Rome, 1521 (New York Public Library, *KB 1526 Silvestri); Cicero, *De philosophia*, Paris, Simon Colines, 1545 (Fulbeck Hall, Lincolnshire); Joannes de Roias, *Commentariorum in astrolabum, quod planisphaerium vocant, libri sex*, Paris, Vascosan, 1550; Lucius Annaeus Seneca, *Tragoediae*, Lyon, Sebastianus Gryphius, 1548. The de Thou volume (with the bachelor arms) is Michael Vosmer, *Principes Hollandiae et Zelandiae, domini Frisiae*, Antwerp, Plantin, 1578 (University of Virginia, Alderman Library, Special Collections, Gordon 1578.V67).

64   Thycidides, *L'Hystoire de Thucydide Athenien de la guerre qui fut entre les Peloponesiens et Atheniens* (transl. from Lorenzo Valla's Latin by Claude de Seyssel into French), Paris, Gilles Gormont, 1530 (PML 125273).

65   Of the Lyon imprints in limp bindings, thirty have paste-downs and only three do not, whereas of the Paris imprints in limp bindings, twenty-seven have paste-downs against sixty-two which do not. This seems to me to be a significant difference, and it will be interesting to see whether other undisturbed examples of French limp binding bear this out. If so, then it might be possible to show that the twenty-seven Paris imprints with paste-downs were in fact bound in Lyon.

66   See Dudin, *op. cit.*, pp. 27–8 and Pickwoad, 'Italian and French sixteenth-century bookbindings', *Gazette of the Grolier Club*, p. 74 and fig. 8. Chambers, *op. cit.*, vol. I, pp. 116–7, also refers to the French practice of passing the slips 'thro three holes'.

67   See Colin Clair, *Christopher Plantin*, London, 1987, pp. 207–8.

68   Godescalcus Stewechius, *In L. Apulei opera omnia quaestiones et coniecturae*, Antwerp, Christophe Plantin, 1586 (PML 125185).

69   Torquato Tasso, *Il Goffredo overo Gierusalemme liberata*, Venice, Giovan Battista Ciotti, 1595 (PML 125290). The binding is probably Italian, though it is difficult to tell, being both heavily damaged and very cheaply put together. Being left-handed, I can confirm that that has nothing to do with it.

70   PML 125155 (Paris, 1535), 125263 (Paris, 1537), 125255 (Lyon, 1546), 125345 (Paris, 1563), and 125310 (Paris, 1569).

71 *Nouvelle guide des chemins*, Paris, 1613 (Lincoln Cathedral, Oo 7.15).

72 *Le Grand calendrier et compost des bergiers*, Lyon, Jehan Canterel, 1551 (Houghton Library, Typ 515.51.258). Another limp parchment binding with external supports in the Houghton library is on a much earlier book (*La Cronique de Gennes avec la totalle description de toute Ytallie*, Paris, Eustace de Brie, 1508, *FC5.A100.507c), but this uses cord as the sewing support material, and I cannot tell how early the binding may be. An incunable edition of pseudo-Bonaventure, *Tractatus de profectu religiosorum,* Paris, Denis Roce, [*c.* 1500], in the Library of Congress (Goff B-888), also has an external-support limp parchment binding, using rolled tawed skin as the support material. This suggests that an early date for the introduction of these bindings is possible, but the presence later in the century of more sophisticated versions, both in the Ramey collection with double supports (Paris, 1537) and in the Houghton 1552 *Calendrier*, also with double supports and slips laced through the parchment cover, suggests that the two earlier texts were put into the bindings somewhat later in the century. Similar sewing structures are found on manuscript notebooks of the fourteenth–fifteenth centuries in the Herzog August Bibliothek (Dag-Ernst Petersen, *Mittelalterliche Bucheinbände der Herzog August Bibliothek*, Wolfenbuettel, 1975, plate xxxvi) and on two late fifteenth- or early sixteenth-century manuscripts in the Bibliothèque municipale in Vendôme (Jean-Louis Alexandre, Genevieve Grand, Guy Lanoë, *Reliures medievales des bibliothèques de France: Bibliothèque municipale de Vendôme*, Turnhout, 2000, figs 118 and 119), suggesting that this unusual structure derived from the blank-book binding tradition, as is the case with so many other inexpensive bindings. Its use on printed books appears to be exclusively French.

73 Lilius Gregorius Gyraldus, *De annis et mensibus, caeterisque temporum partibus*, Basle, Isingrinius, 1541 (Special Collections, St. John's University, Minnesota) and Marcus Valerius Martialis, *Epigrammaton libri XII*, Antwerp, Plantin, 1568 [bound with] Decimus Magnus Ausonius, *Opera*, Antwerp, Plantin, 1568 (Folger Library PA 6501 A2 1568 Cage, illustrated in Frederick A. Bearman, Nati H. Krivatsky and J. Franklin Mowery, *Fine and historic bookbindings in the Folger Shakespeare Library*, Washington, 1992, p. 149).

74 I have seen only one English example of this phenomenon on a copy of Sir Anthony Fitzherbert, *La Graunde abridgement*, London, Richard Tottel, 1577 (Swaffham Parish Library, SWD 4/21, Lyons 229, STC 10957). It is probably either an example of French influence on English binding practice, or the work of a French binder living in England.

75 See note 16.

76 PML 125351 (Venice, 1505, in a French binding), PML 125050 (Paris, 1522, with the name D E M Y N E R A Y gauffered on the fore-edge), PML 125265–6 (Paris, 1524). The only later binding with gauffered edges is the silk binding, PML 125012 (Lyon, 1552, see note 14), a binding of unusually high quality for the collection.

77 The earliest depiction I know of a draw knife in use appears in a fresco in the Salone Sistina in the Vatican by Cesare Nebbia and Giovanni Guerra, 1585–90, illustrated in: Anthony Grafton (ed.), *Rome reborn: the Vatican Library and Renaissance culture*, Washington DC, 1993, p. 45.

78 Jost Amman and Hans Sachs, *Eygentliche Beschreibung aller Stände auff Erden ... aller Künsten, Handwercken und Händeln*, Frankfurt, 1568.

79 See Christoph Ernst Prediger, *Der in aller heut zu Tag üblichen Arbeit wohl anweisende accurate Buchbinder und Futeralmacher*, 4 vols, Frankfurt and Leipzig, 1741–53, vol. II, plate 8.

80 The figures are fifty-three from German-speaking countries, thirty-six from Italy and fifteen from the Low Countries.

81   Bernardo Tasso, *Le Lettere*, Venice, 1580 (PML 125285).

82   Mercurius Trismegistus, *Il Pimandro di Mercurio Trismegisto, tradotta da Tommaso Benci in lingua fiorentina*, Florence, 1549 (PML 125157).

83   See note 23.

84   See note 22.

85   Denise Gid, *Catalogue des reliures françaises estampées à froid XVe–XVIe siècle, de la Bibliothèque Mazarine*, 2 vols, Paris, 1984.

86   Ivo, *Liber decretorum sive panormia Ivonis accurato labore summoque studio in unum redacta continens*, Basle, Michael Furter, 1499 (PML 125030, Goff I-223). This binding uses rolls DCc7 and ENp from Gid, *op. cit.*, p. 429, no. 518, there found on: Erasmus, *Lingua*, Antwerp, Michael Hillenius, 1526, 8° and on Joannes Franciscus Quintianus Stoa (Giovanni Francesco), *Tragedia de passione Domini nostri Jesu Christi*, Lyon, Laurent Hylaire for Pierre Ballet, 1515, 8°. The localisation to Normandy appears to be given without supporting evidence.

87   Aulus Gellius, *Noctium Atticarum libri XX. summa accuratione Joannis Connelli Camoten. ad recognitionem Beroaldinam repositi*, Paris, Jehan Petit, 1511 (PML 125334).

88   Pliny the Elder, *Naturalis historiae libri XXXVII*, Paris, François Regnault, 1511 (PML 125275).

89   Pietro Bembo, *Epistolarum Leonis Decimi Pont. Max. nomine scriptarum libri XVI*, Lyon, Haeredes Simonis Vincent, 1538 (PML 125047).

90   H. W. Davies, *Devices of early printers 1457–1560*, London, 1935, pp. 470–1. The device is also illustrated in L. C. Sylvestre, *Marques typographiques*, Paris, 1853, no. 421. Two other bindings with the Le Preux device have been published, in: John P. Harthan, 'Early trade bindings', *The Book Collector*, 1 (1952), p. 266, and Georges Colin, 'A binding with the mark of Poncet Le Preux', *The Book Collector*, 23 (1974), pp. 213–4; the latter example is illustrated.

91   M. T. Cicero, *Rhetoricorum ad Herennium libri IIII*, Lyon, Vincentius de Portonariis, 1535 (PML 125182).

AROUND THE PADELOUP
AND DEROME WORKSHOPS

Gold-tooled Parisian Bindings
of the Eighteenth Century

Giles Barber

T HE NATURE OF THE STONE may, as some sculptors find, evolve differently from what they first thought. The same can happen to bibliographical research. My material comes largely from work done over all too many years on the very fine library of French seventeenth- and eighteenth-century books and bindings at Waddesdon Manor, a collection put together by Baron Ferdinand Rothschild (1844–1897). The manor and its collections now belong to the National Trust and reopened in 1994 after a total refurbishment masterminded by Lord Rothschild. I owe much to the Trust, to Lord Rothschild and to the late Baronne Elie de Rothschild for help and support in preparing the catalogue of books, a work taken over after the sudden and much regretted death of Graham Pollard, and I would like to express my very warm thanks to them for their encouragement in a work which is now, at last, drawing to a close.[1]

Nicholas Pickwoad's essay on the Ramey collection, published elsewhere in this volume, deals with French binding construction in the sixteenth century. My subtitle is intended to underline a shift to finishing and a later century: the title itself to suggest a concentration on the techniques employed in the leading workshops. It will first however be necessary to set out the general background to the eighteenth century Parisian bookbinding trade, and then to run through the main decorative styles of the period before finally studying the execution of certain works in detail.

The mere mention of Paris in the eighteenth century tends to evoke memories of summer days at Versailles, an atmosphere of sun-lit terraces, gods, goddesses and steeds serving as sparkling fountains in shimmering pools, terraced walks with vast urns of geraniums and large boxes of potted palms, the whole against a backdrop of classical architecture and aristocratic opulence. The bindings we have to consider may have ended up in such a world but they began life in a very different one. The opening passage Patrick Suskind's famous novel, *Perfume* (London, 1985), set in early eighteenth-century Paris, starts with the birth of his hero, fair and square in the fish market of the Place de la Grève, a far more down market location. The scene is described in detail, bringing out every smell, every scrap and pile of rubbish to be associated with the crowded conditions under which the poorer members of the Paris work force had lived for centuries. Victor Hugo too reflected this in a romantic sort of way, the scene with him in *Notre-Dame de Paris* (1831) or even in *Les Misérables* (1862), being crowded but full of life; Suskind underlines the more sordid side. Another writer, the American novelist Janet Lewis, picks up yet another aspect in her book, *The Ghost of Monsieur Scarron* (1959), which is based on a real-life incident in the Paris binding trade of the period when a journeyman printer and an apprentice binder were hung for producing and selling a 'scandalous' publication concerning the marriage of Louis XIV and Madame de Maintenon, the widow of the novelist Scarron. For the poorer members of the trade Versailles and the world of luxury were a long way away, living – and indeed working – conditions were rudimentary and times were hard.

First then, what do we know of the binding trade around 1700? Louis XIV had come to power against the background of the Civil War called the *Fronde*; a recession and the strongly centralist policies of Colbert had led to stricter control of the organisation of many trades and, in particular, of the potentially dangerous booktrade. The government had found itself to have common ground with the bigger printer-publishers in a desire to reduce the number of those engaged in the various sides of the book trades and especially in eliminating smaller, and often less orthodox, operators. As far as the binding trade was concerned there were moves towards this in the 1670s but it was not finally until 1686 that Colbert forced through an edict which decreed the separation of the binders from the other book trades, requiring members of the community to opt permanently for either printing and publishing or for binding. There were evidently minor concessions allowing printers to bind very small items, or those in cheaper paper or vellum covers, but in general and despite a fairly long-drawn out struggle this separated the binders, ever the poorer brothers, into an independent guild of much reduced status. They remained officers of the University and continued to belong to the same religious community as the printers and booksellers but even this latter right was whittled away by 1730.

The *Règlement des relieurs et doreurs de livres* (note the further distinction between trades), issued in September 1686, required the members to reside within the University area and to elect officers.[2] It also controlled admission to the mastership as well as the number of apprentices and the way in which members' relatives could enter the trade on favourable terms. All this was very similar to the regulations for other trades. The new guild started with some forty-five members but, despite apparently rigid controls on admission, it has been suggested that by 1718 there were 184 and that at the mid-century some 300 masters and 400 journeymen were at work in Paris.[3] There are no firm lists until around 1770 but we can say that at that date there were around 250 masters and that for each of the previous five-year periods thirty (or roughly six a year on average) masters had been admitted. In the 1770s therefore it would appear that there were some thirty binders in their seventies or late sixties, thirty-three in their late fifties, sixty-one in their forties, twenty-six in their thirties, and sixty-six in their twenties, the evident oscillation between these groups being due to the intermittent way in which both government and trade regulated the numbers, at times forbidding admissions for five or even ten years at a go. It is of course very evident that many bear similar family names and, although theoretically (and indeed practically) open, the guild was, equally obviously, progressively closing itself to outsiders through both inheritance and intermarriage. The dynasties of Anguerrands, Bradels, Deromes and Padeloups, to name but some, illustrate the point.

The regulations also required the binders to live within the University area of Paris and as a result three quarters of the Parisian binders of the late eighteenth century can be found in five small intercommunicating streets, one a mere forty-five feet long and with only five houses on each side (fig. 1). These were located on the north side of the Montagne Sainte-Geneviève or, in today's parlance, just to the south of the Boulevard Saint-Germain, near the statue of Ronsard next to the Collège de France. They lived very much cheek by jowl, clustered around the guild church of St Hilaire (now destroyed and represented only by a café of that name). The houses were dark and crowded and the cramped conditions, while hardly worse than those of fellow booktrade workers, were clearly rudimentary and unpleasant even if neighbouring streets, such as the evocatively named Rue des Amandiers, then led immediately into open countryside. Moreover the working day was long – a strike in 1776 attempted unsuccessfully to reduce it from sixteen to fourteen hours – and a vivid picture of the

1. The area close to the Sorbonne and the booksellers in the Rue St Jacques where bookbinders had to live. L. Bretez, *Plan de Paris*, Paris 1739.

horrors of an apprentice's life can be read in the poem (one of a series on various trades) entitled *La Misère des apprentifs relieurs et doreurs de livres* [Paris, 1747].[4] The impression to be kept in mind is that the trade, regulated by official decrees and by community rules, watched over by guild officials and police spies, was run by inter-related families living in very close proximity and doubtless sharing many common sources of supply for their materials. Such conclusions cannot but affect our interpretation of certain trade problems.

Following the trade, its location, and the people involved, what do we know about their equipment? Here we are fortunate in having some post-mortem inventories which give us at least a small insight into contemporary binders' houses.[5] One of the royal binders, Luc-Antoine Boyet, died in 1733. He was known as a rich man, owning his house where the workshop was on the ground floor with two large presses, three tables with four finishing presses, and two smaller presses. The living room and bedroom were, clearly unusually, on the first floor. The elder of the more famous Deromes, Jacques-Antoine, died in 1760 at the age of sixty-four but he may well have retired for he lived with one of his daughters and possessed very few tools. He did however own a landscape in oils, a fine clock and certain other luxury items.[6] The most interesting inventory however is that of another royal binder, Antoine-Michel Padeloup, who died in 1758. Padeloup was a leader in the trade and owned eleven paintings, three framed engravings and an inlaid desk.[7] He also owned:

30 gilding rolls, large and small.
34 pallets of various sizes.
48 tools for the *centres* of spine panels, for folios and other sizes.
48 tools for the *corners* of spine panels, folio and other sizes.
36 tools for Rococo 'dentelle' work.
8 alphabets of letters in different sizes and styles.
24 'bandes pour les noms' (a phrase which can be translated as 'lettering pallets', that is cast pallets bearing, on one line, one of the most frequently used lettering words. In French these would typically be 'ALMANACH', 'ROYAL', 'TOME', etc.).
2 boxes full of small decorative tools.
2 gilder's stoves (doubtless for use with charcoal or coke).
2 sets of large gilding blocks (these would have been for works of over folio size).
2 large gilding tables, each with their own sets of drawers and gilding press.

Clearly such a list of tools, representing the stock of an important binder, is of the greatest interest. It indicates, *inter alia,* that he was essentially a finisher, a 'doreur', who, one must assume, had his forwarding work done elsewhere, perhaps regularly in some other shop, perhaps not. Most of these technical terms have been translated from the list originally in French and certain assumptions and explanations may thus have been made in so doing but while the majority are indeed still those in use in the Paris trade today it is worth noting that strict equivalence may not be the case and that tools may relate more particularly to those in use by top Parisian binders of that date.

The rolls and pallets, the spine panel tools, the small decorative tools and the stoves, tables and presses are all typical of the trade anywhere in the eighteenth century. One should however point out that the lettering of titles and so on was still achieved, at least in mid-eighteenth century France and England, by the use of individual letter tools, each applied one after the other by hand, and that it was only from the end of the century that the use of the type-holder, able to letter a whole line of type at one time, came in. Bernard Middleton has shown that the type-holder was known in Germany as early as 1708 but a French binder such as Padeloup seems still not to have had one some fifty years later.[8] What is in evidence in France from the early eighteenth century however is the use of the lettering-pallet, something which may well have been caused by the growth of the learned periodical in the later seventeenth century which would have given rise to the regular binding of a number of volumes with largely identical lettering.

The most interesting items in the list are evidently the two 'assortiments de grands fers garnis de dorure' since these must refer to the special sets of gilding blocks for large engraved works of more than folio size which seem to have been a Padeloup innovation and start with the commission to bind a certain number of copies of the edition of the *Sacre de Louis XV* in 1730, a matter which will be referred to again later. The second set may well have been the blocks for the binding of the *Fêtes de Strasbourg* of 1744, a work equally commissioned from Padeloup.

How were all these tools used and what do we know of finishing techniques? The eighteenth century was after all the century of the Enlightenment and from the Académie royale des sciences's enquiry into the technical processes of the various trades, headed by the Abbé Jaugeon, started in 1693 and containing Desbillettes' article on finishing of 1703,[9] through the *Encyclopédie,* the short work by de

Gauffecourt, Dudin and his *Art du relieur-doreur de livres,* and finally the *Encyclopédie méthodique,* to name but some of the major texts, we hardly lack some form of contemporary description.[10] However these works, strong in detail on forwarding are, almost uniformly, silent on finishing apart from the barest of statements outlining briefly the sequence of movements. The preparation of the leather, the laying-on of the gold and the heating and application of the tools are covered but the sequence of work between the spine, the boards, their edges, the turn-ins, and the whole series of problems arising from the different styles are never touched on. It will be said that these techniques have not changed over the centuries and that the great binders of our day can easily tell us how this work was done and that in any case such attention to detail is not important. This may not be so. There is of course a very strong traditional element in such a manual trade and much modern practice *may* well continue that carried out some three hundred years ago. However the historian of the trade must recognise that the use, first of gas, then of electricity (be it for lighting or heating), the fact that the large industrialised workshops of the nineteenth century have existed, that modern materials are often, perhaps one should add, sadly, different from those used in the eighteenth century, may well have influenced the techniques of the most traditional of binders, who moreover know from personal experience no more than the regular practice of, shall we say, their immediate predecessors of the last hundred years at most. Moreover should we talk of 'the' practice of the eighteenth century or, mindful of Don McKenzie and his 'printers of the mind', preferably of the *practices* of those times.[11]

The approach to the history of bookbinding has been cogently surveyed by Mirjam Foot in an essay printed elsewhere in this volume and in the Bibliographical Society's centennial volume where she has described the shift from 'costume history' to the study of structure and to the more critical identification of finishing tools.[12] She raises many pertinent questions with regard to French bindings and seeks an internationally agreed vocabulary, a wider approach to binding history (taking in many aspects of both the history of the book and of allied disciplines), and, lastly, more information on the cutters or designers of finishers' tools. To such an approach – which I shall be taking further in two forthcoming publications – I would add the careful study of how such tools were actually used.

There are of course tools and tools: they vary in their functions, uses, fashions, prices and many other aspects. Mirjam Foot suggests that the royal arms on the bindings for Henry Prince of Wales belonged to a central source and were allocated from time to time to a number of binders.[13] We know who cut similar armorial blocks at the court of Louis XIV and there seems to be a strong case for suggesting that the blocks accompanied the large binding orders for the royal library, sent to different binders – none of whom then in fact held the title of Royal Binder – some of the orders being regular ones for the binding of current library intake, others being for numerous copies of prestige items like volumes of the *Cabinet du Roi*. The presence on such volumes of certain armorial blocks is therefore no guarantee that they all come from the same shop. These were special items, the royal arms evidently having a special position and indeed legal warrant. Ornaments made for presentation bindings or others with special symbolic connotations, like those so fascinatingly traced by Anthony Hobson within a particular cultural context, probably also share this rather special nature and status.[14]

What should interest us is the standard route for the supply of currently fashionable tools to the trade. Once in the hands of finishers these tools will lead their own life. They may change hands through sale, death, marriage, act of God, or any other cause. They will too become worn and their design may well go out of fashion. In his essay 'English centre-piece bookbindings, 1560–1640', earlier in this volume, David Pearson outlines how it might be possible to record all forms of the centre-piece in use in England between the 1560s and the 1640s, an exact period for a particular fashion. We should not forget either that such tools are probably made from brass and that from this angle alone they will have a distinct commercial value – and that this will be particularly high in wartime when there is a strong demand for bullet cases. The dearth of genuine eighteenth century tools is easily understood in the light both of a revolutionary antipathy to anything symbollically recalling the *Ancien Régime*, and of the armament needs of the Napoleonic wars. The late Monsieur J. F. Barbance, the skilled and learned binder latterly of Avallon, told me that during the Nazi occupation of Paris during World War II extra wine rations were on offer in exchange for old brass tools.[15] The scarcity and thus possible value of such metals need to be appreciated.

What is however clear is that by the 1820s the manufacture of binders' finishing tools was recognised, both in England and in France, as a separately identifiable trade. My research suggests that specialist firms existed virtually all over Europe – and even in America – by the mid-nineteenth century and a volume listing such firms has just been published.[16] It is also evident that some of these firms go back some way into the eighteenth century and, while it is unlikely that one will be able to identify their earlier work and thus possibly the inspiration for their designs, the earlier history of an organised and specialised supply trade in this field will undoubtedly raise fundamental questions in relation to the ascription of bindings to particular binders. An important early document in this field – but one which raises almost as many questions as it solves – is the earliest French tool catalogue, the manuscript volume, *Catalogue des fers qui sont dans la boete à dorer de Tessier à l'époque de 1789*.[17] This is however a somewhat mysterious document for various reasons – not least since it appears to have a supplement dated 1760! Since Tessier was the successor to a well-known workshop, that of Lemonnier, there is promise in this line of research but, in the present writer's view, what is particularly worthy of note is the fact that the catalogue contains so few of the tools needed for the styles in fashion around even 1760. Fashion clearly moves on apace and, without the archaising tendencies brought in by the nineteenth century, old stock seems to have been cleared.

To come to the study of the act of gold-tooling itself. As mentioned, eighteenth century sources tell one little. Louis Sébastien Lenormand, writing in 1827 and producing an important text largely copied by the first English writer J. A. Arnett [pseud. of J. Hannett] eight years later,[18] takes the headcaps of the spine first, then the spine itself, starting with the pallets at the head and tail, followed by the main panel ornaments and then the in-filling tools around. The title lettering completes the tooling of the spine. Then come the upper and lower covers, in that order, the outer work being done first and any armorial in the centre last. The edges of the boards and the turn-ins complete his list, coming just before the pasting down of the end-leaves. Although there is much to be said about the different treatments available for the spine and the other parts named, I will, in the following text, concentrate on the tooling of the main decorative area, the covers. One should however point out that some aspects of the decoration of the spine will have been settled at the outset of the binding process by decisions taken in relation to sewing, themselves sometimes determined by format, and by the subject of the book. The size of the upper panel, controlled by the fold of the sheets, is relatively fixed but that of the bottom one, where there may be considerable variation in the regular length of the deckle edges of the sheets, will be much more uncertain and individual. A single top pallet may therefore be balanced by several at the foot – a practical, not an aesthetic, decision. Much too could be said about the panels but perhaps the important point to make is that before the very late eighteenth century in most cases the treatment of the spine and the covers are two different things. In well and consciously designed bindings there will be stylistic unity to the whole but for much of the eighteenth century one could argue that spines were designed to be seen on library shelves and were therefore somewhat conservative, while books with anything other than a plain armorial stamp on the cover were intended for display and therefore expected to be in a currently fashionable style.

Looking briefly at a selection of major eighteenth century bindings will allow some analysis of the changing styles being produced and of the different methods used to achieve them. First the large late-seventeenth century volumes of propaganda engravings called the *Cabinet du Roi* were widely distributed in a style which seems later to have been mysteriously given the name ('à la Duseuil') of a celebrated binder who, in fact, was only born at the time the style began to come in (fig. 2). This typical official presentation binding has a decorated spine but plain armorial covers, the panel having been made with a triple fillet, more widely spaced between the centre and outer fillet, a spacing fashion which changes through the eighteenth century, as space first moves to the inner gap, then becomes even between the two, before equating itself with the central fillet, finally becoming fatter and more prominent and then ultimately yielding to a totally different Neo-Classical fillet. These are minor points but it is often by such details that we can obtain additional information which may, cumulatively, help to date particular items.

Folio books of printed text from the Imprimerie royale were commonly bound with a wide exterior border created by a carefully and closely placed series of impresions of a single tool (fig. 3). This style, found on these particular books from the royal press in the Louvre, became known as the 'dentelle du Louvre' although today the more correct name of 'Bordure du Louvre' is preferred. Over the years a number of different tools were used in repetition for the border and later, in the eighteenth century, some of these were evidently also available in roll form. Most early versions are however created by repeated and very accurate repetitions of the same basic tool as can be seen by a careful inspection of the point at which they overlap.

2. A. Van der Meulen, *Oeuvres gravées*, Paris, *c.* 1700, *Cabinet du Roi*.
Waddesdon Manor, Aylesbury, B1/16/8.

3. [*Cabinet du Roi*], *Les Conquestes du Roi*, Paris, 1674? (detail).
Waddesdon Manor, B1/9/10.

4. J. Donneau de Visé, *Histoire de Louis le Grand*, Paris, 1668.
Bibliothèque nationale de France.

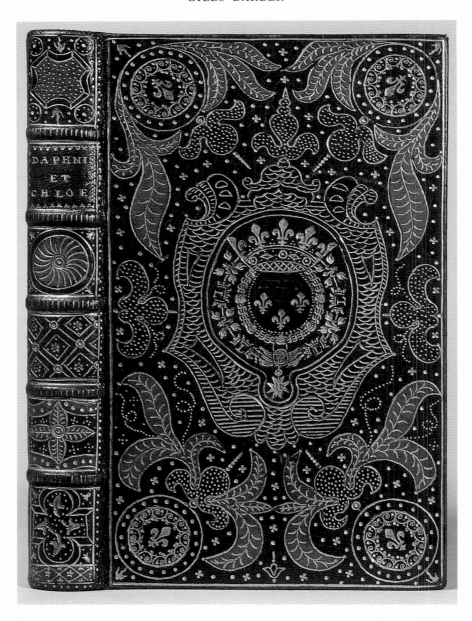

5. Longus, *Les Amours pastorales de Daphnis et Chloé*, Paris 1718.
Waddesdon Manor, B1/23/7.

Binding styles were clearly influenced by general current decorative styles and the use of florid inlay with metals is reflected in an unusual binding, attributed to André-Charles Boulle, who was not a binder but became *ébeniste du Roi* in 1672 and continued to be a major force in the French decorative world up to his death in 1732 (fig. 4). The interlacing, some side decoration and the prominent clasps are all in metal. This binding also illustrates the new colourful inlaid style which came in at the turn of 1700.

Indeed there was something of a reaction against the severe last years of the ageing Louis XIV and in anticipation of the freer spirit which reigned under the following Regency. Longus's faintly erotic novel, *Les Amours pastorales de Daphnis et Chloé,* illustrated by the Regent himself, set the tone. The copy illustrated is from Waddesdon Manor and is one of three known in a mosaic binding with the Regent's own arms (fig. 5). Another similar but different example belonged to the late Sir Paul Getty. They can be attributed to Antoine-Michel Padeloup on the grounds of the characteristic treatment of the spine with divergently decorated panels. They have been acclaimed as one of the most desirable of eighteenth-century French books and bindings. What is important from the design point of view is the total decorative dependence on the mosaic effect, the swirling semi-naturalistic nature of the design, and, above all, the almost complete absence of any special engraved tools, the entire pattern being made up by curves, gouges and dots.

The mosaic was however used in three different manners; it could be of a generally decorative nature as on the *Daphnis et Chloé*, it could be applied within a strictly formal all-over pattern (fig. 6), when it was termed 'à compartiments', or it could be used to produce fairly naturalistic designs, usually floral but sometimes influenced by the taste for things Chinese. The all-over compartment style, produced not with a special 'tile' tool for each compartment, but by the very careful construction of each one with a series of curved, circular and short straight line tools, all strictly within a set and calculated grid, and with the onlays, both blue and red, cut with the greatest accuracy, was very suitable for the small format books on which it is found; it is again attributed to Padeloup. The volume illustrated was probably one of a series of similar bindings at Waddesdon probably made for that great collector, Count Hoym, the Polish ambassador in Paris from 1717 to 1729. Further evidence of the high standard of the work is the fact that the decorative grid and the tools selected to carry it out have been exactly calculated so as to fit the cover area with complete accuracy.

6. G. Bruno, *Spaccio de la bestia trionfante*, [London], 1584.
Waddesdon Manor, B1/23/13.

Another mosaic on a book dated 1689, but probably bound by Padeloup after 1742, also at Waddesdon, has an interlace border recalling that on the metallic Boulle binding but here the interlace is in fact a very carefull red morocco frame laid on top of the olive morocco base, an incredible piece of cutting, but again careful observation under a magnifying glass shows that the outlining of this, the bat's wing and much of the design is all done with gouges and rules, some late seventeenth-century style filigree tools alone occupying the small ovals.

The floral style also relies almost entirely on small tools. The *Eucologue* of 1712, attributed by Michon to the 'Atelier aux Bouquets de Fleurs' (fig. 7), again uses only gouges to build up an elegant, firm and clear design. The different leathers have been carefully chosen for their colours and have survived very well. The work is of a very high level, for not only does the spine match the boards but the two covers are seen as a pair, complementing each other in that the pattern is reversed on the lower cover so that the flowers all face in towards the spine. The result is a small, hand-held book of great charm. All the mosaic bindings described so far have been of a small format: Bandello's *Novelle* of 1740, a very international work where an Italian author, an English printer and a French binder are found together, is a quarto, bound in four volumes, and decorated to a design of a floral centre surrounded by a wide, and interestingly almost three-dimensional, mosaic border (colour plate 3). The floral centre combines multicolour mosaics with gold tooling, using the red morocco ground to show these off. Very close inspection again shows that the design is entirely achieved by the sole use of gouges. The binder, Lemonnier, has signed his name with a pallet both up the central stem and in the centre at the foot of the cover. On this work, where eight covers had to be decorated, the finisher, while following the same general design everywhere, allowed himself the freedom of varying the decorative parts on the inner parts of the flowers from volume to volume, the covers of each one however mirroring each other. This is again characteristic of the freer, more individual, manner of the eighteenth century, since most nineteenth century versions would have insisted on all being asolutely and mechanically alike.

All fashion markets are competitive and for ever seeking innovation. A further novelty added to the mosaic style was the introduction of mica elements, to add sparkle and colour (colour plate 4). Here however trade demarcation came in, the mirror-makers challenging the binders' right to work in this medium.[19] The shaping of the

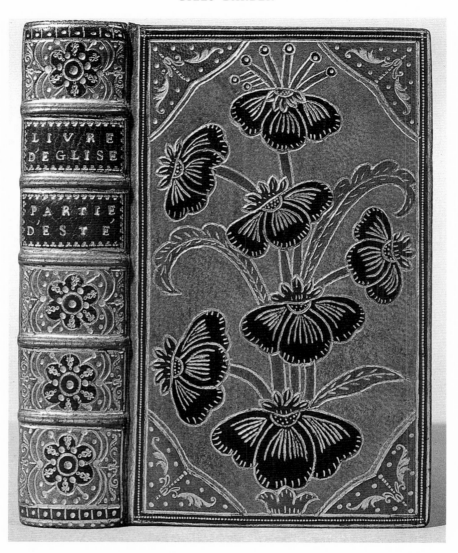

7. *Eucologue*, Paris , 1712. Waddesdon Manor, B1/24/1.

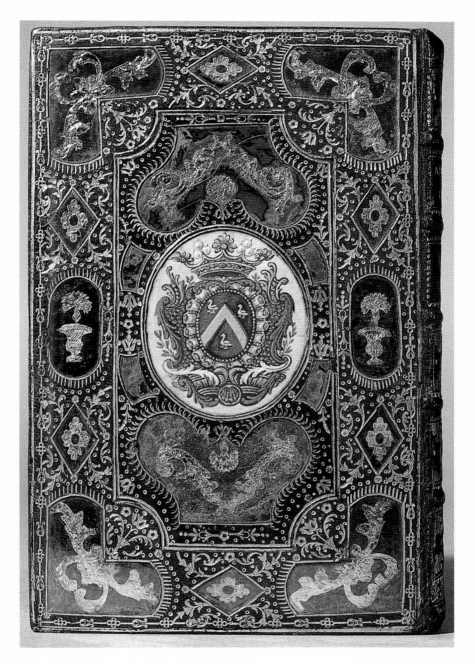

8. *Almanach royal*, Paris, 1769, with the arms of Deume de la Chesnay
(lower cover). Waddesdon Manor, B1/23/3.

9. Longus, *Les Amours pastorales de Daphnis et Chloé*, Paris, 1745.
Waddesdon Manor, B2/8/6.

sophisticated decorative pattern of the underlying silver or coloured paper ground could also involve other trades. Mica was also used as a cover to protect larger areas with painted arms or other decoration (fig. 8). In this case the vase containing a pink shown on the binding is not a gilt ornament but in fact silver paper under mica. One can also note that, while much of the general decoration is still made with simple lines and dots, one or two other tools, of a somewhat older style, also feature thus indicating that one is always likely to find a number of apparently out of period tools even on an otherwise very fashionable binding.

Although more popular in the first half of the eighteenth century, the mosaic style continued to be used in various forms right up to the Revolution. It probably owed its origins to the general fashion for inlaid work in furniture, starting, as we have seen, with Boulle. One might venture however to suggest two other reasons which may have influenced Parisian binders towards working in this style. Both are concerned with the nature of the finishing tools used. First there was the separation of the binders' guild from that of the printers, an action which may well have left them among the poorer members of the book trades. They may therefore have had to rely on the simpler, but very adaptable, forms of tools such as gouges since they were either unwilling or unable to afford to buy more complex engraved ones. Secondly, the split occurred at roughly the same time as the Revocation of the Edict of Nantes with its consequent diaspora of Protestant engravers, some of whom may well have also been the people who engraved decorated tools. There may therefore have been a relative dearth of competent tool cutters in Paris in the early years of the century.

The 1740s saw the introduction of the second great style of the century, the 'dentelle' or lace style (fig. 9). One can see how the name arose but, although wide lace collars were high fashion from the early years of the seventeenth century, the design origins of the so-called 'dentelle' style may in fact really lie in the contemporary early eighteenth-century vogue for decorated ironwork, the main period of this binding style being exactly that of the production of, for instance, the great gates and grilles of the Place Stanislas at Nancy. The binding illustrated, attributed to Louis Douceur largely on the strength of the lambs in the corners, shows the same rather rectangular form of design with, somewhat unusually, a central ornament. Here the borders are now made up, almost free hand, by the systematically regular use of a series of foliate tools in matching style.

The dentelle style broke away from being a straight rectangular border towards a freer, more undulating, edge design, still of course based on corners and swelling mid-points half way up the sides. In the 1757 quarto *Daphnis et Chloé* (fig. 10) the lace border is deeper and more indented while a relatively rare allusive centre-piece underlines the pastoral nature of the work, an allusion on the binding of other than a religious work of the nature of its contents.

In general however the dentelle style relied on leaving the central ground clear and contrasting its highly charged borders with the broad expanse of its high quality leather ground in the centre. A particular virtue of the style was its adaptability to all formats, from duodecimo to folio. The vast folio edition of La Fontaine's *Fables choisies* (1755–1759) was, in every aspect of its production, a deliberately prestige work which had a royal subsidy and copies are thus found in particularly interesting bindings.[20] For this work Douceur had had special tools cut, each illustrating a fable by La Fontaine so that Master Crow, the Crane, the Fox and other animals appear all over the borders of his bindings.

It is worth looking in more detail at the composition and execution of a particularly fine example of this style: for example that on the Waddesdon copy of the manuscript account of the entertainments conducted by the Duchesse du Maine at her castle at Sceaux in the years just before the death of Louis XIV and when the Duchesse hoped that her husband would shortly succeed to the throne (fig. 11). The manuscript is clearly an important one but was only bound up as we know it today in or after 1778, that being the watermark date on the integral endleaves. It also bears the ticket of Nicholas-Denis Derome (called 'le jeune'), for that period.[21] The boards are decorated with a deeply indented swirling dentelle border, highly charged and thus contrasting with the plain leather centre. Like most dentelles the design consists of four corner patterns linked to two different ones at the mid-points of the sides, the whole being joined up by similar but minor work between these elements. Whereas in the 'reliures à compartiments', or in any traditional interlace design, the construction lines are based on a cross in the centre of the cover, here the lines are either bisecting the corners or the mid-points of the sides – two elements which never meet and indeed could only do so on a square book. How then does the binder proceed? Does he work out the whole in blind beforehand? Does he tool it in blind first and then tool over it with gold leaf, as some nineteenth century manuals recommend? There are no traces on the present binding of any previous

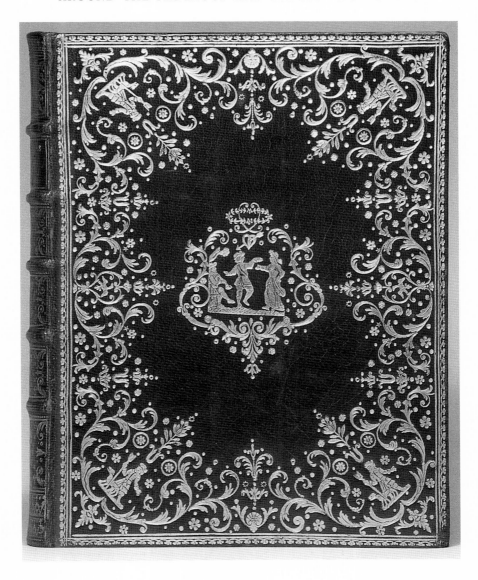

10. Longus, *Les Amours pastorales de Daphnis et Chloé*, Paris, 1757.
Waddesdon Manor, B1/12/8.

11. [Duchesse du Maine], *Les Grandes nuits de Sceaux*, MS 1715, bound *c.* 1780.
Waddesdon Manor, B1/5/8.

Opposite: 12. [Duchesse du Maine], *Les Grandes nuits de Sceaux*, corner detail.

blind tooling nor of any construction lines, other than those mentioned in relation to the corners and the mid-points. Leading binders of today have suggested that over-much planning was a nineteenth-century characteristic and typical of the contemporary obsession with exactitude. A good eighteenth century binder who knew his tools would have had a general idea in mind but have set to work rapidly, starting corner by corner. It has even been suggested to me that such a practised binder could achieve a simple dentelle for one whole cover within an hour. Once one has seen a binder of such a standard at work, the insight gained into the process adds to one's appreciation of the binding.

How then does the binder – in this case the finisher – go about his work?[22] He starts, naturally, with the fillet or other decorative roll round the outside of the covers, usually doing the two long sides first and then the two shorter ones. Then he tackles a corner, working from the inner angle out towards the centre along the bisecting axis. Taking the corner decoration step by step, one sees that the first tool to go down is the triangular corner tool which fits into the depth of the corner and provides a flatter base for the rest of the design (fig. 12). A space is left on the sides of it for branchwork, and the second tool is therefore the oval which will contain the third tool, a symbolic one, here a group of musical instruments. There are two such tools on this book, each being worked in pairs diagonally across the volume. These tools are not in an identical position within each oval and must therefore be separate tools.

A series of five small tools continue the bisecting axis; two W-shaped and across the line, the others prolonging the line towards the centre. These being in, it is now possible to lay them aside and to take

up the nine pairs of branching tools. These tools are in pairs, curving left or right, and can be used alternately, one heating while the other is in use. Thus the base pair go in first, between the corner tool and the oval, and starting a branching form around the decorative oval. A second branch follows on each side and then a third small one. The same second branching tools are then used a second time – but this time swapped over to the other side; thus the first time they are turned in towards the oval, the second time they turn towards the outer frame. A small branch tool follows, continuing the encircling of the central axis. Then come the two large curving tools, the first with a characteristic blob head, and finally a more slender and open scroll with a U shape half way along. This tool comes in two sizes of which this is the smaller. The bisecting axis is therefore now constructed and framed.

Once the outer corners of the cover design have been completed, the empty spaces in the decorated border need to be filled in. The gilder extends the framework of the corners to the centre of the short and long sides of the covers. This is again done by a judicious use of branching tools which give the design a structure and then the sides are further ornamented by the use of other smaller decorative tools, each quarter section design along the shorter or longer side, naturally mirroring each other across the covers.

In total this corner design will have required twenty-seven differently designed tools, eleven of them in both left and right hand versions, making thirty-seven actual tools in all. They will between them have made some 180 tool impressions although many of these – for example the small dots – will only take seconds to achieve. The four corners will thus need some 800 impressons between them and the completion of the sides and the narrower top and bottom edges can be estimated as requiring a further 400, making a grand total of 1,200 for the whole of this one cover. In one sense this would seem to represent a considerable amount of work but, since the mid-point decoration uses much the same set of tools, a practised finisher will in fact be able to work at some speed.

After the study of the sequencing of the gilding it would be logical to look at the actual design of the tools involved. The many eighteeenth century French tools found on bindings at Waddesdon are virtually all being reproduced in the forthcoming catalogue of the library through computer scanning (not rubbings), to actual size and in classified order. Only brief comment on two specific tools will therefore be made here. The tools making up the branching fronds of the dentelle are particular to this style but in general one can, when looking at bindings of this period, break down all the tools used according to three elements: function (often related to overall shape), design (meaning pattern or decorative style), and size. Thus while a binder may use a particular tool almost anywhere on a binding, tools were (and perhaps still are) cut with certain functions in mind. There are spine tools, cover tools, and certain, usually smaller, general purpose tools.

In the latter group perhaps the best known French tool of the eighteenth century is the famous bird, universally, and often rather uncritically, attributed to 'Derome', no distinction being made between father and son nor of the lengthy period in which the two

13. One of the Derome bird tools.

worked. Mirjam Foot has started the ornithological/bibliopegic study of this important creature and I can only offer some minor further observations.[23] The 'Derome' bird, a tool which depicts a bird with a prominent head, outstretched wings and one or two feet, all within a curling frame of lines which curl outwards both above and below, has been mentioned by the Parisian antiquarian booktrade for at least a century and now almost any binding with this tool, of which there is yet no detailed study, is unequivocally attributed to one (unidentified) of the Deromes (fig. 13). The origins of the attribution are less clear: Lesné, writing in 1820,[24] does not mention the tool, nor does the very historically minded Thoinan in 1893. Gruel, a practising binder equally interested in history, makes the attribution a few years earlier but later French writers such as Devaux and Michon are more cautious.[25] In practice one finds that there are a number of tools representing the bird in this design, some of different sizes, some clearly differing in the details of the design. A classic version portrays the bird, body turned to his left but with his head turned to the binding viewer's left, his two feet together and on a central blob. Other versions show the bird with his head turned to the right and a similar central blob, or to the left but with more rudimentary wings and tail, as well as a central blob. Yet another version has the bird with its head against the top of the frame, its tail touching the left hand side of the frame, and a foot touching the right side. Finally another left-facing bird, tail to the side, stands on an elongated ice-cream cone in the centre. The illustration is not to size and for full reproduction of all the birds together with a discussion of how and when they occur it will be necessary to await the Waddesdon catalogue but here the important point is the variety and range of 'this' tool – or rather tools. There may be a case for associating the right-hand facing versions with Padeloup and for suggesting that he initiated the use of this tool, but since some versions are often found on signed Derome (father or son) bindings, there is clearly much yet to be sorted out on this complex subject.

The complexity of these tool designs can also be illustrated by another and, in my experience, even more popular design: that of the bulbous flower vase tool, of which at least eighteen versions have now been recorded (fig. 14). As a brief guide one can say that in some the large flower at the top leans to the left, or sometimes to the right, that this flower is sometimes approached by an insect from the left – or from the right, or even by two insects, one on either side. All these are basically French tools, probably produced and used in Paris, but, just as with printer's ornaments of the period, fashion rapidly led to copies – and often very accurate copies – being made for use in other countries and thus at least English and German versions of these designs are known.

Reference has been made to demarcation problems between the binders and other trades of a very similar nature. Portfolios, boxes and cases for silverware and the like, as well as despatch cases, were strictly the province of the 'gainiers' (box or luggage makers) but

14. Bulbous flower-vase tool.

some ministerial portfolios however were evidently made by top binders and identical tools are sometimes found on items of this sort as well as on books. A case in point is the binding of a volume of engravings on the state arrival of Louis XV at Le Havre in 1753 (fig. 15). Here the binding bears exactly the same rather unusual corner-block and outer decoration as a large and very fine box made for the King's gaming tokens (private collection) and as another box, now at Versailles as a bequest from the late Duchess of Windsor.

Clearly the dentelle style was versatile in application; it was adaptable to different formats and uses; it allowed for either armorial stamps or symbolic tooling. The drawbacks included the need for quite a number of tools and a certain amount of time to achieve the finished product. The latter could be quite a disadvantage in certain markets: large royal orders for outsize festival books or for seasonal items such as almanacs being among them. These specific markets required other production methods and two new techniques were therefore evolved to meet these problems.

15. *Arrivée du Roi au Havre de Grace*, Paris, 1753.
Bibliothèque municipale, Troyes.

The first appears to surface in 1731 with Padeloup's binding of several copies of the souvenir volume of the engravings of the coronation of Louis XV, the *Sacre de Louis XV* (fig. 16).[26] This has been studied by Paul Culot and the case is now a classic one: an ornate but

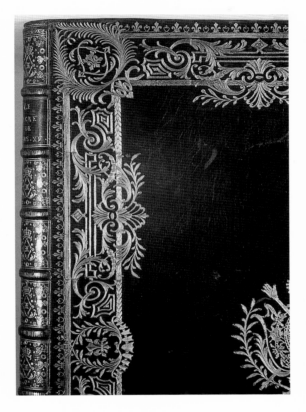

16. *Le Sacre de Louis XV*, Paris, 1731 (detail). Waddesdon Manor, B1/18/3.

restricted border being achieved by the use of a number of well-designed blocks, adapted so as to fit together with each other in a variety of positions, and, because of their size, impressed by means of a blocking press rather than by hand, the slight unevenesses between them can be spotted in the breaks between the different blocks. This technique was further elaborated for later volumes of the same kind and over a dozen sets of designs of this sort are now known.

The solution to the second market problem, that of producing a number of more standard octavo-type bindings in a fancy style fairly

17. J. de La Fontaine, *Contes et nouvelles*, Amsterdam, 1762.
Waddesdon Manor, B2/7/11.

quickly to meet the New Year market for almanacs or the like, was to revert to the old technique of the panel stamp. This probably arose first in dealing with a work, the *Office de la Semaine Sainte,* for the circle around Queen Marie Leczinska about 1730 although the regular use of such panels – with more currently fashionable designs – has generally been associated with the binder P. P. Dubuisson some twenty years later.[27]

All-over ornate designs of these sorts were however close to the end of their day and the advent of Neo-Classicism from the 1760s initiated a desire for a clearer, cleaner, form of decoration with other references. A pivotal volume in this change is the binding found on a number of copies of the 1762 'Fermiers généraux' octavo edition of La Fontaine's *Contes,* once again a very fashion conscious work with remarkable engravings, and often described as having a 'de présent' binding (fig. 17). The design of this binding has usually been attributed to the engraver Gravelot and if this is correct it is an important item, being one of the first binding designs to be definitely attributed to a fairly major artist. It has also sometimes been said to have been produced by means of a panel stamp, presumably because there are several copies with exactly the same design. This is however very far from being the case since there are in fact some sixteen separate units required to build up the cover design and a further twenty-five for the spine, making a total of forty-one in all. The binding is therefore very like earlier work in requiring a large number of tools. It is however at the same time very different, both in general 'atmosphere' where it is the harbinger of the Neo-Classical style, and in the detail and accuracy which its design demands. Thus while from then onwards many binding operations were in general much the same as those in use earlier, the marketing requirements and the techniques evolved to meet them were in fact changing the trade.

Earlier binding history has often aimed, perhaps under booktrade or collector pressure, to attempt to give the names of master binders to particular works. This approach has been more than questioned of late. New historical attitudes and new reproductive techniques should encourage us to experiment with new approaches. The detailed study of just one major collection suggests that there is still much to be learnt, not only about minor styles but even about major ones. In this three things are essential: firstly, we must look as carefully at finishing as we have learnt to do at forwarding; secondly, we must establish an agreed vocabulary for the various areas and styles of tooling – something, ranging over different centuries and styles, but needing to be tackled consequently and not piecemeal; and, thirdly, we need to illustrate the vocabulary with as full a repertoire as possible of the various forms of tools known. References to hard-to-find sale catalogues or statements such as 'a number of the same tools will be found on other bindings' will no longer do.

In trying to take up the problems and techniques of Parisian eighteenth century workshops an approach has been adopted of relying on social history, on finishing techniques, on market forces, and on contemporary decorative styles, something which, it is hoped will not only help to answer some of the technical and historical problems of the period but which will also allow for further exploration of these bindings and, perhaps above all, for a greater appreciation of the undoubtedly fascinating masterworks of this great period of binding.

NOTES

1   The two-volume catalogue of the books and bindings in the James A. de Rothschild Collection at Waddesdon Manor, near Aylesbury, a National Trust property, is in the course of production. It will contain a general introduction, the catalogue of the books and bindings in the collection, and a study of the Parisian binding trade in the later seventeenth and eighteenth centuries, complete with the classified reproduction of most of the tools on the French bindings in the collection.

2   *Edit du Roi pour le règlement des relieurs et relieurs-doreurs de Paris, registré en Parlement le 7 Septembre 1686*. See E. Thoinan, *Les Relieurs français*, Paris, 1893, pp. 60–1.

3   E. Fournier, *L'Art de la reliure en France aux derniers siècles*, Paris, 1888, pp. 255–68.

4   Republished in Cailleau, *Les Misères de ce monde*, Paris, 1783, see Thoinan, *op. cit.*, p. 80.

5   See, for example, Thoinan, *op. cit.*, p. 216.

6   Thoinan, *op. cit.*, p. 251.

7   Thoinan, *op. cit,* pp. 365–6.

8   B. Middleton, *A History of English craft bookbinding technique,* London, 1978, p. 241.

9   See J. Jaugeon, 'Descriptions et perfection des arts et métiers', [Paris] 1704, Paris, Bibliothèque de l'Institut, MS 2741.

10   D. Diderot and J. Le R. d'Alembert, *Encyclopédie*, Paris, 1751 etc., J. V. Capronnier de Gauffecourt, *Traité de la reliure des livres*, La Motte, 1763; R. M. Dudin, *L'Art du relieur-doreur de livres*, Paris, 1772; *Encyclopédie méthodique*, Paris, 1790.

11   D. F. McKenzie, 'Printers of the mind', *Studies in Bibliography,* 22 (1969), pp. 1–76.

12   M. M. Foot, 'The future of bookbinding research' in: P. H. Davidson (ed.), *The Book encompassed*, London, 1992, pp. 99–106.

13   M. M. Foot, 'Bookbinding research', p. 17 above.

14   See A. R. A. Hobson, *Humanists and bookbinders,* Cambridge, 1989.

15 My article 'Towards the study of bookbinders' finishing tools', in a Festschrift volume due for publication in 2003, considers the problems surrounding the survival of genuine pre-1800 finishing tools, attempting to locate major holdings, together with a relevant bibliography.

16 Tom Conroy, *Bookbinder's finishing tool makers 1780–1965*, New Castle, Delaware, 2002.

17 Paris, Bibliothèque des Arts décoratifs, 39094. See R. B. Savigny de Moncorps, 'Un Catalogue de fers à dorer au XVIIIe siècle', *Le Livre et l'image*, 2 (1893/94), pp. 14–23, reprinted Brussels, 1988.

18 L. S. Lenormand, *Manuel du relieur, dans tous ses parties*, Paris, 1827; J. A. Arnett, *Bibliopegia; or, the art of bookbinding in all its branches*, London, 1835.

19 See Thoinan, *op. cit.*, p. 90.

20 See Giles Barber's 1998 Sandars Lectures, *Bibliography with Rococo roses: the 1755 La Fontaine's Fables choisies and the arts of the book in eighteenth century France*, as yet unpublished, but the lecture text, without illustrative material, is available at the Cambridge University Library.

21 P. Ract-Madoux, 'Essai de classement chronologique des étiquettes de Derome le Jeune', *Bulletin du bibliophile*, 1989, pp. 383–92, ticket L1.

22 The following section of the original lecture was accompanied by a video illustrative of the sequence of the tooling of the book. This can naturally not be reproduced and the text has been adapted in consequence. It is hoped that a similar video of the tooling of this work will ultimately be available.

23 M. M. Foot, *The Henry Davis Gift*, vol. 1, London, 1976, p. 200.

24 M. M. Lesné, *La Reliure*, Paris, 1820.

25 L. Gruel, *Manuel historique et bibliographique de l'amateur de reliures*, Paris, 1887; L.-M. Michon, *La Reliure française*, Paris, 1951; L.-M. Michon, *Les Reliures mosaïquées du XVIIIe siècle*, Paris, 1956; Y. Devaux, *Dix siècles de reliure*, Paris, 1977.

26 P. Culot, 'Sur quelques reliures d'époque à décor doré du "Sacre de Louis XV"', *Cahiers de Mariemont*, 1 (1970), pp. 36–51.

27 See Giles Barber, 'Il fallut meme reveiller les Suisses: aspects of private religious practice in a public setting in eighteenth-century Versailles' in: *Religious change in Europe 1650–1914*, essays for John McManners, Oxford, Clarendon Press, 1997, pp. 75–101. It is hoped to use full reproductions of many of these designs found in the 1910 Rahir catalogue in the forthcoming Waddesdon one.

'A MAGNIFICENT AND BEWILDERING VARIETY'

Irish Bookbinding in the Eighteenth Century

Mirjam M. Foot

FINE BINDING IN Ireland in the eighteenth century, needs to be considered in the wider political and cultural sphere that made its production possible. When one looks at the literature about Irish binding, one can easily get the impression that a completely-developed craft, producing highly skilled, splendid and exuberant objects of art, emerged fully-formed during the second and third decades of the eighteenth century, flowered briefly but lavishly, to dwindle and disappear again a century later. This is of course not true. There are accounts of medieval Irish binders and bindings and one of the earliest-known members of the booktrade in Dublin was a book-binder, a certain Simon Walsh who is mentioned in 1485.[1] However, not much has been preserved, and after some indigenous and fairly basic trade binding in the seventeenth century, the manifestation of binding as an art in Georgian Ireland may come as a surprise.

Not only binding reached extraordinary heights of workmanship and taste during the eighteenth century. The striking achievements in architecture, art and craftsmanship, much of which is still in evidence today, find their beginning in the Restoration period.[2]

In 1662 an 'Act for Encouraging Protestant Strangers in Ireland' brought Huguenot immigrants who imported the technique of gold-smithing, but who became also involved in the booktrade. By the end of the seventeenth century professional designers and 'artificers', builders and carpenters had appeared and gained a reputation, even abroad. 'Gentleman's seats were built or building everywhere' wrote William King referring to 1685.[3] Some great town houses were built; there were large extensions to Trinity College, and Dublin became Britain's second city. From 1660 the government had been centralised in Dublin. Ormond (whom we will meet later in a different context) dominated politics as Viceroy; he was Lord Lieutenant from 1644 to 1649, from 1662 to 1669, and again from 1677 to 1685. The accession of James II in 1685 had improved matters for the Irish Catholics, but when Protestant William landed in England in 1688, James fled to

France and thence crossed to Ireland in the following year. In the struggle that followed Ireland became a theatre of European war. The Battle of the Boyne, followed by Aughrim's great disaster, became subjects for historical novelists and painters, as well as historians. These and the siege of Limerick left a divided country in a state of uneasy and exhausted peace. Catholics were debarred from free citizenship and were in effect (due to oaths that had to be sworn against transubstantiation) prevented from joining the guilds, including the Guild of St Luke, that combined cutlers, painters and stainers, and stationers, and that had received its first charter in 1670.[4] Yeats's view of Georgian Ireland as 'that one Irish century that escaped from darkness and confusion'[5] is seen by modern historians more as romantic re-invention than historical accuracy. Nevertheless, during the eighteenth century prosperity was growing, crop failures and famine notwithstanding.

The flowering of architecture, art and crafts in Georgian Ireland took place in a colonial society, an Anglo-Irish milieu of landowners, top-government officials and the richer echelons of the professional classes, a cultural and intellectual elite, whose taste and patronage were important factors in the creation of splendid houses and decorative objects.

Elizabeth Bowen's description of the world of her ancestors is evocative: 'The great bold rooms, the high doors imposed an order on life. Sun blazed in at the windows, fires roared in the grates. There was a sweet, fresh-planed smell from the floors. Life still kept a touch of colonial vigour; at the same time, because of the glory of everything, it was bound up in the quality of a dream.'[6] This vision can still be experienced in the great country houses and in the exquisite town houses in Dublin, houses with halls and staircases of great grandeur, stucco interiors, splendidly decorated plasterwork ceilings and carved mantelpieces, much of which was the work of immigrant craftsmen. At the same time a very competent school of landscape and portrait painting developed; engravers such as John Brooks and his pupils, produced remarkable results; paper making flourished and some really good printing work was produced, especially at the press in Trinity College. Gold- and silver-smithing reached remarkable levels of complexity and beauty, perhaps initially under influence of foreign craftsmen, but developing into a typical Irish style. The same can be said of the decoration of bookbindings.

It is possible that the first finishers to produce finely decorated bindings were immigrants, Huguenots from France, artisans from

Italy, and indeed stationers from London. Joseph McDonnell suggests[7] that the Devotional binder worked in Dublin for a while, possibly for William Norman, a bookseller, bookbinder and auctioneer, who called himself 'Bookbinder' to the Duke of Ormond. A number of books printed in Dublin between 1674 and 1682 were bound by the Devotional binder and a genealogical manuscript of the Duke of Ormond, written by Richard Connell of Kilkenny, c. 1675, was bound by him in black goatskin. However, Ormond, who rose to prominence through his services to the English Crown and who was rewarded with a dukedom by Charles II, was also Chancellor of Oxford University (from 1669) and divided his time between England and Ireland. It is therefore possible that he used the services of the Devotional binder when in London.

The decorative styles of fine Irish bindings may have come from England and France, from Scotland even, but the results of the best efforts have an unmistakable Irish-ness.

The booktrade had developed as part of the general cultural and economic trends. Printing came late to Ireland, the first book to be printed there, a *Book of Common Prayer*, was printed in Dublin by Humphrey Powell in 1551 (STC 16277). From 1551 to 1680 no more than one printer was at work in Dublin at any one time. With the King's Printer's patent, the monopoly of the entire trade in the whole country was given to one man. No one could legally exercise the trade of printing, bookselling, bookbinding or any other function pertaining to the profession of stationer, except the King's Printer for life. As well as the authority to print, the patentee received 'full, sole and complete license and authority as well of binding and covering as of exposing for sale and selling all ... books of whatsoever kind' in any language.[8] The same all-encompassing clause pertained throughout the century and was still in force in 1693. This situation, as well as the continuous wars, severely curbed the development of the whole booktrade. During the seventeenth century the bulk of the books bought and read in Ireland were imported. This is clearly visible in what remains of libraries formed at that time. The books bought for Trinity College by Luke Challoner, James Ussher (whose brother Ambrose was the first librarian of Trinity College, Dublin) and Provost Henry Alvey between 1601 and 1613 were printed and bound abroad, largely in England and France. A few of the books may have been imported unbound and got their binding in Dublin. In 1608 John Franckton, printer, bookseller and bookbinder, King's Printer (1604–1618), was paid 3 shillings 'for bynding Lorinus uppon ye actes'[9] in sheepskin with a border of blind lines, but many of the plain or blind-tooled calf bindings from this period at Trinity College were supplied by the London bookseller Gregory Seton. Those that were decorated with centre-pieces in blind, but occasionally in – by now oxydised – silver and even in gold, are of the familiar types found in London, Oxford and Cambridge. One or possibly two may have come from France. Some are decorated with single tools or with a combination of rolls and hand tools, and are clearly English work.

The King's Printer's monopoly was challenged by Joseph Ray who had a press in Dublin in 1680. In his reply to the King's Printer's petition against him Ray stated that 'it was never the Intention of the sd. Letters patents that the said Complainants should Monopolize the sole Trade of Imprinting, binding, covering, and selling all books wh. soever, in this Realme of Ireland ...'.[10] He added that there were more books needed than one printer could supply. Although Ray lost the case, he remained active and from 1680 onwards other stationers appeared in Dublin. Bookselling expanded and when in 1732 George Grierson became King's Printer, his patent was restricted to certain categories of books, such as Bibles, Books of Common Prayer, Psalms, Primers with the Catechism, Statutes and other government publications. Likewise, bookselling and binding were no longer the prerogative of the King's Printer, although for the binding of official documents, such as *Books of Statutes* and the *Journals* of the Houses of Lords and Commons, the King's Printer or the King's Stationer was paid. This does not mean that he carried out the actual craft himself, but that he arranged for it to be done. This was nothing new, for already in Franckton's patent allowance was made for delegation. It is therefore dangerous to assume that, monopoly notwithstanding, the actual crafts of forwarding and finishing were carried out by the named King's Printer or King's Stationer who was paid for the work.

It may be useful to remember that the Dublin printers, booksellers and binders did not fall into neatly separate categories. Many of the booksellers were also printers and binders, and in a variety of records the term 'bookbinder' appears to have been used instead of 'bookseller', as Mary Pollard has shown in her massive and extremely useful *Dictionary of the Dublin booktrade 1550–1800* (London, Bibliographical Society, 2000), as well as in her Lyell lectures of 1987.[11]

Although the trade loosened up and consequently expanded at great speed during the eighteenth century, the importation of books from the continent and from England continued, witness two late seventeenth-/early eighteenth-century libraries still intact in Dublin.

The library of Narcissus Marsh, former Provost of Trinity College, Archbishop of Armagh (d. 1713), who, dissatisfied with the provision of books to students at Trinity, decided to build a library 'in some other Place ... for publick use',[12] contains mainly English and continental books in European bindings. Marsh was a man of learning and religion; he was interested in science, mathematics, and especially in Oriental languages. He began building his library c. 1701 and, notwithstanding some local opposition, the first part was completed by the summer of 1703. In 1705 he obtained the library of Bishop Stillingfleet, c. 10,000 volumes for which he paid £2500, mainly theology, history, law, medicine, classical literature and travel. Marsh's first librarian, the Huguenot Elias Bouhéreau, brought his own books with him and left them to the library, and John Stearne, Bishop of Clogher (d. 1745) bequeathed about 3000 books to Marsh's library. In 1707 an Act was passed 'for settling and preserving a publick library for ever, in the house for that purpose built by his grace Narcissus, now lord archbishop of Armagh, on part of the ground belonging to the archbishop of Dublin's palace, near to the City of Dublin'.[13] It is still there, virtually as it was in Marsh's day, opposite St Patrick's Cathedral. My own recent research there shows that the majority of the books in bindings of any distinction in Marsh's library were made in England; there are also a number of fine bindings from France, Italy, Spain, Germany and the Netherlands and a few from Eastern Europe. A number of trade bindings made in Dublin are still present, and bills of c. 1740 and 1801–2 in the library's Account Book (1731–1953), refer to binding books in plain calf, sheepskin or in half bindings, but the fine Irish bindings that are now in the library were largely later gifts, most of them presented by the bibliographer Ernest Reginald McClintock Dix (1857–1936) in 1905.[14]

Another eighteenth-century library that is still intact in Dublin, that collected by Dr Edward Worth (1678–1733) and left to Dr Steevens' Hospital, consists of over 4500 books on medical subjects, but also on mathematics, history, topography, theology, classical authors and modern (i.e. 18th century) literature. Worth acquired most of his books at auctions in England, Holland and Ireland and although he did have a number of his books bound in Dublin (a 'Worth binder' has been postulated by Joseph McDonnell, but not yet fully explored),[15] the majority of his fine bindings are of European origin. Many are French and have impressive provenances. Worth bought forty-four books from the Loménie de Brienne sale in 1724 and he owned books from the libraries of de Thou, Baron de Longepierre, Colbert and Grolier. There are several fine English bindings including one bound for Robert Dudley, Earl of Leicester and a small group of eighteenth-century bindings were made in The Hague.

Nevertheless, Irish home talent began to develop and expand, and rose to exceptional heights during the eighteenth century.

Interestingly, the only hard and fast rule for the regulation of the booktrade made in the 130 years of the Guild's existence related to bookbinding. In 1725, in response to a complaint that several brothers 'bind their Books with the grain of Sheep Leather',[16] this practice was forbidden and transgressors were to be prosecuted. To encourage their discovery, a reward of 5s. would be made on legal conviction. At the next Hall a publication was issued to inform all booksellers and binders that every book already bound in grain (of sheep) must be re-bound on pain of prosecution as 'publick Cheats'.[17] The protection of the public from incompetent work or shoddy binding had been one of the reasons for the Guild's foundation and – as was the case with the Stationers' Company in London – some quality control was obviously carried out. We do not know much about trade binding in Ireland. There are a number of binders mentioned by name in Charles Ramsden's *Bookbinders of the United Kingdom* (London, 1954) and, thanks to Mary Pollard's *Dictionary*, we now know of quite a few more, but in most instances there is no way of connecting them with their products. Moreover it is very difficult to distinguish between Irish and English plain work. There appear not to be really significant structural differences and the few features that may be typically Irish, such as large-ish squares, a liking for spot-marbled endleaves and for yellow- or green-stained edges, apply more to fine than to trade binding. We have seen that many books were imported bound and Port book records show that books also entered the country unbound.[18] Booksellers in Dublin, as elsewhere, arranged for binding to be done, both for individual clients and also for their own stock. In 1698/9 John Dunton brought books to Ireland for sale to booksellers and for his own auctions, claiming that he spent £400 in Dublin 'with Printers, Stationers, and Binders and the Servants concerned in my three auctions'.[19]

We know a little more about trade bindings and their prices from a few surviving lists of prices agreed by the bookbinders among themselves or between binders and booksellers, in attempting to establish a common price for various kinds of trade binding.[20] The earliest list referring to prices of trade binding in Dublin dates from *c.* 1620. It is a statement of 'Bookes as they are sold bound' issued by the King's Printer, Thomas Downes, comparing prices for various kinds and sizes of books bound, decorated, with fillets, with bosses, and with clasps, charged in London and in Dublin, the Dublin prices being consistently higher. John Dunton also complained of having to pay in Dublin 'a rate for Binding, ... beyond what was given in London'.[21]

The earliest surviving evidence of the Dublin bookbinders combining forces to establish a minimum rate of pay for various types of work is a broadsheet 'Printed by EDWARD BATE, in *George's Lane* near *Dame's Street*' in 1743. This list, when compared to a London one of a year later, shows that by now prices in Dublin were slightly lower than those in London for the larger formats, or the same for the smaller formats. This pricelist includes 'gilt work' and 'books bound in vellum', as well as 'forril' (vellum made from unsplit sheepskin) in 'yellow' (i.e. natural) and 'green', a phenomenon quite often found in Ireland.

The next price list was issued in Dublin in 1766. It has not been preserved, but the row between the booksellers and binders that followed was reported in the *Freeman's Journal* for 3 June 1766. The booksellers objected to the proposed increase in price amounting to about 9%, recalling the 'former Regulations in the year 1743'. Two years later (25 April 1768) the bookbinders published a third price increase, justifying their action in the *Dublin Gazette* of 30 April 1768, by stating that due to the 'excessive Rise of Calf Leather, (owing to the constant Export of raw Skins to Great Britain) ... we cannot bind any Duodecimo in Calf and lettered, under 10*d.* nor any Octavo under 1*s.*1*d.* per Vol. and all other Sizes in proportion'. Booksellers advised their customers to 'have their Books done up in Boards, or sewed in blue Paper' (*Dublin Journal*, 28 May 1768). This provoked an anonymous letter in the *Freeman's Journal* for 7 June 1768 in defence of the binders: 'In the Year 1743, certain *Rates* were then agreed to by the MASTER-BINDERS, which have ever since been the standard between them and the BOOK-SELLERS. At that Time, Calf leather could be purchased from Twelve to Eighteen Shillings per Dozen, seldom above Twenty Shillings; Journeymen's Wages [were] from Seven to Ten Shillings per Week. Within these Ten Years, the Leather has been extreamly fluctuating, and still on the Rise every Year, according as the Demand was from Great Britain ... Journeymen's Wages likewise encreased ... so that on the whole, Leather is now from Twenty-four to Thirty Shillings per

Dozen, Journeymen from Ten to Fifteen Shillings per Week, together with proportionable Advance on other necessary Articles used in that Brand of Trade, besides these, the Great Advance on Provisions within these last Twenty Years, cannot escape the notice of any Individual.' The writer concluded by advising gentlemen who want their books bound to go directly to the binders without 'applying to Booksellers'.[22]

In 1774 the Dublin booksellers issued 'A Complete catalogue of Modern Books (printed in Ireland) ... Also, The Prices of the Different Bindings of Books'.[23] If one compares these prices with those in a London price list of 1760, the Dublin prices for the larger formats in plain calf match the lowest in the London price range; octavos in plain calf cost 11d. in Dublin, while duodecimos are 10d., both more expensive than prices charged in London (where the binders charged 9d. for octavos and 7–9d. for duodecimos).

Other costs were also rising. During the eighteenth century the cost of binding in boards rose from 2s.6d. in 1787 to 3s. in 1791. Blue paper stayed cheap: 3d. for an octavo and 1½d. for a duodecimo (1791). We know this from the last list of the century, issued in 1791: 'A REGULATION OF PRICES AGREED TO BY *THE COMPANY OF BOOKBINDERS*, OF THE CITY OF DUBLIN, FOR WORK DONE FOR BOOKSELLERS ONLY. *Commencing the 1st Day of December*, 1791. Revised and corrected by a Committee of the Company of Booksellers.'[24]

The folios in plain calf cost the same as in 1774, but quartos have gone up from 1s.10d. to 2s.8½d., octavos rose by 1d. to 1s., while duodecimos remained at 10d. This price list, however, gives a greater choice of leather and decoration. 'Turkey' comes in 'gilt over' as well as 'gilt', calf can be had 'gilt' or 'plain'; sheep is always 'plain'. There is now also the choice of 'half-binding[s]', 'cut and lettered' or not, while 'blue Boards' and 'blue Paper' are available, the latter only for the smaller formats (octavo and infra).

There are separate charges for 'Ornamenting Books', that is to say for tooling previously-bound books, a habit also common in England at the time. A gentleman could have his library enlivened by having the backs of his books gilt or by having the books tooled and filleted; a medium folio 'Gilt back' would set him back 2s.2d., while 'Tooling and filletting' the same size cost 6d., suggesting not all that much tooling. The backs could also simply be lettered, ranging from 2d. for a duodecimo to 5d. for a folio 'If not bound at same Time'. 'Rolling the Edges' (i.e. running a roll along the edges of the boards) of a medium folio cost 10*d*., while '*Rolling round the Boards* with any ornamented Roll, to be double the Price of Edge-rolling'. Edges could also be coloured and burnished which cost 6*d*. for a folio. Armorial blocks could be added, the 'King's Arms, large' for 1*s*.1*d*. and 'the College Arms, or others of that Size, on the sides of Books, per vol. 0 10'. 'Almanacks', 'Memorandum Books' and 'Calendars' could be ordered 'in DIFFERENT BINDINGS', the first category, 'gilt in Turkey', in 'Red Spanish' (i.e. a cheaper goatskin) or 'Red Sheep' either 'gilt' or 'plain', the second also 'Bound in Silk, and Barbary [goatskin] slip Case'. Octavo 'Pocket-Books' came in vellum or in forel, the latter about half the price of the former. A note at the end states that 'White Vellum, gilt extra, [is] charged the same as Turkey gilt extra'. Gold-tooled white vellum bindings are not unusual in Dublin in the eighteenth century. Ann Leathley's binder made them and a fair number of University Press books were bound in this way. On 30 December 1761 Horace Walpole wrote to George Montagu, then in Dublin, asking him to bring back a Dublin vellum binding, 'for I am told that they bind well there in vellum'. He got the 1724 Grierson duodecimo edition of Virgil, in vellum, tooled in gold with a diamond-shaped centre-piece.[25]

As 'Almanacks' and 'Calendars' were usually bound when and where they were issued, they can be used to date and locate other bindings. Maurice Craig illustrated the earliest-known Irish almanac in an Irish binding, that for 1705 printed by the King's Printer Andrew Crooke.[26] The same tools in a very similar lay-out are found on *A New Almanack for the year 1713*, also printed by Crooke, now at Trinity College Dublin (fig. 1). The design and disposition of the tools: drawer-handles, acorns, floral curls, remind us strongly of English work of the post-Restoration period, such as that by the Devotional binder and the Queens' binders, but the tools themselves are different and this binding, as well as three others with identical tools, also mentioned by Craig, are certainly Irish. The quality of the workmanship and of the finishing leaves a certain amount to be desired – there are some crooked lines and uneven spacing – especially when compared with the more sophisticated and precise tooling of the finisher of Queens' Binder B. The *Almanack* for 1713 is sewn on three thongs that have been laced into the boards. It has very small squares, in contrast to Irish bindings later in the century. On the endleaves we find some builders' accounts dated 1736–7, signed by Mick Cullen, but also a 'Receipt to make a liquid for blackening Leather in the Nicest manner'. A comparatively common sight on

1. A Dublin binding, *c.* 1713. *A New Almanack for the year 1713*, Dublin, 1713.
Brown calf tooled in gold. 150 × 92 × 12 mm. Trinity College, Dublin, Armoire.

Irish brown calf bindings are black 'cat's paw' splodges and black is also used from time to time to emphasise tooled compartments on the covers.

Several designs that are frequently found on Irish bindings were quite clearly influenced by English examples, such as sombre bindings in blind-tooled black calf, in Ireland apparently exclusively found on copies of the *Eikon Basilike,* but strongly reminiscent of English work of the same type; cottage-roof designs, with the peak of the gable often touching the edges of the covers and pointed, not cusped: features not unknown on English bindings either.[27] Other designs that are commonly found on both sides of the Irish Sea are panels and lozenges which become scalloped and cusped after 1703; panels and lozenges are often combined in one design, and so are cottage roofs and lozenges.[28]

A typical Irish lozenge design occurs on a copy of Hugh Maffet's translation of Sallust, *The Catiline and Jugurtine wars,* published by subscription in Dublin in 1772 while Maffet was in the Marshalsea prison for debt (colour plate 5). It is bound in blue goatskin with a lozenge onlay in calf and tooled in gold. It is sewn on five cords, three of which have been laced in. As well as a red title label there is a fawn label lettered: 'Right honourable Francis Andrews'. I know of nine copies of this book in fine bindings made for notable patrons, several of whom also subscribed to the book. They were not all bound in the same shop. The binding illustrated on colour plate 5 comes from the shop that also bound the Earl of Ely's copy in red goatskin with a black onlay.[29] Six copies, one at the British Library, one belonging to Maurice Craig and four formerly in the library of Lord Iveagh, are all decorated with the same tools: one, for the Earl of Moira, is in green vellum with a white paper onlay, two very Irish characteristics, one in black goatskin with two small vesica-shaped paper onlays was made for the Right Honourable the Earl of Belvedere in 1773, another one in black goatskin was made also in 1773 for Matthew Forde MP;[30] two much simpler bindings in red goatskin, decorated with a roll and some tooling on the spine, were made for Sir Robert Staples, Bart. and for Dean Swift,[31] while a copy in gold-tooled white vellum has no named recipient.[32] A ninth in red goatskin for Hill Willson Esq.[33] was made in yet another shop. The largest group, consisting of six copies, has tools in common with those on the binding of John Leland, *The Advantage and necessity of the Christian revelation* in 2 vols (Dublin, 1766),[34] which in turn shows a very common kind of Irish eighteenth-century tool, a cross-over loop on a shield, of which there are a number of variants. This particular tool, however, occurs also on Thomas Leland's translation of Demosthenes, *Orationes* (Dublin, 1756),[35] probably one of the most beautiful and strange Irish bindings still in existence. It was made by one of the binders (Parliamentary Binder Bb) who were responsible for the Manuscript *Journals* of the Houses of Lords and Commons, mostly bound splendidly in red goatskin, often with onlays and with a great deal of very accomplished and intricate tooling. When Sir Edward Sullivan, to whom we owe the knowledge of these bindings, discussed the 149 volumes then still in existence he described their designs as of a 'magnificent and bewildering variety', presenting 'an almost complete panorama of the history of decorative bookbinding in Ireland'.[36] Sullivan photographed and made rubbings of these splendid volumes, which went up in flames with the Four Courts in 1922. The rubbings are now in the National Library of Ireland. These 'Parliamentary' bindings have been much discussed in the literature, and not only by Sir Edward Sullivan. Maurice Craig was the first to divide them into three styles (A, B and C) and to allocate them, according to the tools used to effect their designs, to two binders (Parliamentary Binders A and B).[37] Craig was well aware that, although the King's Stationers were responsible for binding these *Journals*, they could and would have given the actual work to the best forwarders and finishers available in Dublin at that time. He nevertheless suggested that Abraham Bradley, King's Printer from 1749 to 1780, was Parliamentary Binder B. More recently Joseph McDonnell has made the interesting, but unproven suggestion that Bradley farmed the work out to a bookbinder who lived in the same street (Fownes Street), called Edward Beattie.[38] Beattie is recorded as a bookbinder in the Guild of St Luke's records. He was freed in 1745, became Master of the Guild in 1760 and died in 1794. In December 1755 he was paid £3.15s.7d. by Michael Wills, the translator of Vitruvius, *De architectura* (an undated MS, *c*. 1750–60) for binding an unspecified book. This manuscript translation of Vitruvius, now in the Chester Beatty Library, is bound in red goatskin with a white onlay, elaborately tooled in gold with the same characteristic feather work that is found on the Leland Demostenes, and with tools said to have been used by Parliamentary Binder B.[39] I have not seen this binding and the reproductions are not detailed enough to identify the tools with certainty.

These Parliamentary binders are by no means straight forward, but the tools that appear to have been used on the manuscript Lords and Commons *Journals,* not forgetting that they can now only be studied from Sir Edward Sullivan's rubbings in the National Library of Ireland, the photographs and reproduced plates being virtually useless, also occur on a number of fine bindings that do still exist. The tools used on those bindings that have been attributed to Parliamentary Binder B fall into three distinct groups (Ba, Bb, and Bc).[40] Another binding, also on the 1756 Leland Demosthenes, and decorated with the famous feather work from which the 'Parliamentary Binder B' earned his reputation, is now in Frankfurt,[41] and may be by the same binder. They all fall into group Bb.

A binder (or finisher) (Ba) who used tools that are extremely similar to those found on the Demosthenes, but with minute differences,[42] bound a copy of E. Barry's *Observations, historical, critical and medical on the wines of the ancients* (London, 1775) (fig. 2); while a third group (Bc), again decorated with extremely similar tools includes a copy of Milton's *Poetical works*, 2 vols (Birmingham, 1760) (fig. 3). Bindings from this last group have been attributed by McDonnell to George Faulkner's binder (formerly the Rawdon binder, so named by Craig), who was responsible for a number of bindings on books with Faulkner's imprints, as well as for a whole group of Baskerville Common Prayers (1760–61).[43]

Parliamentary Binder A is simplicity itself by comparison. One of his bindings belongs to the Henry Davis Gift to the British Library,[44] several are in private collections, and one is in Trinity College, Dublin. It covers S. Clarke, *A Paraphrase on the four Evangelists* (Dublin, 1737) and is in black-stained brown calf with a white calf centre onlay surrounded by black paint (fig. 4). As well as the earlier set of Lords and Commons manuscript *Journals* (1697–1749), he bound several copies of John Hawkey's editions of the classics, printed by the University Press in Dublin between 1745 and 1747, when Samuel Powell was the printer to the University.[45] The Parliamentary Binder A had by no means the monopoly of binding these Hawkey classics and several were bound by the binder who carried out most binding work for Trinity College at that time and who worked for Joseph Leathley, formerly known as the College binder. William O'Sullivan, Keeper of MSS at Trinity College, Dublin from 1949, already knew about Leathley as College bookseller and Charles Ramsden, in *Bookbinders of the United Kingdom* mentions in passing both Joseph and his wife Ann.[46] Joseph McDonnell and Patrick Healy in their *Gold-tooled bookbindings commissioned by Trinity College Dublin in the eighteenth century* (Leixlip, 1987) put the Leathleys firmly on the map. Their thorough research in Trinity

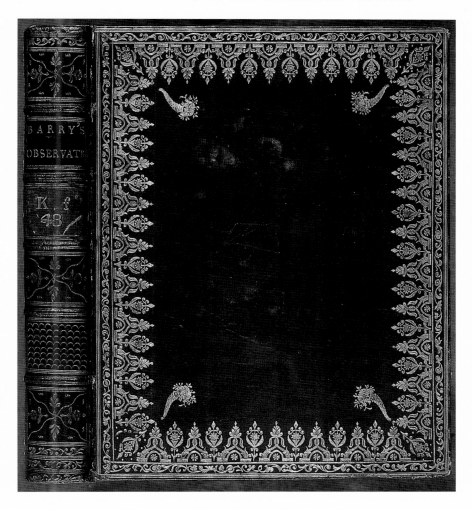

2. A Dublin binding by Parliamentary Binder Ba, *c.* 1775. E. Barry, *Wines of the ancients*, London, 1775. Red goatskin, tooled in gold. 262 × 205 × 41 mm. Trinity College, Dublin, K.f.48.

College muniments, library accounts, other manuscript sources and contemporary newspapers has produced a great deal of information. More was supplied by Mary Pollard in her *Dictionary*. To summarise their findings: Joseph Leathley was a bookseller and bookbinder. He was freed in 1719 and elected Master of the Guild of St Luke in 1745. From 1732 he bound printed books for Trinity College library and for the College, and supplied both with stationery. In May 1732 a heavy rebinding programme started as the library's books were moved into

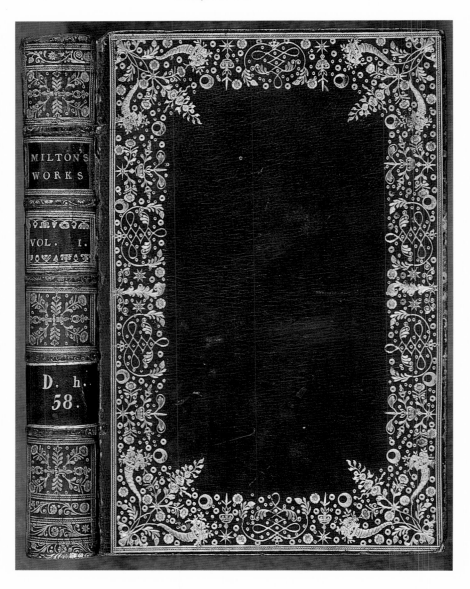

3. A Dublin binding by Parliamentary Binder Bc, *c.* 1760. J. Milton, *Poetical works*, vol. 1, Birmingham, 1760. Red goatskin, tooled in gold. 236 × 155 × 37 mm. Trinity College, Dublin, Dh.58.

4. A Dublin binding by Parliamentary Binder A, *c.* 1737. S. Clarke, *Paraphrase on the four Evangelists*, vol. 1, Dublin, 1737. Black-stained brown calf, onlaid in white calf, tooled in gold. 200 × 127 × 33 mm.
Trinity College, Dublin, Armoire.

the newly built Long Room, and in December Leathley charged £80.17s.7d. for binding 947 volumes. Both McDonnell and Pollard quote from a number of bills at Trinity College, that clearly show his prodigious output. During his twenty-five years as College bookseller, Joseph Leathley appears to have employed the same binder: Craig's College binder. Mary Pollard suggests he may have farmed out the work to Thomas Whitehouse, a binder who married his sister Elizabeth in 1725. His bindings show four main decorative styles: a panel design with or without the Trinity College armorial stamp in the centre; a design of roll-tooled borders and small corner tools, often with the College arms block in the centre; a diamond-shaped centre-piece built up of small tools; and, most frequently, variations on the 'Irish Harleian' style: a diamond-shaped centre-piece combined with roll-tooled borders. In 1738 he supplied the College's presentation bindings on 'Ten Plato's Dialogues of the large Paper in blew Turky Gilt over' for £5.[47] The presentation copy from the Provost and Fellows to the Reverend Dr Claude Gilbert, late Senior Fellow, is illustrated here (fig. 5). A year later he was paid 11s.6d. for 'Binding Pine's Horace blew Turky' for the Library (fig. 6).[48] Many bindings from the shop that worked for Leathley have now been identified and illustrated by McDonnell and Healy. Leathley died in 1757 and was succeeded by his wife, Ann, who was a bookseller. She signed the booksellers' protest against the increase in binding prices in 1766 and was clearly not a binder herself. However, she was responsible for binding work carried out for Trinity College and bills from her are among the muniments there. In 1768 she charged £9.0s.3½d. for six presentation copies of Trinity College's quarto *Statutes* (1768). Ann died in 1775 and was in turn succeeded by her nephew, William Hallhead, who seems to have lived with and worked for the Leathleys. He supplied Trinity College with stationery and the library with books until 1781. In 1777 a copy of Demosthenes, *Orations*, translated by Thomas Leland (2 vols) was presented to the translator by William Hallhead, bound in green goatskin, rolled and tooled in gold (fig. 7).[49] Hallhead employed a very competent craftsman who used tree calf, and green and citron goatskin, as well as the more familiar red and blue. Perhaps his most sumptuous piece is a binding in red goatskin on a Baskerville *Bible* of 1763, which has in the centre a brass plaque with the arms of Sir Richard Cox of Dunmanway, Co. Cork (colour plate 6).

William Hallhead died in 1781, leaving a widow, Sarah, who succeeded him as bookseller and stationer to Trinity College. On 20

5. A Dublin binding by Joseph Leathley's binder, 1738. Plato, *Dialogi*, Dublin, 1738. Dark blue goatskin, tooled in gold. 228 × 135 × 38 mm. Trinity College, Dublin, TT.kk.14.

6. A Dublin binding by Joseph Leathley's binder, 1739. Horace, *Opera*, vol. 2, Dublin, 1737. Dark blue goatskin, tooled in gold. 232 × 142 × 33 mm. Trinity College, Dublin, R.ff.37.

7. A Dublin binding by William Hallhead's binder, 1777. Demosthenes, *Orations*
(transl. T. Leland), vol. 1, Dublin, 1777. Green goatskin, tooled in gold.
218 × 130 × 35 mm. Trinity College, Dublin, 190.r.11.

8. A Dublin binding by William McKenzie, *c.* 1783. *Chartae et statuta Colegii ...
Trinitatis*, Dublin, 1768. Brown marbled calf, tooled in gold.
238 × 189 × 22 mm. Trinity College, Dublin, Armoire.

May 1783 she married William McKenzie, who had worked for her
from *c.* 1781; they stayed at Hallhead's and Leathley's old address,
63 Dame Street. McKenzie really was a binder himself and one of the
most remarkable of the late eighteenth century. He was apprenticed
to William Gilbert, a bookbinder and bookseller and was freed in
1780. Seven years later he was elected Master of the Guild. After his
marriage to Sarah he took over from his wife as bookseller and
stationer to the University, from 1783 until 1795, providing books

and bindings for the library, as well as stationery, and from 1791 till
1795 he was Printer to the University Press. His relations with the
College were not without difficulties. He appears to have supplied
defective sets, made mistakes in numbering series, sent unwanted
material and, on occasion, overcharged. By 1795 he had exasperated
the College librarian to such an extent that he was dismissed.[50] Four
years earlier, in June 1791, he had moved to 33 College Green[51] and
in 1810 he moved to 7 Merrion Row. He died in January 1817. His
work, which is quite often signed with an engraved ticket, is easily
recognisable. As a rule he used green goatskin or tree calf, as on a
copy of Trinity College *Statutes* (1768) (fig. 8) and tooled the covers
with a border roll, occasionally adding a central armsblock. The books
are usually sewn on three sawn-in cords, producing a flat spine,
frequently decorated with coloured labels and onlays and elaborate
gold tooling. He was fond of a distinctive green, yellow, pink and
black spot-marbled paper which he used for endleaves, he sewed his
endbands with red and white silk, and often marbled or stained the
edges of the leaves. Another binding of tree calf, this time with the
Trinity College armsblock, covers Thomas Warton, *The History of
English poetry* in 3 volumes (London, 1774–81) (fig. 9), also sewn on
three sawn-in cords and with a lavishly tooled spine. It has a prize
label for Carolus Gulielmus Bury, Michaelmas 1784 and is signed
with a ticket: 'Bound by McKenzie, 63, Dame Str[eet]'.[52]

A third example of his work, in green goatskin, also with the
College arms and also signed with his ticket, covers Oliver Goldsmith's translation of *The Comic Romance of Monsieur Scarron*, 2
vols (Dublin, n.d.) (fig. 10). It was a College prize for John Duquery,
3rd class, Trinity Term, 1786.

One more category of bindings that has also been documented to
some extent, consists of those on the printed *Journals* and *Statutes*.
The King's Printer kept the monopoly for the printing and binding of
official documents, such as the printed *Journals* of the Lords and
Commons and the *Statutes* passed in Parliament. Complete sets of
the first printed edition of the *Journals of the House of Commons of
Ireland*, in 20 volumes, Dublin, 1753–82, are rare. A set (lacking vols
18 and 20) was presented by Maurice Craig to Trinity College (fig.
11).[53] This first edition of the *Journals* was the biggest single project
so far undertaken by an Irish printer, using Irish paper and locally
founded type. The contract for the first eight volumes was awarded
to Abraham Bradley, King's Stationer and Printer to the House of
Commons. They were finished by November 1753 at a cost of 2*d.* per

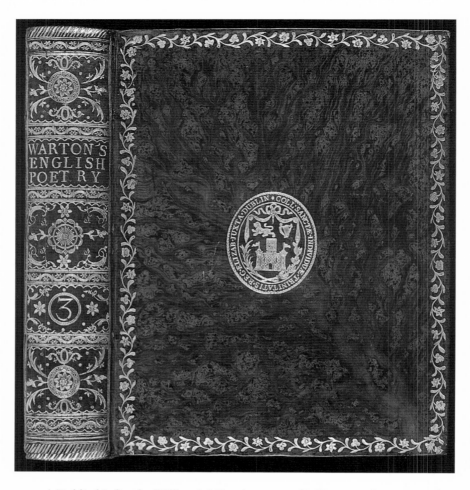

9. A Dublin binding by William McKenzie, *c.* 1784. T. Warton, *The History of
English poetry*, vol. 3, London, 1774. Brown marbled calf, tooled in gold.
272 × 210 × 49 mm. British Library, C.155.a.10.

sheet, while the binding cost 6*s.* per volume. Bradley is known as a
bookseller, stationer and bookbinder. He probably farmed out the
actual printing (Mary Pollard suggests either to George Grierson I or
to William Sleater). In March 1756 the House ordered a ninth volume
from Bradley, printed in 1757, volumes 10 to 13 followed in 1761–65;
and the rest, volumes 14 to 20, between 1771 and 1782, all supplied
by Bradley. As King's Stationer Bradley was certainly responsible
for the binding of the sets. As his period of office as King's Stationer

10. A Dublin binding by William McKenzie, *c.* 1786. O. Goldsmith (transl.), *The Comic Romance of Monsieur Scarron*, vol. 2, Dublin, n.d. Green goatskin, tooled in gold. 173 × 102 × 18 mm. Trinity College, Dublin, OLS. bind. B. 23.

11. A Dublin binding, possibly by Abraham Bradley, *c.* 1753. *Journals of the House of Commons of Ireland*, vol. 1, Dublin, 1753. Brown calf, tooled in gold. 375 × 235 × 72 mm. Trinity College, Dublin, OLS.x.1.81.

co-incides with the bindings of the (now lost) manuscript Lords and Commons *Journals*, that have been attributed to Parliamentary Binder B, Maurice Craig thought Bradley was responsible for what he identified as Parliamentary styles B and C. The only evidence that Bradley supplied bindings at all is an account (now lost), dated 10

October 1773 from Bradley for 'One Bible Royal folio gilt Barbary leather with silk strings and registers, £5.10s', delivered to the House of Lords.[54]

The odd volumes of the first edition of the Commons *Journals* that can be found in various libraries (e.g. at Trinity College, Dublin and in Marsh's library) are usually bound in calf, sewn on six cords, four of which have been laced in, their spines tooled in gold and with goatskin lettering pieces and volume labels. It is probable that this was the common 'trade' binding at a price of 6s. per volume. The set now at Trinity College is much more elaborate and was obviously a presentation copy. Inside volume I is a MS label: 'Commons Iournals 17 Vols. The gift of John, Lord Bishop of Clogher to the Library or Register Office at Clogher 1776'. The donor was John Garnett (1709–1782), who would have acquired his set as a member of the House of Lords.[55] It has been suggested that this set was bound by the Parliamentary Binder B, but, alas, the tools on this presentation set are very closely similar to, but not identical with, any used on either of the three groups into which the work of the Parliamentary Binder B can be divided.

We are on firmer ground with a new edition of the *Statutes at Large, passed in the Parliaments held in Ireland*, in 8 volumes, printed by Hugh Boulter Primrose Grierson in 1765 (fig. 12). Grierson was paid 2d. per sheet for printing and 10s. per volume for binding the sets in standard bindings (at £4 a set). He also supplied twelve sets 'elegantly bound in Turkey, and ornamented with Gold' at £22.15s. a set, or £2.16s.10½d. per volume. The latter were for presentation to the King, the Duke of York, the Lord Lieutenant and other grandees. The set for the King came with the King's library to the British Library.[56] The red goatskin bindings have scalloped onlays of white vellum and a centre onlay of dark green goatskin. The vesica-shaped compartments have been painted black. The same tools occur on other individual volumes of this same edition in very similar bindings. Volumes VI and VII, in red goatskin with white leather(?) scalloped onlays and a centre onlay in dark blue, tooled to the same design and with the same tools, are respectively at Trinity College, Cambridge (it belonged to Lord Rothschild) and the National Library of Ireland.[57] A copy of volume II, belonging to a different presentation set, is in the Henry Davis Gift to the British Library and volume V, once in the possession of Earl FitzWilliam, is also in the British Library.[58] These two volumes are both in red goatskin, decorated with the same tools as were used on the royal set, but without onlays. Boulter Grierson is

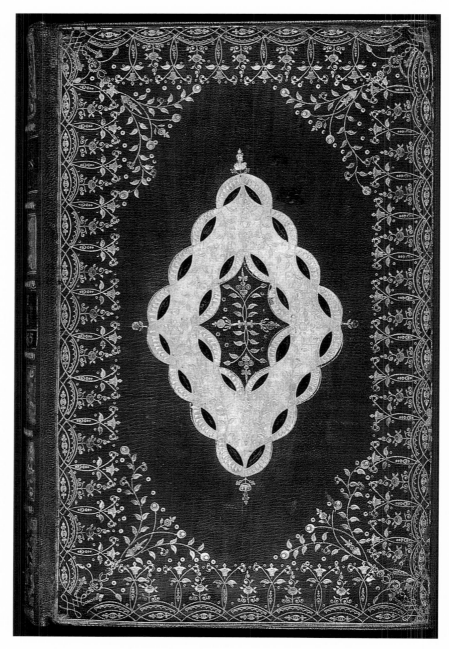

12. A Dublin binding by Boulter Grierson, 1765. *Statutes at large, passed in the Parliaments held in Ireland*, vol. 5, Dublin, 1765. Red goatskin, onlaid in white vellum and dark green goatskin, tooled in gold, decorated with black paint. 370 × 235 × 62 mm. British Library, 21.e.5.

recorded as printer, bookseller and bookbinder. He was freed in 1760, elected Master of the Guild of St Luke in 1769 and held the appointment of King's Printer from 1758 until his death in 1771.[59]

In 1914 Sir Edward Sullivan issued to the 'Members of the Sette of Odd Volumes' a privately-printed *Opusculum*, in 133 copies, entitled: 'Decorative Bookbinding in Ireland'. In this he rather whimsically described 'Bookbinding as the younger sister of the Arts ... [who] has had occasionally in her time all the triumphant satisfaction of a Cinderella. She has, indeed, become rather a favourite at the Court of Kings – and that too without the undignified limitations as to time which were imposed in the fairy tale under a twelve o'clock rule.'[60]

Alas for Sir Edward and the Irish Cinderella, the clock struck in 1800. The Union between England and Ireland meant the end of the Irish Parliament. Abraham Bradley King, grandson of Abraham Bradley and himself responsible for several fine bindings, one of which he signed at the foot of the spine,[61] lost his position as printer and stationer to the House of Commons, although his patent as King's Printer was not revoked until 1831. The British Copyright Act was extended to Ireland and the whole basis of the booktrade was changed.[62]

Fine binding – of a sort – was carried out in Dublin throughout the nineteenth century by the Mullens, Caldwell and Bellew among others, but compared to the magnificence of the previous century, their work was pretty uninspired: pumpkins instead of coaches, mice instead of thoroughbreds.

The rise and fall of the splendour of Irish bookbinding can only be understood against the background of the Irish booktrade as a whole and of Irish political and cultural life at the time. It shows clear parallels with other decorative arts, in style, as well as in the circumstances of its production. Cornucopiae, cartouches, scallop-shells, swathes and garlands, bunches of roses, curling leafy tendrils and palmettes, grace ceilings, cascade along staircase walls, droop over mantlepieces, and adorn the books, commissioned by 'those who lived at the top of that gilded world'[63] during that one century of relative peace and prosperity.

NOTES

1 M. Pollard, *A Dictionary of the Dublin booktrade 1550–1800*, London, 2000, p. 586 (quoted as Pollard, *Dictionary*).
2 R. E. Foster, *Modern Ireland 1600–1972*, London, 1988 (and for the historical account that follows).
3 William King (1650–1729), Dean of St Patrick's, 1689; Archbishop of Dublin, 1703; published in 1691 *State of the Protestants of Ireland*; see Foster, *op. cit.*, pp. 118, 135.
4 Pollard, *Dictionary*, introduction.
5 W. B. Yeats 'Introduction' to *The Words upon the window-pane*, reprinted in *Explorations*, London, 1962, p. 345.
6 Elizaberth Bowen, *Bowen's Court*, London, 1942, p. 172.
7 J. McDonnell, *Five hundred years of the art of the book in Ireland*, Dublin/London, 1997, p. 13, nos 15–17 (quoted below as McDonnell, *NLI*).
8 M. Pollard, *Dublin's trade in books 1550–1800*, Oxford, 1989, p. 3 (quoted as Pollard, *Dublin's trade*).
9 Lorinus (Lyon, 1605) is still at Trinity College, Dublin in its original binding. Pollard, *Dictionary*, p. 226. A. Cains, 'The Long Room survey of sixteenth- and seventeenth-century books of the first collections' in: V. Kinane and A. Walsh (eds), *Essays on the history of Trinity College Library Dublin*, Dublin, 2000, pp. 53–71.
10 Pollard, *Dublin's trade*, p. 7.
11 Pollard, *Dublin's trade*.
12 Marsh's diary, quoted in M. McCarthy, *All graduates and gentlemen*, Dublin, 1980, p. 15.
13 Act transcribed in Marsh's Library MS Visitation Book (1707); see also *The Statutes at large passed in the Parliaments of Ireland*, Dublin, 1765, vol. 4, chap. XIX, pp. 169–79: 6th Queen Anne, 1707.
14 M. M. Foot, *Decorated bindings in Marsh's Library*, Aldershot (Ashgate), 2004.
15 J. McDonnell and P. Healy, *Gold-tooled bookbindings commissioned by Trinity College Dublin in the eighteenth century*, Leixlip, 1987, p. 76, nos 1–3 (quoted below as McDonnell and Healy, *TCD*).
16 The grain-split or outer layer of a skin.
17 For this case see Pollard, *Dictionary*, pp. xvi–xvii.
18 Pollard, *Dublin's trade*, p. 37.
19 J. Dunton, *The Dublin scuffle*, London, 1699, p. 129.
20 Two of which have been published in: M. M. Foot, *Studies in the history of bookbinding*, Aldershot, 1993, pp. 15–67.
21 Dunton, *op. cit.*, p. 357, wrongly paginated as 341 (Ddd5 recto).
22 Pollard, *Dublin's trade*, p. 127.
23 Pollard, *Dublin's trade*, p. 128. See also M. Pollard, 'Plain calf for plain people: Dublin bookbinders' price lists of the eighteenth century' in: A. Bernelle (ed.), *Decantations: a tribute to Maurice Craig*, Dublin, 1992, pp. 177–86.
24 The only known copy belongs to Dr A. R. A. Hobson. I am grateful to Mary Pollard for giving me a photocopy of her transcription of this list.
25 See M. Craig, *Irish bookbindings 1600–1800*, London, 1954, p. 18 (quoted below as Craig, 1954). Craig's statement that Irish vellum bindings are of 'extreme rarity' is not born out by my own observations.
26 Craig, 1954, pl. 18.
27 See, for example, the binder who worked for Pepys, the Centre-Rectangle binder and the Sombre binder.

28   For English examples see the work of Owen, the Queens' Binder A, and the Royal Heads binder.

29   In the collection that formerly belonged to Lord Iveagh, now belonging to the State of Ireland (referred to below as Iveagh collection).

30   All three are in the the Iveagh collection.

31   Respectively belonging to Maurice Craig and in the British Library (587.d.22). I am grateful to M. Craig for showing me this and other bindings from his collection.

32   Iveagh collection.

33   Iveagh collection.

34   Iveagh collection.

35   Iveagh collection. Illustrated in: Bibliothèque Nationale, *Le Livre Anglais*, exhibition, Paris, 1951, no. 422, pl. 15.

36   E. Sullivan, 'Ornamental bookbinding in Ireland', *The Studio*, XXXVI (1905), pp. 52–9.

37   Craig, 1954, pp. 3–12, 14–15.

38   J. McDonnell, 'Parliamentary Binder B identified', *Bulletin of the Irish Georgian Society*, XXXV (1992–93), pp. 52–61.

39   M. Craig, *Irish bookbindings*, The Irish heritage series, 6, Dublin, 1976, pl. 10, describes this binding as 'by an unknown binder' (quoted below as Craig, 1976).

40   Ba consists of Iveagh collection, 20 and Trinity College, Dublin, K.f.48; Bb of Iveagh collection, 1107, 193 and 200; Bc of Iveagh collection, 3, 183, BCP1760, T.C.D., Dh58–9, T.C.D., BCP1760, Pierpont Morgan Library, 2108, and Marsh's Library, Dix 6. These groups are so small that it is perfectly possible that further research will show them all to have come from the same shop. If that turns out to be the case, this shop must have been a large one, employing several finishers, in order to justify the possession of several so closely-similar tools and pairs of tools.

41   Illustrated by McDonnell, *art. cit.* and Mc Donnell, *NLI*, no. 32.

42   E.g. the pair of cornucopia tools used by Bb have four hatchings along the top; the left-hand version of the pair of cornucopia tools used by Ba has three hatchings, while the right-hand version has four hatchings, but differs in other detail from that used by Bb; both versions of the pair of cornucopia tools used by Bc have three hatchings and are again slightly different from those used by Ba and Bb.

43   J. McDonnell, 'The Coote armorial bindings', *Bulletin of the Irish Georgian Society*, xxxvii (1995), pp. 4–12.

44   M. M. Foot, *The Henry Davis Gift*, vol. 2, London, 1983, no. 252.

45   See Pollard, *Dictionary*; McDonnell and Healy, *TCD*, chapter III; McDonnell, *NLI*, no. 30.

46   C. Ramsden, *Bookbinders of the United Kingdom*, London, 1954, p. 396 under 'Hallhead'.

47   Pollard, *Dictionary*, p. 359. See also McDonnell and Healy, *TCD*, no. 20.

48   McDonnell and Healy, *TCD*, no. 14.

49   T.C.D., 190 r 11–12. On the end-leaf of vol. 1 in ms: 'Wm Hallhead (one of the Editors) with gratitude for favours Received entreats Dr Leland to accept this Edition of his translation of the Orations of Demosthenes'.

50   Pollard, *Dictionary*; McDonnell and Healy, *TCD*, pp. 58–67; Ramsden, *op. cit.*, pp. 241–2; Craig, 1954, p. 21. See also Wilson's *Dublin directory*, 1794 and 1811.

51   A trade card describing him as 'Wm McKenzie Printer Bookseller & Stationer 33 College Green Dublin' was item 88 in Patrick King's *Bulletin* 28.

52   Charles William Bury won two more prizes in the same Term, both bound by McKenzie, one in the Iveagh collection, the other belonged to Maggs Bros, 23 Oct. 1986.

53   V. Kinane, 'A fine set of Irish Commons' *Journals*: a study of its production history', *The Long Room*, 30 (1985), pp. 11–28.

54   G. D. Hobson, *Thirty bindings*, London, 1926, p. 68, pl. 30. There is no reason to believe that the account quoted relates to the binding illustrated, which dates probably from the late 1790s.

55   Kinane, *art. cit.* There was a reciprocal arrangement between the Houses, mentioned in the Lords' *Journals* on 23 May 1785.

56   British Library, 21.e.1–8.

57   Craig, 1954, pl. 40 and Craig, 1976, cover. McDonnell, *NLI*, no. 35. The two odd volumes, VIII and X, in the Henry Davis Gift to the British Library (Foot, *Henry Davis Gift*, II, nos 259 and 260), although both by the same binder, have not been decorated with Grierson's tools. Vol. X is of the same design as the royal set, but was produced after Grierson's death.

58   Respectively, Foot, *Henry Davis Gift*, II, no. 261 and British Library, C. 108.i.13.

59   Pollard, *Dictionary*, pp. 258–9.

60   Sullivan, *Opusculum*, 'Decorative Bookbinding in Ireland', pp. 10–11.

61   On a *Report from the secret committee of the House of Commons*, Dublin, 1798, Lord Castlereagh's copy, see Craig, 1954, plate 56.

62   Pollard, *Dictionary*, p. xii.

63   Foster, *op. cit.*, p. 167.

BENJAMIN WEST
1805–1883

Esther Potter

THE BOOKBINDINGS OF Benjamin West caught the eye of a book collector whose name, by coincidence, was also West, and over a period of some ten years he put together a collection of sixty-six volumes bound by Benjamin West which was acquired in 1994 by the National Art Library of the Victoria and Albert Museum and has been kept together as a collection of bindings.[1] While they do not rank with the finest work of the best nineteenth-century binders they are nevertheless neat morocco bindings attractively decorated in gold and blind and the opportunity of studying a fair number of them all together makes it possible to trace the interesting development in bookbinding technique which was designed to meet a growing demand from an expanding middle class for books that looked sumptuous but were not too expensive.[2]

Benjamin West was born on 10 May 1805.[3] Although his father Joseph and his grandfather Richard were established silversmiths and Freemen of the Goldsmiths' Company, Benjamin was apprenticed to a bookbinder, Davis Cox, at Stationers' Hall on 4 May 1819 for the usual period of seven years, his father paying £10. There is some conflict of evidence here: his obituary notice in the monthly trade journal, *The Bookseller,* states that he served his apprenticeship with Francis Westley, one of the principal trade bookbinders. There can be no doubt about the apprenticeship entry in the memo book at Stationers' Hall and when he took his freedom on 4 October 1859 he is still described as 'apprentice of Davis Cox'. It may be that he worked for Francis Westley as a journeyman after completing his apprenticeship. Certainly he worked in the trade for a short time as a journeyman, a necessary qualification for membership of the journeymen bookbinders' trade society, the Friendly Society of Journeymen Bookbinders of London and Westminster, which he joined in April 1829.[4] He was a member of Lodge 2 for a year or so and then resigned to set up in business as a bookbinder on his own account.

He was sufficiently well established to appear in Robson's *London directory* for 1832 (which would have gone to press in 1831). His

237

address is given as 2, St James's Walk, Clerkenwell, and he is described as 'arabesque bookbinder', a term which will be considered later. His neighbour at no. 1 was J. L. Barritt, a die sinker for the silversmiths, and, since Benjamin West came from a family of silversmiths, it is conceivable that the two young men were already acquainted before they found themselves neighbours in St James's Walk. *The Bookseller* tells us that Benjamin West was James Barritt's brother-in-law and as their business relations were also closely linked it is necessary to trace Barritt's intriguing career as well.[5]

James Littler Barritt was born in 1801 and so was three years older than Benjamin West. He was apprenticed in 1815 to the royal goldsmiths, Rundell, Bridge and Rundell, to learn the art of sinking dies for silversmiths. If he served the usual term of seven years he would have been free in 1822. He must have established himself in business soon afterwards for Pigot's *London directory* for 1825 (which would have been compiled in 1824) shows him as Jas. L. Barrett [sic], engraver and die engraver, at 60 Tabernacle Walk, Finsbury. Ten years later he was a wholesale bookseller. This transformation is chronicled in the trade directories. In 1832 and 1833 Robson's *London commercial directory* describes him just as die sinker, already at 1, St James's Walk, but in 1834 Robson gives him two entries, J. L. Barritt, die sinker, at 1, St James's Walk, and Barritt & Co., booksellers, at 2, St James's Walk. What lies behind all this explains the connection with Benjamin West.

In about 1825 one of the principal bookbinders, Frederick Remnant, having been shown some bookbinding leather embossed by a process that had recently been developed in France, saw its potential for his own business and he and his partner, Jacob Edmonds, set about devising a method of making it. Embossed leather is impressed with a design in relief, before it is put on the book, by placing it between an engraved die and a counter die on which is the design in reverse and applying heavy pressure.[6] A neighbour was William Eley, a silversmith, and the heavy fly press that he used for stamping spoons and dish covers suggested a means of applying the necessary pressure, while they employed, to cut their dies, Eley's die cutter who was James Barritt.

Embossed leather was a great success. Remnant used it in his own business and sold pieces of embossed leather to other bookbinders. The first of Remnant's embossed leather was patterned with dies engraved by Barritt and signed 'REMNANT & EDMONDS'.

However Barritt's initiative and enterprise outran his discretion. He invested in a press and sold pieces of embossed leather to the trade in competition with Remnant, signing his dies 'BARRITT / LONDON' at first and then 'BARRITT & CO'. When Remnant discovered this he ceased to employ Barritt who then turned to the stationery trade and sold embossed paper and card alongside his embossed leather. The stationers took to embossed leather with enthusiasm for their albums of blank paper which were then high fashion and often incorporated leaves of embossed paper.[7] Barritt also employed some pocket-book makers to make up blotting books and card cases from his embossed leather.

The transition from J. L. Barritt, die sinker, to Barritt & Co., booksellers, must have taken place before the publication of Robson's *London directory* for 1834 where he appears as Barritt & Co. booksellers. His partner was William Eley, the silversmith for whom he used to cut dies, who had given up his silversmithing business in order to develop a new cartridge. With the capital that he brought into the business they were able to buy prayer books, Bibles and hymn books in sheets, bind and sell them, and establish a warehouse in Fleet Street. A bill head they were using in 1836 is headed:

'BARRITT & ELEY, wholesale Bible & prayer book warehouse. 173, Fleet Street, London. Manufactory 2, St James's Walk, Clerkenwell.'[8]

Meanwhile Benjamin West was building up his bookbinding business, also at 2 St James's Walk, and the implication must be that his was the manufactory for Barritt & Eley.

James Barritt was undoubtedly an astute businessman; he was quick to appreciate the possibilities in embossed leather and his move into the wholesale Bible trade was well judged. In about 1839 he obtained a share in the agency for the Queen's Printer's Bibles which had previously been exclusively in the hands of Longman. The Bible trade in the nineteenth century was very big business indeed and the demand accelerated in 1840 when the Bible printers reduced their prices to the trade in sheets. *The Bookseller* recorded that 'Messrs Barritt also introduced a cheaper kind of binding, so that an enormous impetus was given to the business. A Ruby Bible bound in morocco extra was in January sold to the trade at 10s.6d. while in the following April a book, just the same in appearance, was offered for 3s.6d. ... The credit of introducing this cheap morocco and morocco extra binding is due to Mr. B. West of Clerkenwell, a binder who had long been trying to get his cheap binding taken up, but without success till the Bibles themselves were cheapened'. This leaves us with two problems. If Benjamin West had little success in getting his cheap bindings taken up until 1840 when the printers reduced their prices, how did he build up a substantial bookbinding business before then? And exactly what were the magic bindings that looked like hand-tooled morocco but cost only a third as much?

Benjamin West was never among the largest of the nineteenth century binders but he managed a medium-sized innovative business for some fifty years and was active in trade affairs. When, in 1837, the London bookbinders, in anticipation of a confrontation with their journeymen about the number of apprentices they were taking, formed as a defensive measure, or rather re-formed, the Master Bookbinders' Association, West was a founder member and served on the committee.[9] His obituary notice mentions that when the Bible monopoly was broken up in 1840 he was of infinite service to Dr Campbell in providing him with prices and facts in order to support his argument. In the 1830s he was building up a steady business. In 1837 he was paying a rate of subscription to the Masters' Association appropriate for someone employing fewer than ten men; for 1839 we have the names of 26 people (13 men and 13 women) who worked for him, and this may not have been the whole of his workforce.[10] His name occurs from time to time in the records of the binding trade charities: in 1870, for example, sixty-two of his employees subscribed to the Pension Supplement. This build-up was not without its tensions. When the small masters, who had some sympathy for the journeymen, formed a separate association, the Friendly Society of Master Bookbinders of London and its Environs, and asked their members to sign an undertaking not to take more than three apprentices, 'all those present then signed their names with the exception of Mr B. West – too confirmed a sweater of apprentices to submit quietly to such resolutions'.[11]

Although his cheap bindings may have been slow to sell he was obviously finding a market for bindings of some kind. His training and experience as apprentice and journeyman between 1819 and 1830 would have been in the traditional full and half calf and morocco that were the staple work at that time. Evidently he started with these and was working to a high standard since *The Bookseller*, in its obituary notice of him, tells us that he 'commenced business on his own account about the year 1830 and speedily obtained a good connection as a binder of Bibles with a reputation second only to that of Mr Hayday'. That was a reputation worth having: Hayday was one of the foremost extra morocco binders of his time and it was said that a note 'bound by Hayday' added 25% to the value of a book.[12] The 1830s was a period of rapid economic and technical development in bookbinding and West, like Barritt, was quick to exploit it. Embossed leather was just coming in as he finished his apprenticeship and his brother-in-law next door was making it. There can be no doubt that West was using it: the description of him in Robson's *London directory* for 1832 as 'arabesque bookbinder' indicates as much. John Hannett, a bookbinder who published in 1835 a classic manual of bookbinding under the pseudonym A. J. Arnett, uses the term 'arabesque' to describe embossed leather, no doubt because arabesque designs were the most popular.[13] He later used 'arabesque' to refer to blocked decoration. The description of Benjamin West as 'arabesque bookbinder' in Robson's *London directory* for 1832 must refer to embossed binding – it is a little too early to mean decorative blocking.

There would have been a steady demand for embossed leather for some twenty years until it was, to a large extent, superseded by elaborately gold-blocked cloth. Gold blocking on cloth was introduced in 1832 and by 1850 was common on publishers' bindings and generally acceptable. At what stage Benjamin West embarked on cloth binding is unclear. His little binder's ticket is found in a book published by the Religious Tract Society in 1859 (fig. 1).[14] The cloth has been heavily grained and is blocked in blind with on both covers a decorative frame and the title in gold on the upper cover only – a typical run-of-the-mill cloth binding of the period. If confirmation were needed that in the latter part of his career he was engaged in publishers' cloth binding it can be found in an edition of John Bunyan's *Pilgrim's progress,* published for him in 1876, the cloth binding unsigned but decorated with a border which was also used by him on a signed leather-bound book in the 1850s.[15]

Though West did not confine his business to Bibles and prayer books he must have had considerable experience in binding them before 1840 if he was able to provide Dr Campbell with useful statistics, and in 1840 he was certainly producing his cheap bindings for Barritt. He was, however, to become further involved in Barritt & Co. Barritt's partner Eley had left the company in 1835 and was succeeded by Frederick Wilson who managed the warehouse in Fleet Street while Barritt toured the country building up a connection with local booksellers. Sales grew rapidly: it is recorded that on more than one occasion Barritt & Co. had printed for them editions of 100,000

1. *Life's morning*, Religious Tract Society, [1859].
Cloth, blocked in blind. (Author's rubbing).

prayer books and 50,000 Bibles. Frederick Wilson retired after seven years, which would be in about 1842, and at the same time James Barritt 'having acquired a sufficient sum to live upon in comfort, left the business'[16] and this flourishing concern was disposed of to his brother-in-law Benjamin West. All the evidence suggests that he had been closely associated with it from the beginning. He continued it as a Bible wholesaler, at first alone and then in partnership with another bookbinder, Hector Baxter, whose speciality was cloth binding for the Religious Tract Society. West retired from Barritt & Co. in 1860 and the business was continued by Baxter. Robert Stevenson, a bookbinder who had been associated with Barritt & Co. almost from the beginning, became manager. In 1868 Baxter found that Barritt & Co. occupied too much of his time, wound up the company and sold the stock. Robert Stevenson, with his brother Henry, then established a company, H. Stevenson & Co., to operate along the same lines.[17]

Both Benjamin West and Hector Baxter continued their own book-binding businesses separately from Barritt & Co. Baxter's entry in the *Post Office London directory* became Baxter & Son after 1886. West had a son, also Benjamin, who was apprenticed to him in 1853 'to learn his art of bookbinding'.[18] Nevertheless the name Benjamin West disappears from the trade directories after the death of West senior in 1883. His retirement from Barritt & Co. did not unfortunately imply a commitment to develop new bookbinding techniques. His obituary notice says sadly 'For some years past he had paid less attention to bookbinding than to the dissemination of cheap Testaments and religious books in English, French, and Spanish'. This refers to a projected series of illustrated polyglot editions of Bunyan's *Pilgrim's progress* to be published by Benjamin West; it was inspired by a speech of Gladstone's and its declared purpose was partly educational and partly evangelical. The first part of this programme was realised by the publication of an edition with English and French text on facing pages and the imprint: 'London: printed for Benjamin West and sold by Elliot Stock, 62 Paternoster Row'. The binding of the British Museum's deposit copy is described above.[19]

After James Barritt's retirement the business of Barritt & Co. was continued by these two booksellers, West and Baxter, along the same lines. The letter head used by Barritt & Eley in 1835 describes the business as 'wholesale Bible and prayerbook warehouse: ... Pocket books, blotting cases, albums, scrap books, card cases &c. &c.' Their advertisement twenty years later in *Hodson's Booksellers', publishers' and stationers' directory*, 1855 is essentially the same: 'A large variety of Bibles, Prayer Books, and Church Services, ... in every style of binding ... Papier Maché and Leather Blottings, Porte-Monnaies, Travelling Cases, Papeteries, Wallets, Music Boxes, and Folios, in great variety'. In 1835 they were described as booksellers and embossers and in 1843 'wholesale Bible and prayer book warehouse and embossers of book covers'.[20] Embossing of book covers is not mentioned after James Barritt's retirement, though Bibles and prayer books in embossed roan were still being advertised in 1858.[21] The range of fancy stationery was continued and enlarged to keep up to date: photograph albums were added in 1862.[22]

How the binding was divided between Benjamin West, Hector Baxter and Barritt & Co.'s own bindery is a matter for speculation. West no doubt continued to provide the decorative morocco bindings that made such a stir in 1840, and may even have continued to do some binding for Barritt & Co. after he retired from the company: a lyrical description in *The Bookseller* of a Barritt edition of Church Services, 'one of the most elegant books we have seen, bound in olive-coloured morocco, and with an intermixture of blind-tooling and gilding', strongly suggests a West binding.[23] Hector Baxter is otherwise known only as binding for the Religious Tract Society.[24] I have seen only cloth bindings with his ticket and if Barritt & Co. sold cloth bound Bibles and prayer books they did not advertise the fact.

It does seem as though much, and probably most, of the Barritt binding was done in their warehouse at 173 Fleet Street. It will be recalled that when James Barritt was dismissed by Remnant he employed some bookbinders to make pocket books and the like for him and that Robert Stevenson, an experienced bookbinder who later managed the business for Hector Baxter, had been with Barritt since the early 1830s. From then onwards Barritt seems to have had his own bindery, although it makes little showing in the trade directories, apparently because binding was done only on the books he sold and not for the trade generally. A trade card describes the company as 'Bible warehouse, 173 Fleet Street, ecclesiastical bookbinders'.[25] Sundry advertisements in *The Bookseller* make the claim 'Having their own bookbinding and mounting establishments, they are enabled to produce novelties and general binding with the greatest facility'.[26] That this did not mean simply that Barritt & Co. had an arrangement with a local binder is demonstrated by documents of the trade societies which show that qualified, working bookbinders were indeed employed on the premises. The anticipated struggle between the masters and the journeymen (they always called it 'The Struggle') came in 1839 and in preparation the journeymen made a list of the masters and the number of their employees. A working list has survived and has duplicate entries for Barritt & Co. One reads; 'Barratt [sic] Fleet Street – 2 men 3 apprentices' and the other 'Barrits [sic] – 3 men 3 apprentices'.[27] Not a large unit but the high proportion of apprentices indicates growth. We even know who some of these people were from the annual lists of contributors to the Bookbinders' Pension fund in which a few people gave their employer's address instead of their home address. William Kelly and Mrs Kelly were at 173 Fleet Street from 1837 to 1840; William Kelly jr was there from 1836 to 1843 and William Brock from 1838 to 1843 and again in 1847.[28]

The Fleet Street bindery seems to have been capable of high-class work, good enough to win an award at the Great Exhibition of 1851. The Juries reported: 'Specimens of carefully and well-executed work, among which is a royal 4to Altar Service, ultramarine border round the pages, and carved boards covered in Turkey morocco; the electrometal corners and centres deserve mention. Mr Barritt had also numerous small Common Prayers and Church Services, perforated and engraved; solid metal covers'.[29] Benjamin West can surely be exonerated from responsibility for carved wood and perforated metal which could not be further removed from his dainty morocco. It is difficult however to identify Barritt bindings because his signed bindings are almost unknown. By no means all binders used little printed tickets and then not on all copies. Barritt's embossed covers are signed but this name is engraved in the die and is the signature of Barritt as die cutter: the volume might have been bound by anyone to whom he sold the leather. Douglas Ball notes a stamp 'BARRITT, London' on a Bible and prayer book of 1833 in a slip case.[30] Bibles and prayer books do not have a good survival record and we can only assume that those Benjamin West was making for Barritt in 1840 were like the bindings he made for his own trade which can be seen in the Victoria and Albert Museum. The description of Barritt's Bibles in *The Bookseller*'s obituary of Barritt tallies with the bindings in that collection.

What then were these bindings that caused such a stir in 1840? *The Bookseller* gives us two clues. Benjamin West 'was the first to introduce the seconds [sic] style of binding, and the first to introduce moveable ornaments in blocks for gilding the sides of books'. The term 'second style' seems to have been well known in the trade. When the bookbinder James Kitcat wrote to a certain Mr Robertson offering him an engagement as foreman he listed the classes of work done in his shop among which were: 'morocco work second stile, blocked and plain / morocco work best stile'.[31] Warren de la Rue in a note in the official catalogue of the Great Exhibition observed: 'hand tooled designs are usually employed in the higher class of binding.' The 'second style' then appears to be good quality morocco binding but one in which blocking might be substituted for hand tooling.

The 'first to introduce moveable ornaments in blocks for gilding the sides of books' suggests that Benjamin West played a leading part in the development of blocking in the 1830s. Blocking on a wooden press was a tedious business: a revival of interest in blocking was prompted by the introduction in 1832 of the metal framed arming press which had a lever action instead of screw and was quicker and easier to operate. At first it was used in titling the spines of cloth cased books, like the well-known edition of Byron's works of 1832–3, and decorative blocking, on the spine and on the sides, soon followed.[32] John Hannett in the first edition of *Bibliopegia* (1835), records the early development of decorative bindings using the arming press. 'These are executed with designs cut in plates of brass the size of the sides of the book; they were at first only used plain [i.e. blind], but have latterly been adopted in gilding.'[33] The disadvantage was that cutting a separate plate for each work was time-consuming and expensive. One solution was provided by Morris & Co., one of the major bookbinders' tool makers, by the invention of their 'Typographical Accelerator' which allowed the binder to proceed from one design to another without waiting for a new plate to be cut. It is described in the *Transactions* of the Society of Arts: 'It is the present practice of bookbinders, where a label, consisting of a line of letters alone, is wanted, it is composed of moveable types fixed in a case, but for a label consisting of letters and ornaments combined, the custom is to have the whole cut in one brass block, leaving only space for the insertion of movable pieces indicating the number of the volume.

Such blocks, it is obvious, can only be used for lettering that particular work for which they were first intended and are no longer of any value when the immediate purpose has been answered. Mr Morris's contrivance consists in composing the ornaments for labels, such as foliage and scroll work, of separate pieces in the manner of common types. When, therefore, a design of this kind, together with the required lettering, has been arranged, it is to be put into a strong brass frame, and secured in its place by screws.' A square frame is then illustrated with the title 'SCOTT / VOL. 1', set in type and surrounded by four movable ornamental pieces, held in place by four screws, which form a scroll border. The description continues: 'When the work is finished the design is broken up, and the pieces of which it consisted are distributed, and thus are ready to form part of any other label that may be required'.[34] Although this account refers only to titling Hannett makes it clear that it was also used for the complete sides of a book: 'the design is formed with a number of separate ornaments fitting exactly into each other: thus when the number of any design is worked off, it can be taken to pieces, and any other from the size of a folio to a 32mo executed'.[35]

This was not the only attempt to speed up the blocking process. The tool cutter Alexander Bain produced an adjustable frame on which corner- and centre-pieces can be positioned to tool the whole of the board at once, for which he received the silver Isis medal and five pounds from the Society of Arts[36] (John Morris was merely given thanks). The principle of interchangeable blocks was not entirely new. Embossed leather was usually made with a single plate for the sides of the book, but there were some dies that had a separate central medallion which could be exchanged for another of the same size but a different design. Bain's and Morris's devices imply more flexibility than this but neither of them seems consistent with the much greater flexibility of West's designs. Perhaps he made, at an early stage, the discovery, noted by Hannett in his sixth edition of 1865, that rather than fiddling about with metal frames and little screws it is altogether simpler just to stick the individual pieces in place on a piece of cartridge paper or millboard (they were only 6mm high) and fasten that to the plate of the press.[37] Some such device he must have used to explain the claim that he was the first to introduce movable ornaments in blocks for gilding the sides of books.

The description of the bindings he made for James Barritt is consistent with the bindings in the Victoria and Albert Museum and some other very similar bindings in other collections, and, while there is only a single Bible and one prayer book in the West collection, they do not differ in style or technique from the others.

The development of the technique can be followed in the West collection. The books are shelf marked 42.KK.55 to 42.KK.120 and will be referred to here just by the last digits. There are sixty-six volumes of which eight are part of multi-volume sets so that fifty-eight binding designs are represented. The books are dated or datable between 1826 and 1851; most of them date from the 1830s and 1840s. The bindings could, of course, be later than the date of publication, and some of them obviously are (e.g. nos 78, 94 and 105), but twelve of them can be dated by inscriptions on endpapers to within a year or two of publication. The earliest volumes with inscriptions of the same year as publication are no. 67, *The Poetical works of Robert Burns*, published and presented in 1839 and no. 70, Scott's *Marmion,* also published and presented that year. Another copy of the 1839 edition of Scott's *Marmion* was presented in 1840 and an 1838 edition (no. 68) also has an 1840 inscription. It is clear then that the technique used to such effect on Barritt's Bibles in 1840 was already fully developed.

Thirty-four volumes are signed, the earliest ones with a blind embossed stamp in the bottom left-hand corner of the lower paste-down, and the later ones with a little printed paper label, rectangular or lozenge-shaped. Three volumes have designs on the covers, the spine, or on both, identical to those on signed bindings.[38] The remaining thirty are unsigned but attributable to West with reasonable certainty because they use combinations of the same tools which appear on signed bindings, and because they handle like West bindings. He may have taken short cuts with his finishing but there is nothing slipshod about his forwarding. The books are bound in morocco and they are nearly all bound, not cased.[39] They are mainly small books, almost certainly sewn two up, as was usual at the time, on three cords of which the middle one had its ends cut off and the other two laced into the boards. Two larger volumes have five cords with three of them laced in. He used good quality millboard, thin but hard, the squares are small with trim headbands, some hand worked and some made from canvas, but all fitting tidily into the small squares. There is normally a narrow silk marker, the gilt edges are solid and there is a general air of great neatness. The endpapers are of the pale yellow paper that was much used for endpapers at that period.

All these bindings are for the most part blocked but there is a certain amount of hand tooling as well. There is usually a single line forming a border just inside the edges of the cover and this is sometimes run in by hand as in nos 60, 64 and 102 while in no. 74 the border is blocked. Where there is a narrow roll on the edges of the boards or on the turn-ins that would have to be done by hand. To block the covers the whole book, closed, may be put in the press to block one cover and then turned over to block the other. When it comes to the spine there are problems. It can only be put into a blocking press if the whole binding can be laid flat, that is to say if the spine is blocked before the binding is attached to the book, and then the book has to be cased and not bound. But nearly all these volumes are bound. The spine can then be tooled by hand and some, like nos 59 and 103, are.[40] The panels can be tooled with a small block impressed by hand which Mr Middleton calls a butter stamp.[41] Or the leather of the spine can be blocked before the book is covered, in which case the binder has to be very careful not to flatten the pattern. Lining the leather with thin paper helps to preserve a crisp impression.[42] Even if most of the decoration on the spine is blocked some additional small tools can be put in afterwards, such as the dots on no. 112 and the centre tool in the panels of no. 116.

The decoration of these bindings progresses from somewhat restrained blocking in blind to bolder designs partly or wholly gilt. Three early bindings, with the blocking on the covers entirely in blind, although the spines are gilt, are on various works in Scott, Webster and Geary's *English classics* series.[43] The design on one of them, no. 56, is repeated, also in blind, on no. 57, John Newton's *Cardiphonia*, published by Hamilton, Adams and Co.; the two spines however are different. The layout of the designs is much the same as that of no. 59, another of the *English classics* series, illustrated in fig. 2, which has progressed to a combination of blind and gold blocking. They all have a design of light scroll work extending across the cover and reversed at the bottom: sometimes these motifs are connected by one or two long lines down either side. These designs are built up from small pieces which are used again and again in different combinations on other bindings.

Apart from these early ones nearly all the covers are blocked in gold or gold and blind combined. The design is identical on both covers and the spine is nearly always gilt.[44] In later bindings the general layout of the design is frequently varied by using four corner-pieces (fig. 3) again often linked across the top and bottom (figs 4 and 5) and there is usually a large centre-piece, as in figs 3, 4, 5 and 6, so that the design fills the whole cover. Bolder tools were introduced such as the palmette seen in fig. 4. A tool that West used frequently (or is it that it is over-represented because it would be difficult for a collector to miss it?) is the fan which appears in figs 3 and 5. West also had this motif in two smaller sizes as in fig. 7(d). Another favourite was rather like the 'drawer-handle' tools of the later seventeenth century and also comes in several sizes: it can be seen in two sizes in fig. 4 and it appears again in fig. 7(a). One common technique was the use of dotted instead of solid lines, sometimes straight but often curved. They may be seen curved in fig. 5 and straight in fig. 6 and

2. M. de Bourrienne, *Memoires of Napoleon Bonaparte*, Scott, Webster & Geary, 1836. Morocco, blocked in gold and blind. National Art Library, 42.KK.59.

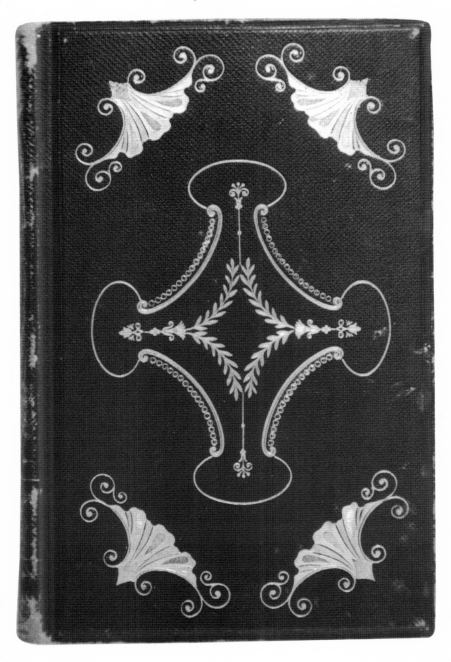

3. James Montgomery, *The West Indies and other poems*, Longman, 1828. Morocco, blocked in gold. National Art Library, 42.KK.78.

4. Sir Walter Scott, *Marmion*, William Smith, 1839. Morocco blocked in gold.
National Art Library, 42.KK.70.

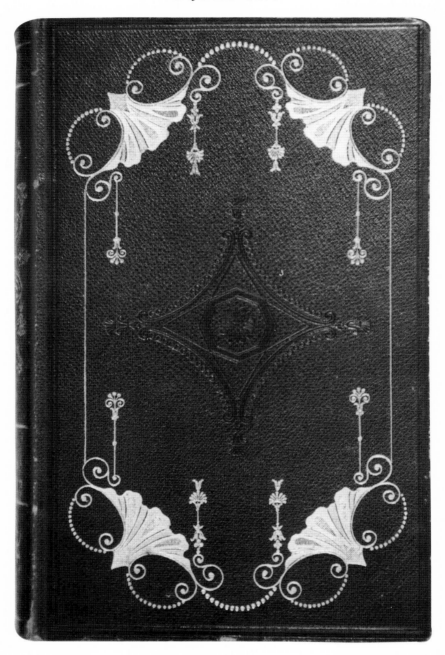

5. Felicia Hemans, *Works*, 7 vols, Wm. Blackwood & Sons, 1839. Vol. 1.
Morocco, blocked in gold and blind. National Art Library, 42.KK.81.

6. William Robertson, *The History of the reign of the Emperor Charles V,*
Scott, Webster & Geary, 1840. Morocco, blocked in blind.
National Art Library, 42.KK.97.

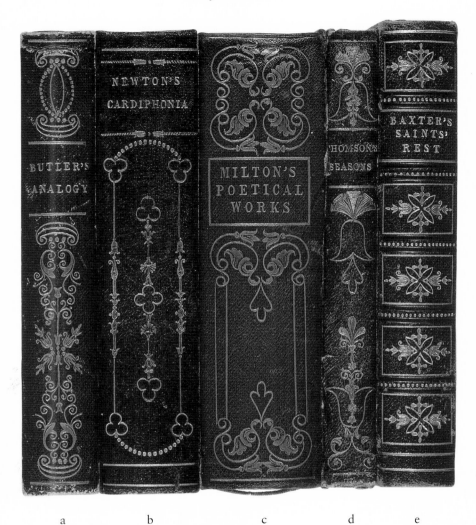

a b c d e

7. Spines of:
a) Joseph Butler, *The Analogy of religion*, Scott, Webster & Geary,
[*c.* 1834]. National Art Library, 42.KK.55.
b) John Newton, *Cardiphonia*, Hamilton, Adams & Co., n.d.
National Art Library, 42.KK.57.
c) John Milton, *The Poetical works*, Scott, Webster & Geary,
1839. National Art Library, 42.KK.58.
d) James Thomson, *The Seasons*, Scott, Webster & Geary, 1837.
National Art Library, 42.KK.61.
e) Richard Baxter, *The Saints' everlasting rest*, Scott, Webster & Geary,
1840. National Art Library, 42.KK.106.
All in morocco, blocked in gold.

appear on spines in fig. 7(a), (b) and (e). These dotted lines had long use; they are still found, in a very crude form, on the cloth binding in fig. 1. Another trick is his use of tools with a stippled ground which gives, especially when gilt, a two-colour effect. It is seen, not very clearly because it is in blind, in the large central diamond and in the corner-pieces in fig. 6, and more obviously, because gilt, in the corner- and side-pieces of fig. 8 and the border of fig. 9.

What is especially characteristic of Benjamin West's bindings is his use of some little tools with which he emphasises the ends of a line or the junction between two lines. There are two trefoils, one in outline ♧ and a smaller one blocked solid ♣. The larger trefoil can be seen in fig. 7(b) and the smaller one in fig. 6. There is a quatrefoil, about the same size as the larger trefoil, ♧ which may be seen in the middle of the panel of fig. 7(b) and a cross formed from four narrow petals ✢ seen in figs 8 and 7(e). The fifth is a three-lobed figure ♡ used in fig. 6 at the top and bottom of the oval frame and again in the lower panels of figs 7(c) and 7(d). They all occur frequently on the spine as well as on the covers of Benjamin West's bindings and in the way in which he uses them they are almost as good as a signature.

As these bindings have hollow backs they do not have raised bands which divide the spine into panels. In a few of the earlier ones the spine is divided into panels by false bands or decorative lines with the same tooling in each of the panels that is not occupied by a title, but more often West treats the spine as a whole, as did many of the cloth binders. A frequently used formula is a small decorative block at the head of the spine, the title below it and then a long panel made of two or three impressions of the smaller block, one of them perhaps inverted. There are infinite variations on this pattern some of which may be seen in fig. 7(a) to (d)

There is something of a gap in the West collection in the later 1840s: there is nothing dated later than 1845 until 1850. Sixty-six volumes are a very small sample on which to base any theory, and the gap may only show the chance of survival, but one is tempted to recall that in 1842 West assumed responsibility for the Barritt wholesale Bible business and was perhaps so busy keeping up with changing fashions in the binding of prayer books that his output of pretty little volumes of poetry dropped a bit.

There are not so many later bindings in the West collection, and then there is a marked change of style. They no longer consist of a mosaic of small blind and gilt blocks; they tend to have a border or frame with a centre design and a spine divided into six evenly spaced

8. Oliver Goldsmith, *The Vicar of Wakefield,* John Sharp, 1828. Morocco, blocked in gold. National Art Library, 42.KK.105

9. *The Keepsake*, Thomas Nelson, 1850. Morocco blocked in gold and blind. National Art Library, 42.KK.113.

panels. Fig. 9 shows a binding on *The Keepsake* for 1850 which is not signed but its border is also used on a signed binding (no. 112). It has some links with the earlier bindings; the border has the stippled ground with the two-colour effect, and two of the characteristic little tools, the trefoil and the three-lobed figure also appear but this time with a heavy black outline. To some extent the change in style appears to reflect a general change in bookbinding design in the third quarter of the century.

We must assume that Benjamin West himself made or supervised the designs of his bindings; he, like several other bookbinders, registered bookbinding patterns under the Board of Trade's Design Acts. But who designed and made the tools from which they were built up? There were several tool makers working in London in the 1830s who could have supplied pallets and gouges and perhaps some of the scroll work but the more individual tools do not look like ordinary commercial work. They could well have been provided by James Barritt; he had the expertise and experience to make them and it was usual at that time for tool makers to be responsible for their own designs. It is possible to trace a stylistic link between dies cut by Barritt for Remnant and West's blocked designs. We know that Barritt cut the first dies used by Remnant for embossed bindings, and Hannett tells us that Remnant's first embossed binding was a cathedral design which he illustrates, embossed in blind on white paper, in several editions of his *Bibliopegia*.[45] It incorporates the trefoil and the quatrefoil, wholly appropriate in this context, which are scattered so plentifully over Benjamin West's bindings. This is far short of proof but, given the close business association between West and Barritt, it does seem plausible.

It remains to consider the market for which these bindings were intended. The great advantage of blocking is that elaborate decoration can be produced quickly and more cheaply than hand tooling and is ideal for bulk binding. Along with the development of book cloth in the 1820s it allowed publishers to supply a whole edition in a uniform binding or to provide a part of an edition in blocked leather for those who wanted a more expensive or a more durable binding. But this is not what Benjamin West was doing; these are not edition bindings. The odd thing about the West collection is that there are no duplicates. Where there are two copies of the same book they are in different bindings; where there are two identical bindings they are on different works from different publishers. The design on the covers of the *Poetical works of Collins, Gray & Beattie*, Scott, Webster & Geary,

1835 (no. 56) is the same as that on John Newton's *Cardiphonia* published by Hamilton, Adams & Co. (no. 57), though the spines differ. There are two copies of an 1839 edition of Cowper's *Poetical works,* published by William Smith, with different blocking, and the design on the covers of one (no. 88, vol. 2 only) is repeated on Felicia Heman's *Vespers of Palermo,* Edinburgh, 1840 (no. 89), while the design on the other (nos 91 and 92) appears again on Robert Pollock's *Course of time,* Edinburgh, 1841 (no. 93). An intriguing variation is found on two sets of the seven-volume edition of Mrs Heman's collected works. Nos 81–89 form one complete set and there are two volumes (nos 79 and 80) from another set. Both sets have the same design on the covers but whereas the outer frame is in gold and the centre lozenge in blind on the complete set (fig. 5) the other set has a gilt centre and blind frame, and the effect is quite different. The two sets also have different spines.

A clue to this contrived variation may be found among the highly informative trade advertisements in *The Bookseller.* As Christmas approached publishers and wholesalers would head their advertisements 'Books for prizes and presents' or words to that effect, and offer an immense variety of suitable books in new and elegant bindings. The rationale behind this was explained in a paragraph in *The Bookseller* of July 1859 which reported that William Gardner had opened a depot, separate from the Oxford Bible agency of Gardner & Son, 'for the sale of elegantly bound books suitable for presents: here the country bookseller may come and make his selection from more than three hundred of the most popular books of all the leading publishers, bound by Hayday and other first class workmen, in every variety of plain and ornamental bindings.' It rashly claimed that 'this business ... is the only one in London specially for the supply of handsomely bound books to the trade', and had to retract in the next issue when the publishers R. & A. Suttaby and Hamilton, Adams & Co. retorted that they had long been supplying nicely bound books to the trade on the usual terms. Suttaby, publishers of devotional books, bound their own publications in leather; Hamilton, Adams are not known as bookbinders but, as three of West's bindings are on books published by them, he may have done binding for them.

Benjamin West and James Barritt were then catering for a recently evolving market for books chosen at least in part for their bindings. The 1820s and 1830s were a period not only of technical development in bookbinding but also of economic change. There was a rapid increase in the output of books to meet the needs of a rising population and the expansion of a literate middle class which demanded a wider range of subjects and a greater variety in the styles of binding available. The introduction in the 1820s of the literary annuals and gift books gave them a taste for pretty bindings. The response of the trade began with Bibles and prayer books; a buyer is going to choose a Bible for its size and binding – the text is standard. From literary annuals and gift books they progressed to general works of literature suitable for New Year and Christmas presents. And so developed a wholesale trade which included, besides Suttaby and Barritt, the Oxford agent, Gardner & Son, and two more bookbinders, Ramage and Co. and Peacock, Mansfield & Company. The importance of the binding as a selling point accounts for the preponderance of binders.

Benjamin West and James Barritt were then working along parallel lines. Barritt seems to have concentrated on religious books and, to judge by his advertisements, was producing a wide range of bindings at 173 Fleet Street in addition to the bindings West made for him. West was developing his own speciality in books for presents and the works in the West collection fit nicely into that category. More than a quarter are reprints of works by popular poets, another quarter are religious works, one in three has a presentation inscription. *The Bookseller* implied that this trade was directed at country booksellers and David Pearson has pointed out the high proportion of volumes with the little printed labels of country booksellers.[46] Of thirteen volumes with a bookseller's ticket only three have London labels while ten come from around the country – two from Liverpool, two from Bristol and one each from Edinburgh, Glasgow, Carlisle, Bath, Wallingford and Eton.

Benjamin West showed great ingenuity in adopting new techniques for this promising trade. As with the brass dies for embossing leather, the problem was to spread the great cost of making the blocks over a large number of volumes. This was solved by the little interchangeable blocks which could be re-used time and again in different combinations. Again, setting up a press for one design takes time and therefore costs money which would, in an edition binding, be spread over a large batch. But West did not want large numbers of identical books; his aim was a range of different books each with a choice of bindings: and so he seems to have built up an economic batch for one design from a few copies each of several different works – perfectly feasible if the volumes were all of the same size – as they were. Most books come in standard sizes and only two sizes of block would be needed to fit 80% of the volumes in this collection. Yet more variety could be obtained by ringing the changes on the spines, as he did. Since blind and gilt blocking is done separately there would be no difficulty in providing some copies of Mrs Heman's *Works* with a gilt outer frame and blind centre and reversing the process on the others.

  Benjamin West's career as a bookbinder spanned half a century which saw notable economic and technical changes to which he successfully adapted his business, from hand-tooled morocco extra to embossed leather, then blocked leather and finally publishers' cloth, but his greatest period of creativity was the first decade when he was developing, perhaps with some inspiration from James Barritt, the bindings documented here, which remained in demand for at least thirty years and were admired by his contemporaries.

NOTES

1   They are shelved at 42.KK.55–120. No. 121 a binding signed by John West of Hatton Garden, and no. 122, a cloth binding, have not been considered.
2   I am most grateful to David Pearson, who introduced me to the West bindings, for a great deal of help which included taking the photographs for figs 2–6, 8, 9; to the staff of the National Art Library who made it easy to study the bindings; to Bernard Middleton for expert advice, and to private collectors who showed me their Benjamin West bindings.
3   Although his obituary notice in the monthly trade journal *The Bookseller* of March 1883, p. 223, gives his age as 78 when he died on 22 February 1883, the parish register of Saint Luke Old Street, Finsbury, records his baptism on 17 July 1805 and his date of birth on 10 May 1805.
4   *Annual audit accounts of the Friendly Society of Journeymen Bookbinders of London & Westminster*, 1828–29 and 1829–30, British Library, JAFF 91.
5   The long and detailed obituary notice of James Barritt in *The Bookseller* for August 1863, pp. 494–5 is also very informative about West. Biographical details about Barritt and West that are not otherwise attributed come from this obituary notice and from that for Benjamin West in *The Bookseller* for March 1883.
6   There is a good description of the process in the *Cyclopaedia of useful arts and manufactures*, edited by C. Tomlinson, London, 1854, under BOOKBINDING.
7   There are many albums with embossed covers among the books in the Bodleian Library, Oxford, John Johnson collection.
8   This bill head, used for an invoice in the Bodleian Library, John Johnson collection, Book Trade, London, must have been old stock; a note at the foot is signed Barritt & Co. Eley had left the partnership in 1835.
9   Master Bookbinders' Association, *Fundamental rules with a list of the members, officers and committee*, London, 1837.
10 *Ninth annual report of the Bookbinders' Pension Society*, London, 1839, Addenda.

11   *The British Bookmaker*, VII, 78, December 1893, p. 139.
12   *The Bookseller*, April 1872, p. 284.
13   [John Hannett] *Bibliopegia; or, the art of bookbinding, in all its branches*, London, 1835, using the pseudonym John Andrews Arnett, pp. 126–7.
14   I am grateful to John Collins for discovering it.
15   *The Pilgrim's progress in English and French*, n.d., but with a preface dated 1876. On the lower cover is the bud-and-leaf border which West had used on the signed leather binding of a copy of *The Christian wreath of prose, poetry and art*, London, Religious Tract Society, [c. 1853], illustrated in Maggs Bros Ltd catalogue 1075, part II, no. 315.
16   *The Bookseller*, August 1863, p. 495.
17   *The Bookseller*, January 1869, p. 5.
18   Although West senior did not take up his freedom of the Stationers' Company until 4 October 1859 he was able to bind an apprentice at Goldsmiths' Hall by patrimony, since he had become free of the Goldsmiths' Company on 2 February 1848, his father having been a Freeman of that Company.
19   British Library 4415.cc.1, received 19 January 1877.
20   *Post Office London directory*, 1835 and 1843.
21   *The Bookseller*, January, 1858.
22   *The Bookseller*, September, 1862.
23   *The Bookseller*, February, 1862.
24   Douglas Ball, *Victorian publishers' bindings*, London, Library Association, 1985, p. 171.
25   British Library, JAFF 156.
26   For example, *The Bookseller*, April 1858.
27   British Library, JAFF 151.
28   Annual reports of the Bookbinders' Pension Society, 1836–43, 1847.
29   Great Exhibition 1851, *Reports of the juries*, pp. 424, 451.
30   Douglas Ball, *op. cit.*, p. 171.
31   British Library, JAFF 156.
32   Michael Sadleir, *The Evolution of publishers' binding styles 1770–1900*, London/New York, 1930, chapter VI.
33   *Bibliopegia*, 1835, pp. 119–20.
34   Vol. 50, part II, 1836 for the session 1834–35, pp. 92–4.
35   *Bibliopegia*, 2nd ed., 1836, pp. 171–2.
36   *Bibliopegia*, 1836, pp. 119–20.
37   *Bibliopegia*, 1865, p. 383.
38   Signed bindings are nos 55–57, 59–61, 70, 72, 74, 75, 77–87, 91, 92, 95–100, 102, 112 and 115–117. No. 76 has covers as 74 and 75; no. 93 has covers and spine as 91–92; no. 71 has spine as 72.
39   No. 65, exceptionally, is cased.
40   In no. 68 the letters of the title were set in a typeholder so that the title could be impressed with a single movement of the wrist; in no. 102 the letters of the title have been impressed individually.
41   Bernard C. Middleton, *A History of English craft bookbinding technique*, 4th ed. London, 1996, p. 180.
42   *Ibid.*, p. 336.
43   Nos 55, 56 and 58.
44   No. 98 is an academic prize and the gold blocking in the centre of the upper cover only is the school's stamp added afterwards.
45   For example, in the 6th edition, 1865, facing p. 156.
46   *The Book Collector*, vol. 45, no. 1 (Spring 1996), pp. 83–6.

COLLECTOR, DEALER AND FORGER

A Fragment of Nineteenth-Century Binding History

Mirjam M. Foot, Carmen Blacker
& Nicholas Poole-Wilson

I. DEALER AND FORGER: MMF

THE BRITISH LIBRARY holds on deposit a file containing 154 letters: autographs, transcripts, telegrams and a few photocopies. The correspondence, mainly in French, dates from October 1875 till December 1896, and the majority covers the business dealings between Bernard Quaritch and Monsieur J. Caulin of Paris and – later – Brussels.[1]

Quaritch and Caulin had done business since 1871 or 1872. From 1875 Caulin, at Quaritch's request, wrote two kinds of letters, those that came in envelopes marked 'private', written in Caulin's own hand and meant for Quaritch's eyes only, and those that survive in transcripts in Quaritch's hand and were meant to be shown to prospective buyers. The bulk of the correspondence shows the supplier offering books in splendid Renaissance bindings, the bookseller trying to place them, sometimes with difficulty, but usually successfully, and only occasionally having to return books that remained unsold. It makes fascinating reading. Books belonging to every important French sixteenth-century collector, Grolier, Mahieu, Anne de Montmorency; French kings and their wives and mistresses, François I, Henri II and III, Catherine de Medici, Diane de Poitiers; popes and cardinals, owned by Caulin, were sold to Quaritch and passed on by him to discerning clients (colour plate 7 and fig. 1).

For the first ten years Caulin specified the price, Quaritch invariably finding it too high and – after some irritable correspondence – usually obtaining it for his client for less. The haggling about the price of the bindings runs as a steady thread through the correspondence. In late March 1882 Caulin wrote that he was tempted to believe that the rarer the bindings were that he had on offer, the more

1. A binding by Hagué. Pius IV, *Pontificale Romanum*, Venice, Giunta, 1561. Fol. Brown calf over wooden boards, tooled in gold and decorated with black and red paint, with the arms of Cardinal François de Tournon. (Blacker sale 77). British Library, C.108.l.2.

Quaritch tried to push down the price. Quaritch's opinion was that 'It takes a lot of skill to please both you and the buyers ... bibliophily has gone in decline these days, all great collectors having died' (8.4.82). He considered Caulin's prices far too high: 'I would do well if I could sell them for half'; this à propos two books, one with the arms of Odet de Chatillon at fr. 4000, the other 'a very rare book, a juris prudence with the arms of Anne de Montmorency' for fr. 4500 (1.6.83). Instead Quaritch enclosed fr. 4000 on account. Caulin found it 'impossible to accept such a low price. The minimum for both volumes is fr. 5000 and at that you know full well that they go below their value. I await your cheque' (6.6.83). Seven months later Quaritch acknowledged receipt of two books, a copy of *Consuetudines* with the arms and cypher of Queen Catherine de Medici, and Guazzo's *Astolfo Borioso* with the arms of Count Mansfeld, for which Caulin had asked fr. 4500 and fr. 3000 respectively. Quaritch, sending fr. 3000 on account stated: 'It will be difficult to sell the Catherine de Medici, even at a low price: it is in very doubtful taste and resembles too much a German binding of bad style' (31.1.84). He then managed to place both volumes for fr. 4500 but Caulin's retort was far from happy. 'I cannot accept such a derisory price – about half of what I asked for such a consignment? Particularly when what I did ask was so extremely reasonable ... Please realise: I do not want to spoil my good relation with you, but take note that I am selling you my books cheaper than I would if I sold them to America ... You must not get into the habit of selling my books at such low prices. I cannot imagine which ignoramus took the Charles IX [sic] for a German binding. When one does not know, one would do better to remain silent. I hope you will think about all this very carefully. Meanwhile I am awaiting your cheque' (27.2.84). Quaritch replied somewhat haughtily: 'I see with keen regret that you are not satisfied with the price. The Catherine de Medici seems to me and to all my clients of doubtful taste and of a price well above its value. The Borioso without the binding is not worth more than fr. 50 and I believe to have acted in your interests by selling them for fr. 4500', but then adopted a more conciliatory tone: 'I cannot send you back the books and whatever I were to send you over and above the fr. 4500 comes out of my own pocket ... If I have made a mistake, I hope you will not ask for such an enormous sacrifice ... and I hope that, with your habitual kindness, you will accept fr. 2000 to settle the business. It is bad enough to work for no profit – as I often do – but it is much worse if I work hard in your interest to suffer such a large loss. The modest commissions I have earned previously [Quaritch charged 10%, then for a while 5%, on any sale], do not make up for this loss. But it is my own fault not to have consulted you before selling the books and I shall have to suffer the consequences ... It will be a good lesson for me. In the hope that your further consignments may compensate me a little for this gross loss, I remain ...' (8.3.84). In March 1884 Caulin sent a splendid Henri II binding and specified the price as 'not less than fr. 5000. If you cannot sell it at that price within two weeks, please send it back' (14.3.84). Quaritch felt 'It will be difficult for me to sell it for fr. 5000' (26.3.84). Caulin pursued the matter with two telegrams, one simply asking 'why no news', the second – apparently in reaction to a revised price proposed by Quaritch: 'Diminution impossible, renvoyer object avec soin' and followed this up in early April with a letter: 'I am still awaiting the book in question' (10.4.84), and again later in the month: 'Will you please send me your cheque as usual – and another fr. 1000 on account of the latest Henri II' (30.4.84).

Meanwhile some correspondence about a binding for Julius III triggered off an exchange about the value – or diminished value – of restored bindings and Caulin stated 'I will take fr. 500 off the price of Julius III. I cannot do more for such a beautiful book. I would like to persuade you to realise that you are a most sincere friend of mine, more so maybe than if I had been your brother' (n.d., but received by Quaritch on 9.5.84). However, this mellow mood changed when in June 1884 Quaritch had difficulties in selling a copy of Champerius bound for Louis de Bourges and a *Traité d'artillerie* from the collection of Gaston d'Orléans for the required fr. 7000, books that Caulin had described as extremely rare and precious, 'deux merles Blancs'. 'If you do not have a client who is capable of appreciating these two volumes, send them back' (5.6.84). Quaritch's reply that 'The Gaston makes it difficult. Fr. 6000 net (fr. 5500 without commission) is the best I can do. I keep trying, but if I cannot succeed, believe me, it is not my fault' (24.6.84), elicited Caulin's wrath: 'I do not understand that it took you twenty days to tell me that the Gaston d'Orleans is difficult to sell. I do not understand that you, as an eminent bookseller do not know that Gaston bindings are of the utmost rarity and, in such wonderful condition, are practically unique. In any case *I cannot accept a lower price*. You know full well that in a public sale you could not get fr. 500' (as commission) (25.6.84). Two days later Quaritch wrote: 'The two volumes are under consideration as you will not accept anything below fr. 7000, I cannot do anything else but take them at my own risk ... to end this business that is *irretrievably* disastrous for me' (27.6.84).

From early in 1885 onwards Caulin asked Quaritch's advice about obtaining the right price for the books on sale. 'Please sell them as expensively as possible. Tell me what I should write to you' (i.e. to show to your clients) (9.2.85), and a few months later: 'I want fr. 8000 [but] tell me how much do I demand from your client. I will send you the letter for your client as soon as I have received yours' (11.6.85). In a letter dated three days later, meant for the client, he asked fr. 10,000.

The relationship between supplier and bookseller appears fraught with irritation and veered between flattering intimacies and bullying contempt. Not only the prices caused discord. Quaritch from time to time expressed his dissatisfaction with the condition of the items sent on approval. On occasion books were damaged: 'the gold on the spines has partly lifted off, because they have rubbed against the lining of the case. It would be better to place the volumes between two planks of soft wood' (17.6.82). Some books were sticky on arrival, Caulin explained: 'The reason is the sulphuric Ether used to dissolve the wax. If you rub it first with a cloth that is a little greasy and then with an old silk cloth the inconvenience will go away. Virgin wax is the best way to preserve old bindings. The inconvenience disappears as soon as the Ether has evaporated' (7.3.82). And, after a further complaint: 'My books are just the same as they always were. Nevertheless you complain about wax or varnish even if there is none ... If I had not looked after the books in the way I have done they would not be in such good condition nor so fresh. Moreover wax or varnish does not diminish the beauty of the design, nor its splendour, I challenge you to show me in any library the equivalent of the bindings I have sent you' (21.3.82). More serious doubts were expressed by Quaritch about the binding for Julius III: 'I much regret that you have sent this back to me, because I repeat what I wrote on 19 March: The book must in no way see the light of day here again, especially not in the state it is in. My clients have already difficulty enough accepting a volume recently re-varnished, but a volume so obviously restored throws serious doubts on its provenance and on the original purity of your previous and future consignments' (5.5.84). Caulin countered three days later: 'I only sent you back the Julius III after having done nothing more to it than remove the bad quality varnish that made it sticky. Now it is in its original state, *without any retouching*. You judge things too often as restored that have not been restored. Books, like pictures, need to be treated with intelligence so as to preserve them for the future. Have you ever found a picture that has been re-varnished every eight or ten years lose its value? It is the same with books. Look at those that have passed through twenty sales, handled by all and sundry and see what state they are in. This is not the case with my books – thank God. If some of your clients were connoisseurs rather than amateurs they would not complain that the bride is too beautiful' (8.5.84).

There was worse to come. In September 1885 Caulin sent a *livre des Tournois* for which he wanted fr. 10,000. Quaritch expressed his doubt about the volume and on 6 October Caulin wrote: 'The explanations you ask from me are easy to give. First of all, I do not have, nor have I ever had a remboîtage. This is absurd. In order to effect a remboîtage one has to cut the headbands. If you look at the livre des Tournois you will see that they have been laced into the wooden boards and therefore make a remboîtage *absolutely impossible*. As far as the damp stains are concerned: the book has been for a long time in a wall cupboard ... If it were a remboîtage one would have washed the book and there would not have been any stains.' He continued to explain how the damp had affected the paper but not the binding, which could be dried and polished, and then turned indignant: 'How can a bookseller like you call this a second-hand book, if this is in order to lower the price, you can save yourself the trouble. I will take nothing off. If you cannot sell it, I will take it back, but I do not like to have books returned and if this one comes back to me I shall have to stop sending you books and look for another less difficult and more knowledgeable buyer' (6.10.85).

Both Quaritch and Caulin referred in the correspondence to the clients who were to be the recipients of the treasures offered for sale. Before 1886 Caulin usually referred to these in the plural, but on 7 March 1886 we read: 'If it does not please your habitual client you will have to send it back. Could you not sound out your client' and in October of the same year when sending a case containing a 'magnificent folio' (unspecified) for fr. 6000: 'Let me know what I can ask, in order not to let the business drag on under the pretext of the difficulty of placing it, because we both know to whom you will address the offer ...' (20.10.86) and one day later Quaritch replied: 'My client who buys your books has become too strong for me. There are so few collectors at present in England that I have surrendered myself to him without conditions. It is my client now who directs my correspondence with you ...' (21.10.86).

Who was this important client, who has bought so much and who had started to call the tune?

2. THE IMPORTANT CLIENT: CB

The important client, who was so infatuated by the bindings that he spent a fortune on them and who, against all evidence, stubbornly until his death continued to believe them to be genuine treasures from the libraries of kings, queens, popes and royal favourites, was my great-grandfather, John Blacker (fig. 2). When I was a child in the 1930s I remember, and so do my sister and brother, how on the death of our grandparents in France dozens of strange purple leather boxes arrived in our house from their estate. We were told that these boxes had once contained a wonderful library of books which our great-grandfather had collected during the 1870s and 1880s. He had spent huge sums on these books, but not a single one of them remained. Something about them had been found to be flawed, and the entire collection had been sold years ago. Only these empty boxes survived, which had been made to measure by an expensive firm in Bond Street to contain the books. No expense was spared to keep the books safe from dust and prying eyes. Some boxes are small, made of morocco leather lined with velvet and with bronze clasps. But some are far less portable. Several are the sizes of trunks or silver chests, others are broad and flat, as though they once contained elephant folios; others are a curious oblong shape. They were soon put to use in our house as containers for old letters or silver spoons, and there the matter rested.

About twenty years ago we came across an interesting file of papers. There was a bundle of sixteen letters and an exercise book containing a hand-written account by our grandmother, Caroline, entitled: 'Mr Blacker's Books.'[2] Caroline's account suggests that this story is not only about bibliography, but also about the psychology of Victorian obsession, particularly as directed to books. It is about the strange power or glamour which books can exert over the human mind. They can become comparable with holy relics, with wives or mistresses in a harem, or with magic talismans which must be kept secret and never divulged to anyone else. Caroline's account is worth paraphrasing. Her claim to special knowledge of the affair was that she was the daughter-in-law of the 'important client', married to Carlos, our grandfather, who inherited the library. Alas, she did not date her statement, but it was probably written about 1898.

She begins by saying that she was soon told about the wonderful library, said to be worth at least £70,000, but warned that she must never mention the books in the presence of old Mr Blacker. He could

2. John Blacker (seated) and his son Carlos.

not bear to have them talked about, much less looked at, and indeed was so obsessionally attached to them that for years he refused to leave London. No one in the family had ever seen the books. They were shrouded in mystery, and kept in the aforementioned leather and velvet boxes, specially made to measure by 'Leuchars, the most expensive place in Bond Street.'³ Some of the books were kept in even more sumptuous 'caskets' for which he had gold keys made, all fitted with Bramah locks. But alas, none of these have survived. In these rich containers the books were hidden away from all eyes but his own. Once, Caroline says, he had to have a man in to mend one of the clasps, but said afterwards that he would have 'given £50 to prevent that man seeing the book.' Every evening he would sit alone in the dining room after everyone else had left, and would bring in one of the boxes and gloat over his treasures. But if anyone came into the room, he would throw a square of silk over the book to prevent it being seen. Indeed, 'his passion for his collection was like a man's love for his mistress.' An idea supported later, when Carlos came to examine the books after John Blacker's death and discovered Atkinson's sachets of perfume inside the boxes. All the books, she goes on to say, had been sold to Mr Blacker by Quaritch, who was 'unquestionably the greatest bookseller and book expert in the world ... esteemed and respected by everyone.' The books themselves were old, but of no particular value. Their importance lay in the bindings of the Renaissance period that were among the finest in the world. It has already been mentioned that the collection included books said to have belonged to François I, Catherine de Medici, Diane de Poitiers, Anne de Montmorency and to various popes and cardinals, but, until John Blacker died suddenly in 1896, no one except Quaritch had any idea what wonderful items might lie inside the leather boxes. It seems strange to us today that John Blacker did not want to discuss his treasures with experts similarly passionate about book collecting. But here undoubtedly we have someone in the grip of collector's mania of a peculiarly possessive kind.

In 1896 John Blacker died and Carlos and Caroline went at once to London to deal with the estate. Carlos soon 'went round to Mr Quaritch's place' to talk about the library. He returned 'looking very shocked and queer.' He then told the following extraordinary story.⁴ From 1873 Mr Blacker had all but monopolised the purchase of bookbindings coming through one 'Caulin' at Blois. It was Caulin who sold the books from the libraries of kings and queens to Quaritch, demanding huge prices, and Quaritch who sold them to Mr Blacker at 5% commission. But apparently no one asked this 'Caulin' how he had acquired these treasures. 'I do not know if the provenance of the books was ever enquired into', Caroline writes, 'but Mr Quaritch thought they were stolen, and he and Mr Blacker and Mr Kearney, who was Mr Quaritch's expert, believed them *all* to be genuine.' It seems extraordinary that no one should have enquired more precisely into the history of these books; that no one should have asked 'Caulin' how he acquired these treasures which belonged to Diane de Poitiers and Catherine de Medici. But apparently no one did. It was not until 1885 that anything happened to check the flow of wonderful bindings from Caulin, which after a little haggling were always bought from Quaritch by the 'important client'. But in the summer of 1885 Mr Blacker suddenly went to Blois, not having left London for years. He did not apparently suspect the genuineness of the books, but was anxious to learn more about them. 'At Blois he learned that "Caulin" was no other than a notorious forger called "Hagué" … who had already perpetrated some big fraud on one of the Museums.'[5] On his return from Blois John Blacker told Quaritch of his discovery. Quaritch was apparently 'horrified' and wished to stop all further transactions. But so infatuated was Mr Blacker that he insisted that Quaritch should continue to supply him with books from Caulin. He refused to believe that they were not genuine treasures of the Renaissance period, from libraries of French kings and queens, and decided that it was all a ruse on Caulin's part to get the books back cheap so that he could sell them again at a profit. Quaritch, despite his 'horror', agreed to continue the transactions, but on the extraordinary condition that in future he should charge not 5% in commission, but 10%,[6] i.e. he should charge more rather than less for books which everyone except the besotted collector now knew must be forgeries. To this condition Mr Blacker agreed, and for no less than five more years, until 1890, continued to pay even huger sums than before to Quaritch.

In 1890 the story took another turn. Hagué took the extraordinary step of coming to London, and 'met Mr Blacker at Quaritch's place 15 Piccadilly', incredibly confessing that 'he himself had made and forged *all* the books sold by him to Quaritch and Mr Blacker.' His action, Caroline notes, is inexplicable. He killed the goose that laid the golden eggs, because he could certainly have continued to sell his forgeries to Mr Blacker, such was his blindness and infatuation. And indeed, John Blacker, though he had heard the confession with his own ears, still obstinately refused to believe the story he had heard; the books could not be forgeries, and Hagué was simply trying to buy them back cheaply in order to resell. But from this date until his death in 1896 there are no records of any more purchases from Caulin-Hagué.[7]

This was the story which Carlos heard from Quaritch in 1896, and which made him look so 'shocked and queer'. Carlos was at the time in dire straits for money. He had dabbled foolishly in a bogus American company and had in fact been declared bankrupt. He was relying on recouping his finances from the sale of this dazzling library. Well might he have looked shocked and queer. Quaritch then came to the house to examine the books, Caroline continues. 'The bindings were of extraordinary beauty … Some were very large volumes, and enormously rich and elaborate in workmanship and detail. I watched Quaritch's face when he looked at them, and I could plainly see that he was under their glamour, and could not quite accept them as forgeries in spite of all the evidence.' Mr Quaritch then advised them to take a selection of the bindings to the British Museum to be submitted to the experts there. They were not to breathe a word of doubt, just to ask their value, so that the experts could 'decide in a perfectly unbiassed manner as to their value.' They chose four or five of the books, one small and simple, the rest 'in varying degrees of size and gorgeousness … In due course Carlos and I drove with them to the British Museum, where we were shown into the presence of the experts, very courteous, elderly gentlemen, and extremely learned looking. We told them we wanted their opinion with regard to the bindings with a view to probate. We were followed by a footman carrying several of the handsome morocco cases … They were put down, the footman withdrew, and the experts first picked up the modest small book, and at once became enthusiastic over it. They immediately assigned it as period François 1er … and seemed interested and delighted with such a specimen. Our hearts rose. They then opened the first case, and looked with silence at its contents, exchanging looks. Without any remark they opened the second case. One of them then picked up again the first modest binding he had seen, examined it more carefully, shook his head, and then made a remark to his colleague about something being incorrect in the binding. Some part of the design not being in keeping with the supposed period. After this they lost interest and did not need much more than one look to pronounce the whole lot forgeries. The whole thing had not taken much more than ten minutes. They admired the bindings, the workmanship etc., but entertained no doubts whatever of their spuriousness.'

So, she concludes, 'it did not take these two experts more than a quarter of an hour to pronounce as forgeries these bindings which Quaritch claimed to have deceived him and his expert Mr Kearney in a period of nearly twenty years. When we told Quaritch the result of the British Museum's "expertise", I asked him "But Mr Quaritch, *why* did you not get the opinion of an expert during all the time you were selling the books to Mr Blacker?" He drew himself up and replied "There is *no* greater expert in the world than our Mr Kearney." I suppose I made the obvious retort, but forget what ensued. This really ends the story of Mr Blacker's collection.' But she adds a comment or two: 'it is hard to believe that Mr Quaritch, a hard man of business, accepted them all at the hands of the so called "Caulin", apparently with no knowledge of his antecedents, as the source of this *immense* supply of bindings and caskets, growing more gorgeous and unrestrained as time went on. When enquiries were made at Blois, it seemed quite easy to identify "Caulin" with the notorious "Hagué", yet Mr Quaritch continued to sell these books to Mr Blacker at huge prices, taking first 5%, and then 10%, without apparently making any such enquiry.' Would not an honest man, she asks, have refused to go on acting as intermediary for what he knew to be forgeries, much less have charged *more* than before in commission? Would not an honest man have shrunk from being party to such a gigantic swindle?

So, alas, the entire library was sold at Sotheby's on 11 November 1897. It was described as: 'A Remarkable Collection of Books in Magnificent Modern Bindings, formed by an Amateur (Recently deceased).' They fetched a grand total of £1907.16s.6d., a fraction of what had been paid for them, and in an annotated copy of the catalogue, the names of Maggs, Sotheran and Quaritch appear a good many times, paying £10, £15, even £25 for these glittering prizes. How bitterly we regret that not even one volume was left in the family as a memento of this 'gigantic swindle'. Or as a work of art in its own right. But Caroline writes that Carlos was anxious that the affair should not be made public, lest his father, who had been made to look an utter fool, should become a public laughing stock. And, she adds, 'if the story had become known, with Quaritch's share in the transaction, it would have meant ... his utter ruin as an expert and even as an honest man.' Though to Quaritch's credit let it be added that, had he chosen to hush the whole matter up, no one would have been any the wiser. John Blacker told no one, and died cherishing his illusions. Quaritch, though he had to give Carlos some explanation, could if he liked have put quite another and less compromising complexion on the affair. So the puzzles still remain – of Quaritch's honesty and John Blacker's credulity. And the empty boxes still testify to the gorgeous and beautiful bindings they once held.

3. DEALER AND FORGER (2): MMF

How was it possible that the 'elderly gentlemen' of the British Museum spotted the forgeries instantly, while the experienced bookseller and the great 'expert ... our Mr Kearney' had not recognised them as such? First of all, Michael Kearney, a great linguist and polymath, but not a specialist in historical bookbinding, had indeed smelled a rat. In May 1884 Caulin asked Quaritch: 'tell me how to behave towards the person who writes to me in French, so that I do not involuntarily say foolish things in reply. Is he your employee or your associate?' (n.d., but received by Quaritch on 9.5.84.) Three years later this 'associate' caused Caulin near-panic: 'After the return of my books by your associate, *I must absolutely have a private conversation with you*. This conversation is of *capital* interest to you. I do not want to have anything to do with your associate, nor do I wish to receive his letters. The latest was signed with your name, but not *by you*' (19.9.87). And less than two weeks later: 'You have without doubt not understood the meaning of my letter, nor the word *capital* underlined ... I really must have a long conversation with you ... After our conversation, during which there will naturally be question of your associate (whom I do not know) I will see what I can do with him. I shall have to tell you many things that you do not know and that touch greatly on your personal interest' (1.10.87). It is tempting to surmise that Kearney had become suspicious of the continuing flood of near-perfect looking bindings, their forwarding impeccable, the quality of the leather so fresh, and their tooling so perfect, even if Kearney may not have realised that in some cases the tools themselves occurred in anachronistic combinations and may not have been in a position to compare M. Caulin's 'Groliers' and 'Mahieus' with those that had actually belonged to those collectors. But, he may have set in train an investigation. In early October 1887 Quaritch received a letter enclosing a description by the Belgian bookbinder J. Schavye of a binding for Catherine de Medici, offered in June 1885, pronouncing it, according to the opinion of two Paris binding restorers, as 'very fresh but of modern manufacture' (6.10.87).

Caulin, notwithstanding his need to have his private conversation with Quaritch, and also possibly in reaction to either Quaritch's or Kearney's doubts, continued to protest: 'Concerning the fabrication of bindings other than adding coats of arms, I do not believe a word, because it is simply impossible. One can never have seen an old binding in order to make such a mistake. That is my opinion in two words' (25.5.88), and again: 'on the subject of the Maioli and the Grolier, I can only repeat what I have said already: everything I have sold you over the past sixteen years is *perfectly authentic*. These are not copies, but originals. I challenge anyone to prove the contrary. I do not care for gossip, tittle-tattle and lies ... and I have nothing to do with it. Moreover I do not know a Mr Haguet or Hagui of whom I have never heard. But if this person makes such beautiful copies, where are the originals? I understand the rage of those gentlemen. You have beautiful things and they have none ... Is this not an attempt at getting to know your sources of supply?' (12.7.88.)

It is not clear whether Quaritch, although he knew from November 1885 Caulin's real name and although he knew from October 1887 that the bindings were faked, and although he and/or Michael Kearney had had suspicions from at least May 1884, realised the full enormity of the situation – at least not before late in 1885. His 'insurance policy' of 15 December 1885, in making Mr Blacker sign the agreement not to hold him legally and financially accountable, speaks for itself. Moreover, as late as October 1886 Quaritch wrote to Caulin, 'if my offer does not suit you then either demand the return of the book or its public sale in London' (21.10.86). Would he have run that risk if he had believed the bindings to be forgeries, or was it bluff?

Some questions remain: what was (and was not) acceptable in the way of varnishing, retouching, or even 'improving' a binding? Where did authenticity stop and forgery begin? What was it like to be a bookseller in the 1870s and 1880s, how many genuine Renaissance bookbindings would Quaritch and Kearney have seen and where from could they and did they derive their knowledge?

4. QUARITCH AND THE TRADE IN BOOKBINDINGS: NP-W

Not much has been published on the selling of bindings and the culture of the binding market in England in the last years of the nineteenth century. There are essays on the growth of the cult of the first edition, the autograph letter, etc., but much less has been written on the history of the marketing of the book as binding. The vogue for collecting Renaissance bindings grew at a much greater rate than knowledge of the subject itself, and Quaritch's first binding catalogue issued in 1883 represents an age of innocence. All is optimistic prose with never a word of worry, like remboîtage, re-casing, re-gilding, or new endleaves. A cast-iron snob provenance, like the Sunderland library, will win a mention, but otherwise there is hardly a word about a book's source, history, bookplate or ownership inscription. A binding for Henri IV is simply 'olive morocco, *super extra*, covered with fleurs-de-lis (the King's Arms forming the centre ornaments with his crowned H at each corner)'; a binding for Pope Innocent XII is 'bright old red morocco, the sides completely covered with exquisitely fine and brilliant gold tooling ... There is no *commercial* binding here: it is all hand-work of the most exquisite finish and was probably executed by someone who had acquired his skill in Paris.' Grolier's copy of the Subiaco Lactantius – the first dated book printed in Italy – is called 'a combination of excellency seldom if ever attainable: a rare volume of the highest value and importance, clad in the precious robes of Grolier's library.'[8] The book is now in the Pierpont Morgan Library and the binding has for long been recognised as a fake – a fake from the so-called Bologna school, active a decade or two earlier than Hagué. Another fake in the same catalogue, probably also by the Bologna school, was Grolier's copy of the Tuppo Aesop.[9]

Quaritch issued two further major binding catalogues in 1889 and 1897, by which time we have entered the real world, and the vocabulary and diction have become more restrained, even cautious. The aggressive self-confidence is tempered. A description now will confess that 'the gold is a little refreshed'; that the Grolier ownership inscription is 'an addition of later date'; that a binding for Charles IX is 'evidently a close imitation of one of the artistic bindings done for that monarch, so close indeed that it has deceived many eyes'.[10] Another Grolier binding gets a longer note:

'The wonderful freshness and perfect preservation of this beautiful binding have led to doubts being thrown upon its genuineness, some persons even going so far as to allege that it is a modern fabrication. I have taken careful opinions from three English binders of great experience, who ridicule the notion that it would be possible to invent such a work at the present day, and who allege that there is nothing modern about it but a possible refreshing of the gold in some places, and perhaps a renewal here and there of the colouring in the painted compartments.'[11]

Meanwhile Grolier's Tuppo Aesop was still on Quaritch's shelves, but – revealingly? – the price has been reduced from £320 to £250. In the same catalogue of 1889, in a section at the end devoted to nineteenth-century bindings, Quaritch does list and describe eight acknowledged bindings by Hagué.[12]

The 1883 binding catalogue contains a section of 'Books on Binding' which demonstrates the paucity of reference material available. It consists of just ten titles of which the two most valuable in scholarship terms are P. G. Brunet, *La Reliure ancienne et moderne* (Paris, 1868) and Marius Michel, *La Reliure française* (Paris, 1880). And even Brunet illustrates one almost certain fake dating from the 1850s. Within the next twenty years the specialist literature on binding was to grow and grow, but there is one factor about these reference books which gave rise to a very distorted perception of bindings and which contributed seriously to the mania for restoration and so-called improvement. The plates in Brunet's *La Reliure* are photographs, perhaps a little drab, but essentially faithful; they illustrate bindings more or less warts and all. But very soon, especially in English reference works, such as R. R. Holmes, *Specimens of ... bookbinding ... from Windsor Castle* (London, 1893), W. Y. Fletcher's *English bookbindings in the British Museum* and his *Foreign bookbindings in the British Museum* (London, 1895 and 1896) and the privately printed Hoe binding catalogue (two vols, New York, 1895), the warts have vanished and the reader is presented with embossed and varnished chromolithographs with all disfiguring marks brushed out. These are plates of impossible visionary ideals; and the paradox is that what they resemble most closely is not the original sixteenth-century binding, but the nineteenth-century pastiche. A lot of over-restoration of bindings at the turn of the century can be put down to these highly deceptive images.

Although the Blacker correspondence and the indemnity which Quaritch required of Blacker in 1885, if he was to continue trading in Hagué bindings, are on deposit in the British Library, some records are still at Quaritch. The accounts, for instance, for the Sotheby sale of the one-hundred-and-ten Hagué bindings in 1897 indicate that Sotheby's also had the sale of Blacker's 'Private Library'; that Sotheby's and Christie's were entrusted with the sale of some of the jewel caskets; and that twenty bindings were committed for sale in Paris. Some books were also sold by Quaritch by private treaty to the American collector Rush Hawkins, best remembered for his collection of incunabula illustrating the spread of printing. Also at Quaritch is an inventory of the complete Blacker library evidently compiled by Bernard Quaritch in 1896. This gives details of the Blacker bindings not found in the Sotheby sale catalogue but sold elsewhere, some committed to Paris: the Emperor Charles V's Plautus; François I's Pausanias, his Ptolemy, and his Medina, *L'Arte del navegar*, and, perhaps best of all, Pope Julius III's copy of More's *Utopia* and Mary Queen of Scots' Plato, *Symposium*. The inventory also shows Blacker as a reader. It lists his Ainsworth and Dickens first editions and his Mark Twains; and then there is his reference library. This last shows Blacker as serious would-be connoisseur. There are the Dibdins, etc. from a former age; but also the modern up-to-date specialist works: the Firmin-Didot catalogues, the Morgand catalogues and – most important from our point of view – the first major study of Grolier's library, A. J. V. Le Roux de Lincy's *Recherches sur J. Grolier* (Paris, 1866). When Blacker studied this, did he not wonder about the status of his own thirteen Grolier bindings? It is ironic that Blacker also owned a copy of one of Brunet's lesser-known works, his *Fantaisies bibliographiques* (Paris, 1864).

The Blacker inventory goes on to list fourteen Renaissance jewel caskets with brief descriptions; a 'book sarcophagus' of inlaid metal; and a 'shrine', again of inlaid metal, 'temp. François I'.

The contemporary parallel to Hagué's bindings is the medieval revival chalice of Limoges enamel or rock crystal fashioned for a 'style Rothschild' *Schatzkammer*. This was the era of the 'style Rothschild', and a sudden imbalance between supply and demand. In the 1930s one Hagué binding was almost good enough to deceive G. D. Hobson. Today they are that much easier to spot because of the way the leather has aged and faded. Today's clever fakes are constructed from period leather and period boards, cut down and stripped from older bindings. The cleverest? These are probably still unrecognised.

NOTES

1   I am grateful to Dr Carmen Blacker and to Messrs Bernard Quaritch for allowing me to quote from these letters. The letters in French have been translated by me. Underlined passages have been printed in italics. The date of the letter is given in parentheses after the quotation. For a more detailed account of this correspondence, see: M. M. Foot, 'Double agent: M. Caulin and M. Hagué', *The Book Collector* (special number for the 150th anniversary of Bernard Quaritch, edited by R. Linenthal), 1977, pp. 136–50.

2   These items spurred me to find out more about this library. I am grateful to Dr David McKitterick for drawing my attention to catalogues and articles that have helped me in my research.

3   Quotations are from the MS of Caroline Blacker's statement in the possession of the author.

4   What follows is Caroline's account. It is not wholly borne out by the surviving correspondence (see above, p. 264).

5   Thus according to Caroline Blacker. In the Caulin-Quaritch correspondence is a letter from Bernard Quaritch to John Blacker, dated 15 December 1885, in which Quaritch writes: 'After your discovery last month at Castel Maré of the real name of Mr. J. Caulin, which you communicated to me ... I feel bound to cease to act as the intermediate agent between you and the individual who corresponds with me under the name of J. Caulin.' For Hagué see: H. M. Nixon, 'Binding forgeries' in: the proceedings of the *VIth International Congress of Bibliophiles, Vienna, 29 September–5 October, 1969*, Vienna, 1971, pp. 76–81.

6   The letter quoted in note 5 continues: '*unless* you agree as follows:

> 1) You give me a guarantee in writing that henceforth I solely act as your servant
>
> 2) that you agree to hold me good against any legal or financial claims of whatsoever nature and from any person or persons whatsoever
>
> 3) that you pay me ten percent commission on any future transactions which I may conduct on your account.'

A signed and sealed agreement to this effect, dated 9 January 1886, was sent by John Blacker to Quaritch.

7   Hagué died in March 1891.

8   B. Quaritch, *Catalogue of books in historical or remarkable bindings*, London, 1883, respectively nos 12885, 12871 and 13010.

9   *Ibid.*, no. 13011.

10   B. Quaritch, *Catalogue: examples of the art of bookbinding*, London, 1897, nos 430 and 460.

11   B. Quaritch, *A Catalogue of fifteen hundred books remarkable for the beauty or the age of their bindings*, London, 1889, no. 124.

12   *Ibid.*, nos 923–30.

WOMEN BOOKBINDERS
IN BRITAIN
Before the First World War
Marianne Tidcombe

AT ONE TIME, the 'lady bookbinder' was a novelty. A woman binding books was considered as improbable as a woman preaching, which, Samuel Johnson said, was 'like a dog walking on his hind legs. It is not done well; but you are surprised to find it done at all.'[1] Indeed, it was not until the 1970s that trade union regulations allowed women to work alongside men in English trade binderies.

Although this essay is about British women binders, the first woman binder whose work I came across was an American, Rachel McMasters Miller, later known as Mrs Hunt, the famous book collector, who founded the Hunt Botanical Library in Pittsburgh. Rachel Miller was taught bookbinding by Euphemia Bakewell, a pupil of T. J. Cobden-Sanderson, and became a very accomplished binder.[2] Many other women in Britain took up the craft in the decades before the First World War. Some, like Katharine Adams, did all of the work themselves, while others concentrated only on design or decoration, or less commonly, carried out the execution of bindings designed by someone else. Together, these women produced a great variety of beautiful and interesting bindings.[3]

The first stage in binding a book is to sew the leaves or sections. Because women have been associated with the use of thread and needle from time immemorial, they have probably been involved with bookbinding for a very long time. There is little evidence as to who did what in the early days of bookbinding, but there are references to women binders from the early fourteenth century, when 'Dionisia le Bokebyndere' worked in a house in 'Flete Street in the Suburbs of London'.[4] In the fifteenth century women bookbinders were mentioned in connection with work for royalty and nobility in England and France, and in convents on the continent nuns were engaged in bookbinding.

In England, superb embroidered bindings were made throughout the Elizabethan and Jacobean periods. Most of these were by professional embroiderers, who were men, but occasionally there is evidence that a binding was the work of a woman. The calligrapher Esther Inglis was probably responsible for some of the embroidered bindings on her own manuscripts, which were produced from about 1591 to 1624. She was born in Edinburgh to French Huguenot parents, and although she married and had six children, she continued to use her maiden name all her life. Her purpose in producing the manuscripts, which emulated printing, was to reap rewards from the wealthy patrons to whom she dedicated and sent them. As she was also known for her fine needlework, and was always in straitened circumstances, it seems likely she did the embroidery on the bindings of her own books rather than having to pay professionals. Her bindings, like many other embroidered bindings of the period, were sewn with silk and metal threads, and pearls were often added.[5]

One of the most interesting episodes in the history of bookbinding involved the women at Little Gidding, a seventeenth-century semireligious community in Huntingdonshire. The community was set up by Nicholas Ferrar, who had been Deputy Governor of the Virginia Company and a member of Parliament until he retired from the world to lead a religious life. In 1626, he settled in the manor of Little Gidding with about thirty members of his family, including his mother, his brother John, his sister Mrs Collet, and her fourteen or fifteen children. Ferrar believed that everyone in the community should learn a trade, and in addition to decorative needlework for the church, many of them worked on preparing and binding books called 'Harmonies'. These were a sophisticated sort of scrapbook, made by cutting out biblical texts such as the four gospels, arranging them, and adding pictures to form a new book. The daughter of a Cambridge bookbinder, who was a skilled binder herself, was employed to teach bookbinding to members of the community. As the work was carefully done, the result was somewhat better than it sounds, and when a 'Harmony' made and specially bound for King Charles I was well received, there was a demand for many similar books, establishing the community's reputation for 'paste-printed' books and bookbinding. It is not known who did the cutting and pasting, or who was primarily responsible for the binding of the books at Little Gidding. However, Mary Collet, Ferrar's niece, was the chief woman binder, and some of the 'Harmonies' have notes in them saying she did the binding.[6]

Most of the bindings produced at Little Gidding are in goldtooled velvet, leather, or vellum. A volume in the British Library, sewn on nine vellum tapes, is bound in vellum stained a bright roseorange (fig. 1); it originally had matching silk ties. The centre- and

1. A 'Harmony of the Gospels', bound by Mary Collet at Little Gidding. Stained
vellum, pierced vellum onlays and gold-tooling. 485 × 355 × 45 mm.
British Library, C.23.e.2.

corner-decoration consists of pierced white vellum onlays and delicate gold-tooling. Some of the finishing tools used on this binding were used on other Little Gidding bindings. After Nicholas Ferrar died in 1637, the community continued for another twenty years, until John Ferrar and Mrs Collet both died. However, Mary Collet, who lived until 1680, is said to have been binding as late as 1669.[7]

In the late eighteenth and early nineteenth centuries, the daughters of Robert Southey were responsible for covering, if not actually binding, a large number of volumes. Southey, reluctant to spend money having his cheaper books bound in leather, asked his daughters to cover them with various printed cotton fabrics. They were helped in this task by other women who came to stay with the family, and between 1200 and 1400 volumes were bound in this way, completely filling one room which Southey called his 'Cottonian Library'. The collection was eventually sold, and these volumes in their colourful chintzes with handwritten paper labels can now be found in a number of libraries. A similar volume in the British Library, which belonged to Wordsworth, has a note on the paste-down stating that it was 'Bound in a piece of one of Mrs Wordsworth's old gowns.'[8]

In the 1870s, a few wealthy Englishwomen began to cover their books with attractive papers brought back from Italy. At first one or two and then a few more of these women tried their hand at book-binding. Until the trade unions became strong enough to enforce restrictions, there was nothing to stop a binder giving lessons to or training someone outside the trade. Several middle-class men and a few women were trained in this way. Aglaia Coronio, a friend of William Morris, was one of the first women to take up bookbinding at this time. Jane Morris, William Morris's wife, also did some binding, although she seems only to have bound little booklets. It was undoubtedly her earlier interest in binding, however, that led her to propose to T. J. Cobden-Sanderson a decade later that he should take up the craft.[9]

The example of Cobden-Sanderson, which showed that one could take up binding in mid-life and make a success of it after only a short period of training, inspired a number of women to try to do the same. Cobden-Sanderson thought women would be particularly good at bookbinding; he encouraged them, and took a number of pupils himself. He also gave lectures on the subject. Women flocked to public lectures in those days, and when they watched him don his apron and explain that 'after the sheets are folded, collated and sewn, a 'book' is essentially bound, and it only remains to add and embellish the covers',[10] it is no wonder so many were tempted to have a go.

The leading London trade binder, Joseph W. Zaehnsdorf, taught bookbinding to Sarah Prideaux, Lady Ribblesdale, and a few other aristocratic ladies. In 1890, Zaehnsdorf made arrangements for Sarah Prideaux to teach a three-month course at his premises in Cambridge Circus, but the men in his shop feared competition from middle-class women binders, quite unnecessarily, and opposed the idea. The binders' union, which was very strong by that time, would have supported the men, and the course never took place. However, Sarah Prideaux did go on to give private lessons, which became the usual way for women to learn bookbinding.

At the same time, a number of women were approaching book-binding from a different direction. Their interests were in embroidery, painting and designing, and leatherwork. The Home Arts and Indus-tries Association had a number of centres where rudimentary book-binding was taught in leatherwork classes. These were set up by a woman with a little knowledge, which she could share with others in her home or in a hired room; if the class was successful and the participants wished to learn more, a professional or better-trained person was brought in to continue the instruction. Such bookbinding classes were offered in Leighton Buzzard, Kirkby Lonsdale, Porlock Weir, and a few other places. The Home Arts and Industries Associ-ation also held exhibitions in the Albert Hall in London, where various crafts were demonstrated. At other times, rooms around the inside of the Hall were let to craftspeople for teaching; in one of them two ladies taught bookbinding. The Royal School of Art Needlework and organisations for 'distressed' gentlewomen offered training in needlework and design, and some of the groups provided outlets for selling work such as embroidered or painted vellum bindings and boxes.

Strictly speaking, embroidered, painted vellum, and most of the modelled leather bindings are not bookbindings by women, as only the decoration was by the woman; the actual binding was done by a professional firm. However, the end result, the beauty of the binding, was due to the woman's artistic ability or craftsmanship. William Morris's daughter May taught embroidery and produced some embroidered bindings in the early 1890s. One of the bindings designed and worked by her (colour plate 8) was commissioned by Morris's publisher F. S. Ellis; it was bound by Cobden-Sanderson. In 1888, Ellis planned to get a number of women to produce embroidered

2. Vellucent binding designed by Jessie M. King, bound by Chivers of Bath.
Thomas Lodge, *The Story of Rosalynde*, 1902. 201 × 132 × 22 mm.
Wormsley Library, Oxfordshire.

book covers for him, which he would later put up for auction at Sotheby's, but it is not known whether the scheme was carried out. The booksellers Mary and James Tregaskis publicized bookbindings by women by showing several of them in their 1891 exhibition of forty-two copies of Charles Kingsley's *The Water babies*; and a similar exhibition in 1894, of seventy-five copies of the Kelmscott Press *King Florus and the fair Jehane*, also featured some women's bookbindings.[11] The embroidered bindings in the Tregaskis exhibitions were by Edith Bloxham, Mrs Walter Crane, Mrs Harry Brownlow, May Morris, and Miss Rigby.

A number of painted vellum bindings, sometimes called illuminated bindings, were produced by women between *c.* 1888 and 1898. These books had stiff boards and were bound in full vellum by trade binders such as Zaehnsdorf's or Morrell's. The painting was usually done only on the surface of the upper cover and spine. Painted vellum bindings cannot take much handling, and sometimes part of the design, in particular the gold which was often used for borders, has rubbed off. There are many examples by the Royal School of Art Needlework, whose members were trained to produce similar designs for embroidery. Aymer Vallance, the artist and critic, designed some striking painted vellum bindings, which were executed by Bessie Huggett of Brighton. A few women who produced painted vellum bindings sent them to be sold by Frank Karslake at the Guild of Women Binders bookshop in the Charing Cross Road. Very little vellum binding was done in the Guild's own workshop, although some of the Guild bindings, mentioned below, do have painted vellum doublures. A variation on painted vellum was pen and ink drawing on vellum, examples of which can be seen on bindings made by Mrs Herbert Railton, and Jessie King.

Jessie M. King was a Scottish artist who attended the Glasgow School of Art. In 1899, when still really only a pupil, she was offered a teaching post in the School's Department of Book Decoration and Design. Although not a bookbinder, she designed and bound examples for her class; a copy of Rossetti's *Ballads* with her pen and ink design on the cover appears to be one of her bindings. She was one of the most talented designers employed by Cedric Chivers of Bath, who produced twenty-five copies of a 'vellucent' binding on *The Story of Rosalynde*, which she designed and painted (fig. 2). Chivers became interested in the eighteenth-century transparent vellum bindings of Edwards of Halifax, in which a design is painted on the underside of the vellum that had been made transparent. In 1897 Chivers decided to re-introduce the process, with the significant difference that the design was painted on paper, under the transparent vellum. Chivers also produced leather bindings with vellucent panels; and some later examples have mother-of-pearl and other exotic materials added as highlights under the vellum. A large proportion of the vellucent bindings were designed by H. Granville Fell, but many others were by Dorothy Carlton Smyth and Miss J. D. Dunn. Chivers had a separate department where he employed five women to work on designing, illuminating, colouring, and embossing leather. Alice Shepherd, best known for her cut and embossed leatherwork, was in charge of the department.

Nineteenth-century leatherwork bindings were often called 'embossed', but that term is now reserved for those embossed by machine. Modelled leather was used for all kinds of leatherwork bindings. The work on calf involved making little cuts, and working the design on the leather before the book was bound. The women who did this work generally had little experience in binding, and unless the work was for something simple like a blotter or scrap album, the book was sent to a professional binder. Modelled calf bindings were produced by Frances Bartholomew and Susanna Firth at Kirkby Lonsdale, M. Sophia Lyndon Smith at Cheltenham Ladies College, and Mary Ann Bassett at Leighton Buzzard. Miss Bassett started teaching leatherwork to give employment to crippled girls in the town, and by 1898 she had six or seven girls working regularly at such binding. Her speciality was colouring, gilding, and varnishing the design on the leather after modelling. A binding by two of her pupils, Hilda Goodall and Minnie King, was illustrated in the Guild of Women Binders' *Bookbindings of tomorrow* (London, 1902, pl. 16). Alice Shepherd was trained by Miss Bassett and worked with her before being employed by Chivers. Her designs for Chivers were almost always floral, and any gilding, colouring, or finishing was done after the book was bound. She also made address books, blotters, card cases, and other small items, and was responsible for the designs on some of Chivers' gold-tooled bindings. Mary Houston was one of the more original modelled-leatherworkers at the turn of the century. As well as her own modelled-calf bindings, she produced modelled panels for gold-tooled bindings by Johanna Birkenruth.

The women working at the Chiswick Art Workers Guild were trained at the Chiswick School of Arts and Crafts, the first school where women (and non-trade men) could learn bookbinding. They produced a distinctive style of modelled-leather binding in native-dyed

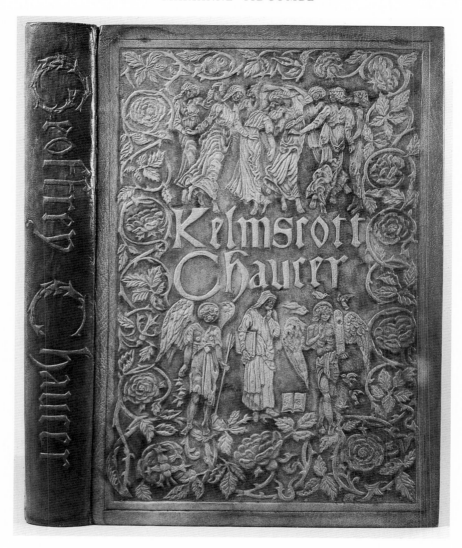

3. Modelled goatskin binding by Annie S. MacDonald, 1899. Geoffrey Chaucer, *Works*, Kelmscott Press, 1896. 432 × 302 × 62 mm. Private collection, England.

Nigerian goatskin, and were probably the first binders in England to use this very durable leather, now known as native-dyed niger.[12] The Chiswick designs often have a Spanish or Italian flavour, reflecting the style of other leatherwork taught at the School. The background of the design, or part of it, was tooled with gold dots, and some of the larger books have a wide border treated in this manner. The bindings are signed 'Chiswick Art Guild'. Some of them were sold at the Guild of Women Binders shop, and some later Guild bindings are in a similar style.

In the early 1890s, Annie MacDonald in Edinburgh began to make a different kind of modelled binding. She used goatskin, full thickness, in its natural state; no cutting was involved, and the leather was worked on the book after it was covered. When the book was finished, the leather was a pale ivory colour, but it gradually darkened with age. Her designs incorporate angels and other figures, and her initials and the date appear in the lettered borders. She bound quite a number of books, including several copies of the Kelmscott Chaucer (fig. 3). She also taught her method to, among others, Willa St George Moore and Anna Phoebe Traquair, who both did fine work in this style. Although she was Irish, Traquair was married to a Scottish palaeontologist and lived in Edinburgh. She was a versatile artist, known for her embroidered panels, mural decoration, painting, book illumination, enamels, and jewellery, as well as her bookbindings. A few of her twenty or so modelled-leather bindings have a little colouring or gold-tooling added. Her distinctive mark, three linked circles containing her initials, a woman leatherworker, and the date, usually appears on the lower cover.

A few women binders of this period used another technique known as pokerwork or pyrogravure, which involved using a hot point to produce a design on light-coloured calf or on wood such as sycamore. A German device called a pyrograph was used: this consisted of a glass bottle half-filled with benzine to provide a flame, to heat a platinum stylus. Pyrographic designs or lettering could be made directly on a bookbinding or on panels which were then glued onto the book. The designs of many pokerwork bindings were simply copied from the title-pages or illustrations in books, but some original work was also done. Queen Victoria's granddaughter, Princess Victoria of Wales, daughter of Edward VII and Alexandra, designed and executed pokerwork bindings at Sandringham, but it is not known whether she ever did any other kind of bookbinding.

Occasionally, bookbindings are made of materials other than embroidered fabric, leather, or vellum. One impressive example, an electro-silver binding for an album commissioned by the Art Union of London, was designed and made by M. Lilian Simpson (fig. 4). The silverwork consists of three hinged panels and a clasp over a binding of dark green hard-grain goatskin. The design, composed of angels and flowers, is symbolic of the growth of life. Miss Simpson was

4. Electro-silver binding by Miss M. L. Simpson. Blank album, for the Art Union of London, 1896. 245 × 187 × 60 mm. British Library, C.108.aaa.1.

awarded a gold medal for the binding in the National Competition for Schools of Art in 1894, and it was exhibited at the Royal Academy in 1896. Lady Mary (Molly) Noble, who had a studio called St Veronica's Workshops, designed a magnificent silver clasp for one of her bookbindings with oak boards. She was taught bookbinding by Douglas Cockerell, and probably also by the American woman binder L. Averill Cole, during the time Miss Cole was in England. Molly Noble created some interesting designs for her gold-tooled leather bindings. After she was divorced from Sir George Noble in 1916, she married the architect A. Randall Wells. She later excelled at decorative plasterwork and other crafts.

The Guild of Women Binders was not a guild in the usual sense, but a business venture of the London bookseller, Frank Karslake, who was a tragi-comic character with a shop at 61 Charing Cross Road. He was later associated with the Antiquarian Booksellers' Association and *Book auction records*, but for a short period, from 1898 to 1904, he was involved in bookbinding. His interest in women binders stemmed from his visit to the Victorian Era Exhibition, held in May 1897 to celebrate Queen Victoria's Diamond Jubilee. There he saw a number of books bound by women, and he wrote to each of the binders to ask them to send examples of their work to an 'Exhibition of Artistic Bookbinding by Women' at his bookshop a few months later. In May 1898, he started the Guild of Women Binders as a way of selling the books produced by these women. At the same time, Karslake was financial backer of the Hampstead Bindery, where male trade binders were employed. Alfred de Sauty worked for Karslake at the Hampstead Bindery, and also for the Guild of Women Binders.

Initially, the 'Guild of Women Binders' stamp on bindings was no more than a bookseller's stamp, but in the summer of 1899 Karslake set up a Guild workshop near his home, also in Hampstead. Karslake's daughter Constance was in charge of the workshop, a bindery where women could be trained and where some of them stayed on to work. Karslake charged fifty guineas for a year's training, which was really only six months since during the second half of the year a learner was expected to turn out work for the Guild. If at the end of the year a newly-trained binder was not able to set up for herself, she could continue to work in the Guild workshop at a fixed wage, depending on her ability. Women who stayed were put either to forwarding or finishing, as in a trade bindery. The forwarding was done by the newcomers and less skilled women. Those who set up on their own tended to be finishers, as this work took up less space at home, and they could send out their books to the Guild workshop to be forwarded. The early work of the Guild was fairly traditional, mostly simple designs, tooled in blind or gold. Lettering, which is difficult for an inexperienced finisher, was often built up with dots or gouges. Constance Karslake and the young sisters Edith and Florence de Rheims were responsible for much of the Guild's best work (fig. 5).

Frank Karslake began to use the name 'Guild of Women Binders' for all his businesses, which included some printing and publishing ventures. In 1902 he published *The Bindings of tomorrow*, a book of fifty colour plates of bindings by the Guild of Women Binders and the Hampstead Bindery. For a short time, when a few excellent tradesmen were employed at the Hampstead Bindery, some high quality bindings were produced, and interesting and innovative designs were developed. However Karslake's enthusiasm knew no bounds. He expected the male binders to teach the Guild women, but he knew little of the ways of bookbinders, and had trouble keeping his professional workers. He also exaggerated the ease with which women could be trained, and the amount they could earn. In fact, there was little demand for the work of semi-skilled women binders, and it was not

5. Onlaid and gold-tooled goatskin doublure, designed by Constance Karslake for the Guild of Women Binders. Robert Browning, *Poems*, London, 1897. 216 × 136 × 33 mm. Duke University Library, Willis Collection.

long before the Guild's bindings began to pile up in Karslake's shop. In 1900 and 1901, he was forced to dispose of them in sales at Sotheby's.[13] The Hampstead Bindery also closed about this time. What started as a noble experiment began to collapse, and soon Karslake was declared bankrupt. The Guild continued for a few more years, the remaining bindings being sold at Sotheby's in 1904.[14] It has been rumoured that some of the bindings Karslake signed 'Guild of Women Binders' were actually the work of the Hampstead Bindery, and later most binders denied ever knowing Karslake or having worked for him. Frank Karslake liked to praise the women's work for its high quality, but the forwarding techniques taught at the Guild were those used at the cheaper end of the trade. Books were sewn on too few cords, and stuck-on headbands and tipped-on endpapers were used, all contrary to the high principles taught by Cobden-Sanderson, Douglas Cockerell, Sarah Prideaux, and Katharine Adams. Gwladys Edwards was one of the few Guild members who continued binding after the Guild closed.

In the 1890s, traditional techniques of hand bookbinding were taught in technical evening classes run by a few schools in London, such as the Central School of Arts and Crafts, but these were open only to tradesmen. Cobden-Sanderson trained about a dozen women, mostly Americans, at the Doves Bindery between about 1895 and 1909. After setting up his own workshop, Douglas Cockerell, a former apprentice of Cobden-Sanderson, also took women pupils, including Anastasia (Annie) Power, Audrey Ricketts, and Sylvia Stebbing. In 1901, Francis Sangorski and George Sutcliffe set up on their own after working for Cockerell, and they too taught a number of women pupils. Sarah Prideaux and Johanna Birkenruth were among the first women to give lessons in bookbinding. Soon, however, some women who had themselves only just learned to bind began taking pupils. Shortly after the turn of the century, the number of women amateurs probably reached its peak. From the top of society to the bottom, all over the country, women were learning bookbinding. The Bloomsbury set had its binders, Virginia Stephen (later Woolf) and her sister Vanessa. Enid Bagnold took up binding for a while; and Winifrid Stopes, younger sister of Dr Marie Stopes, the pioneer of birth control, was a surprisingly good binder. At the other end of the social scale, the Salvation Army had a workshop in Hackney, in the East End of London, where women rescued from the streets who were considered 'unsuited for domestic service' were taught bookbinding. In several towns and cities outside London, local arts and crafts groups held

6. Gold-tooled goatskin binding by Sarah Treverbian Prideaux, 1902.
Omar Khayyám, *The Rubáiyát*, Vale Press, 1901. 216 × 166 × 10 mm.
Wormsley Library, Oxfordshire.

competitions and mounted exhibitions. However, only the work of the better, more established women binders was selected by the Arts and Crafts Exhibition Society in London or sent to international exhibitions abroad.

Sarah Prideaux first learned to bind from Joseph W. Zaehnsdorf in London, and later arranged through the French binder Léon Gruel to go to Paris to have lessons with his former finisher, M. Joli. Her early bindings were modest and restrained: she produced several in blind-tooled pigskin and morocco, and others with delicate gold-tooled designs. In the mid-1890s, however, she began to produce some strikingly original designs, many of which required the use of large solid tools, that would have been difficult for an amateur to use. From this time her bindings were executed by a professional binder, Lucian Broca, who worked for her. She liked panel and border designs, and clean, crisp floral motifs. Her less elaborate bindings are gold-tooled, with delicately marbled endpapers; her more elaborate bindings sometimes have onlays, gauffered edges, and tooled doublures. She designed a number of large 'Persian' tools from patterns on Turkish and Syrian tiles, for use on four elaborate bindings of *The Rubáiyát*, and she also used these tools on other bindings (fig. 6). In 1900 she printed a *Catalogue* of her bookbindings, but continued to bind for a few more years, producing altogether more than 300 bindings. She was an intelligent woman, and knew a great deal not only about the bibliography and history of bookbinding, but also about printing and photography. After giving up binding she wrote several books on bookbinding and other subjects. She died in her 80th year, in 1933.

One of Sarah Prideaux's first pupils, Elizabeth Mathieson MacColl, was born in Glasgow, where she had been trained at art school. Her brother was D. S. MacColl, the artist and critic, who later became Director of the Tate Gallery and the Wallace Collection. D. S. MacColl was responsible for nearly all the designs on his sister's bindings. He had designed edition bindings, but as a designer of hand-bound books he was ahead of his time. They have the quality of free-hand drawings, and would normally have been gold-tooled with several sets of gouges to produce all the different curvatures and lengths of line needed (fig. 7). To speed things up, the MacColls devised a small wheel, with a diameter less than one centimetre, with which all Elizabeth's tooling was done, except for 'a few links and joints'. A small fillet wheel of this sort loses heat very rapidly, and so would have been of little use to a professional finisher; professionals

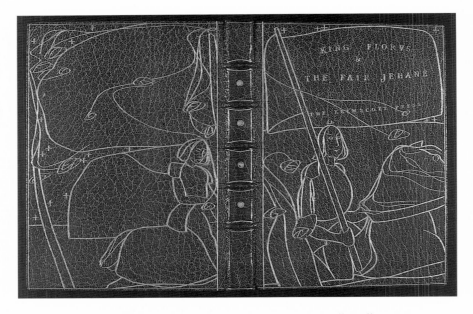

7. Gold-tooled goatskin binding by Elizabeth M. MacColl. William Morris (transl.), *The Tale of King Florus and the fair Jehane*, Kelmscott Press, 1893. 148 × 108 × 14 mm. John Rylands University Library.

worked very fast, keeping a range of tools hot at the same time, so there was no need for waiting. However, such a skill was difficult for an amateur to master. Elizabeth MacColl produced nearly fifty gold-tooled bindings, some with coloured onlays. The intense concentration needed for the work, and her brother's lack of time, forced her to give up binding in 1924.

Katharine Adams was probably the most successful and productive English woman binder. Her father, the Reverend William Fulford Adams, was an old friend of William Morris and vicar of Little Farringdon, and she grew up with the Morris girls who were practically next door at Kelmscott Manor. She was interested in books and bookbinding from an early age and used to go to the Oxford binder Morley to buy scraps of calf and seek advice. In 1897, when she was 35, she found she had to try to supplement her income, and it was then she decided to become a bookbinder. She could only afford to spend three months as a pupil with Sarah Prideaux, and one month with Douglas Cockerell, but by early 1901 she had done enough work to hold an exhibition of fifty-six bindings at Worcester House,

8. Gold-tooled goatskin binding by Katharine Adams, *c.* 1912. Elizabeth
Waterhouse (ed.), *A Little book of life and death*, London, 1910.
148 × 95 × 25 mm. Bodleian Library, Broxb.52.21.

Oxford. Katharine Adams tried a variety of materials for her bindings: in addition to calf and morocco goatskin she used
straight-grained and niger goatskin, dyed and alum-tawed pigskin,
and vellum, which she sometimes painted. Although she is especially
known for her delicate *pointillé* tooling, she was equally adept at
gougework and lettering (fig. 8). When her father became Rector of
Weston-sub-Edge in Gloucestershire, she took a small house nearby
in Broadway. The house was called Eadburgha, after the old church
there, and so she gave this name to her bindery. She sold her bindings
at small exhibitions and through the bookseller Bain in London, and
some were commissioned by friends in the Morris circle. She bound
books for Emery Walker, Sydney Cockerell, and St John Hornby, all
of whom gave her useful criticism and encouragement; and through
them she was introduced to important collectors, such as Dyson
Perrins, Fairfax-Murray, and Yates Thompson. She did a great deal
of plain binding on early books and manuscripts, and bound many
private press books, including her famous Doves Press Bible for
Dyson Perrins.

In 1907, Katharine Adams taught the nuns at Stanbrook Abbey to do simple binding – quite a challenge, because as an enclosed order all instruction had to take place through the grill. In 1913, at the age of 50, she married Edmund James Webb but continued to use the name Adams for her binding. She carried on working in Broadway, with two girls whom she trained, until 1916, when she moved to the tiny village of Noke in Oxfordshire. Later she and Webb moved to St Briavel's, a remote area in Gloucestershire, where she continued to do a little work. She exhibited regularly and widely until the 1930s, and won many awards. Her last few bindings were finished for her at Sangorski & Sutcliffe in the late 1940s. She died in 1952 at the age of 90.

Sybil Pye, born in 1879, was one of the younger pre-First World War women binders. Her father was a successful wine merchant who collected contemporary and oriental art, and the family lived in a large house, Priest Hill, at Limpsfield in Surrey. Sybil suffered from poor health during her early life, but she became a nursery school teacher in a small private kindergarten for a few years. Her sister Ethel, youngest of the three Pye daughters, attended the Slade School of Art and became first a painter and then a sculptor. The two sisters, neither of whom married, lived and worked together throughout their lives. Sybil's father invited artists and writers to Priest Hill, and Laurence Binyon and Thomas Sturge Moore were regular visitors. Sybil discussed drama and poetry with Rupert Brooke and art and design with Sturge Moore. Sturge Moore, who produced some very modern designs for trade book covers, would have liked to marry Sybil, but she decided against marriage and children, probably because of her delicate health. He wrote the poems in *The Little school* for her, and they remained friends and critics of each other's work until his death in 1944. Sturge Moore also introduced Sybil to Charles Ricketts, who in the 1890s designed some bookbindings to be executed by hand by professional binders.

Although Sybil Pye maintained she was entirely self-taught, she was aided by Douglas Cockerell's manual, *Bookbinding and the care of books* (London, 1901). She kept her forwarding very simple, but it was appropriate for the fine press books she usually bound. She always sewed on raised cords, and never cut, coloured, or gilt the edges of her books. Her designs were all her own and made a complete break from what was accepted in bookbinding at the time. At first, she produced a number of bindings in pigskin and morocco, with blind- or blind- and gold-tooling. The dramatic and colourful

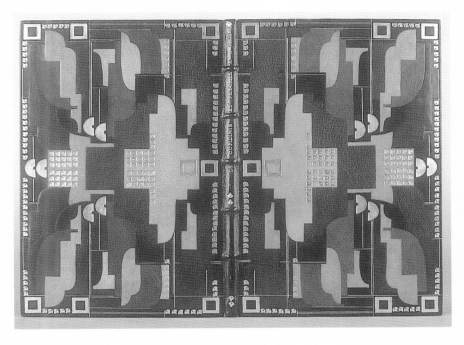

9. Inlaid and gold-tooled goatskin binding by Sybil Pye, 1929. Lucius Apuleius,
De Cupidinis et Psyches amoribus fabula anilis, Vale Press, 1901.
298 × 197 × 9 mm. Wormsley Library, Oxfordshire.

inlaid bindings that became her trademark came a little later (fig. 9).
She was one of the few binders at any time to do inlaid work, rather
than using onlays, and she did it with great skill. For tooling, she very
sparingly used a few tools given to her by Ricketts; later she added
some simple geometric designs of her own, which she preferred. Vale
letters were used for titling, but she never used figures, always
resorting to roman numerals. Her designs have been called 'cubist',
perhaps because they were introduced soon after the Picasso exhibition of 1907. They are, however, very architectural, and she suggested she was inspired by the designs of Michaelangelo and by
Islamic bindings.

Sybil Pye worked slowly but steadily on each of her bindings, first
preparing a rough sketch on vegetable parchment and shading in the
inlaid areas with pastels. Following her early bindings in pigskin, to
which she started adding vellum inlays, she soon settled on working
almost entirely in goatskin. She produced her first inlaid binding in
1910; as her work progressed, her designs tended to get more daring

and more colourful. She also liked the dramatic look of natural inlays in black or nearly black bindings. This combination was a favourite of the important collector Major Abbey, who bought and commissioned many of her bindings. In 1949, Abbey showed thirteen Sybil Pye bindings at the Arts Council in London.[15] After their father's death in 1933, Sybil and Ethel moved to Newick in Sussex, near one of their brothers. There Sybil continued to do a little binding until 1955, three years before she died. Although she produced only about 164 bindings in fifty years, she started a revolution in bookbinding design.

In 1906, in her final book on bookbinding, Sarah Prideaux wrote about modern binding in England and France.[16] No longer a binder herself, she felt free to write frankly about her contemporaries, including women binders. She concluded her remarks on the younger women who were trying to make a living out of the craft, with some intelligent and sensible advice. If a woman wishes to become a bookbinder, she said, three conditions are absolutely necessary: 1) a reasonable period of systematic workshop training; 2) the physique for standing and working at a bench all day; and 3) imagination, controlled by good taste, so that the binder's work has a note of individuality without eccentricity. She believed that properly trained women could bind as well as men, except for large and heavy work, and that those who could do it well enough could earn a fair wage. However she felt those who failed to reach a high standard should leave well alone. For while there was always a market for the best, there was no market for second best – good advice for binders of both sexes.

NOTES

1   James Boswell, *Life of Johnson* (L. F. Powell's revision of G. B. Hill's edition), Oxford, 1964, vol. 1, p. 457 (31 July 1763).

2   For an account of her career see M. Tidcombe, *The Bookbinding career of Rachel McMasters Miller*, Pittsburgh, The Hunt Institute, 1974.

3   Only a small selection of bindings are reproduced here. Many more are illustrated in colour and in black and white in M. Tidcombe, *Women bookbinders 1880–1920*, London and New Castle, Delaware, British Library and Oak Knoll, 1996.

4   Joseph Cundall, *On bookbindings, ancient and modern*, London, 1881, pp. 14, 54.

5   A. H. Scott-Elliot and Elspeth Yeo, 'Calligraphic manuscripts of Esther Inglis (1571–1624): a catalogue', *The Papers of the Bibliographical Society of America*, vol. 84 (March 1990), pp. 21–3.

6   British Library, C.27.d.13; Bodleian Library, Arch. A d.3. See also David Pearson, 'Cambridge bindings in Cosin's library, Durham', in P. C. G. Isaac (ed.), *Six centuries of the provincial book trade in Britain*, Winchester, 1990, pp. 41–60, notes 32 and 35.

7   *Clare College 1326–1926*, Cambridge, 1930, p. 499.

8   BL, C.61.b.14. Illustrated in colour in Tidcombe, *Women bookbinders, op. cit.*, pl. 1. See also H. M. Nixon, *Five centuries of English bookbinding*, London, 1978, pp. 194–5.

9   See M. Tidcombe, *The Bookbindings of T. J. Cobden-Sanderson*, London, British Library, 1984, p. 7.

10   T. J. Cobden-Sanderson, 'Bookbinding', in the Arts and Crafts Exhibition Society, *Catalogue of the first exhibition*, London, 1888, pp. 81–92.

11   The bindings in the 1894 Tregaskis exhibition are illustrated in colour in M. Tidcombe, *Tregaskis centenary exhibition*, London, Designer Bookbinders, 1994, with a facsimile of the original catalogue; bindings in the 1891 Tregaskis exhibition are described in the introductory essay.

12   Douglas Cockerell, who promoted the use of native-dyed niger, was at one time secretary of the Chiswick Art Workers Guild.

13   10 December 1900 and 16 December 1901.

14   7–8 November 1904.

15   See H. M. Nixon, *Broxbourne Library: styles and designs of bookbindings from the twelfth to the twentieth century*, London, 1956, p. 228; Philip James, 'Modern bookbinding', *The Studio*, vol. 138, no. 679 (October 1949), pp. 97–103.

16   Sarah Prideaux, *Modern bookbindings their design and decoration*, London, Archibald Constable and Co. Ltd., 1906.

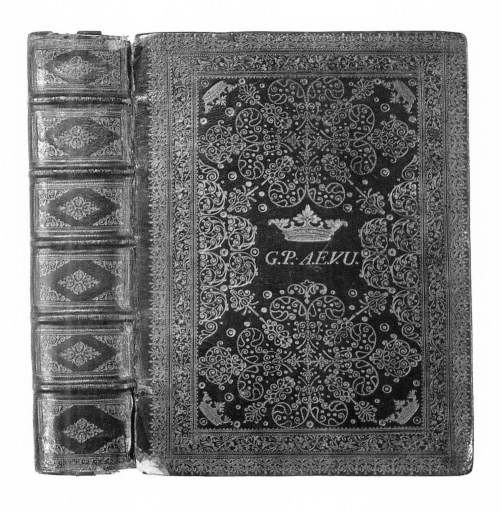

Colour plate 1. Binding by Albert Magnus, Amsterdam, 1679. Red morocco, tooled in gold. I. Cats, *Werelts begin, midden, eynde, besloten in den trou-ringh*, Dordrecht, Matthias Havius, 1637, 4to. The Hague, Royal Library, 1791 B 1.

Colour plate 2. Binding in gold-tooled sprinkled calf by the First Stadholder
Bindery, the Hague, *c.* 1730. Paulus Merula, *Politijck handboexken, van de
Staet van 't Nederlandt*, Leyden, Abraham van Geer-Vliet, 1650, 12mo.
The Hague, Royal Library, 138 G 29.

Colour plate 3. Binding by Lemonnier. M. Bandello, *Novelle*, London, 1740.
Red morocco with multi-coloured onlays, tooled in gold (lower cover).
Waddesdon Manor, B1/24/4.

307

Colour plate 4. Paris mosaic binding, *c.* 1746. *Ordinaire de la messe*, MS 1725.
White calf with multi-coloured onlays and mica, tooled in gold (lower cover).
Waddesdon Manor, B1/22/9.

Colour plate 5. A Dublin binding, *c.* 1772. Sallust, *The Catiline and Jugurtine wars* (transl. H. Maffet), Dublin, 1772. Blue goatskin, onlaid in cream calf, tooled in gold. 209 × 125 × 25 mm. British Library, C. 67.e.15.

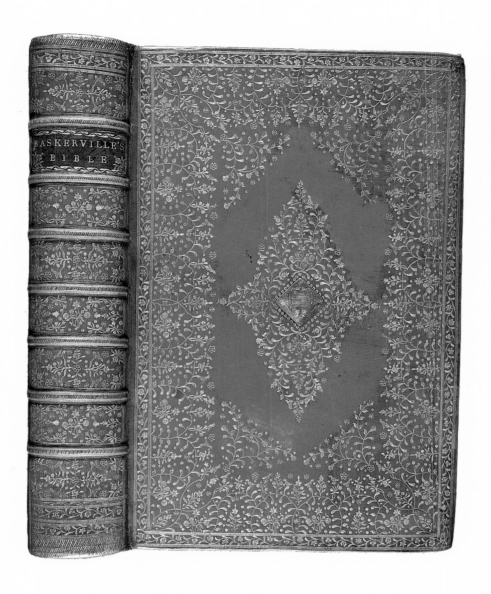

Colour plate 6. A Dublin binding by William Hallhead's binder, *c.* 1775.
The Holy Bible, Cambridge, 1763. Red goatskin, tooled in gold, with the
arms of Sir Richard Cox of Dunmanway on a brass plate in the centre.
504 × 324 × 97 mm. Trinity College, Dublin, Armoire.

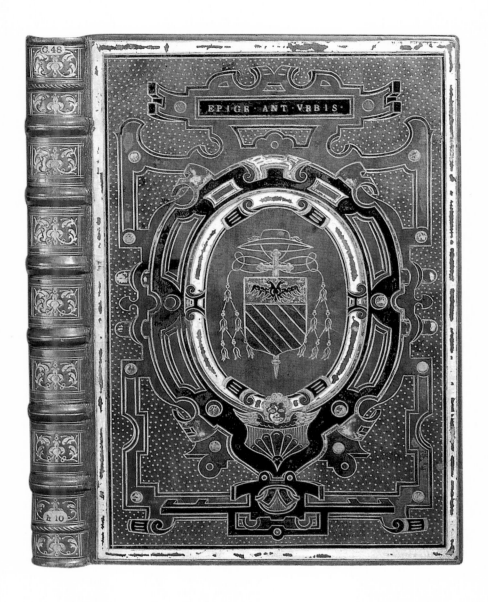

Colour plate 7. A binding by Hagué. *Epigrammata antique urbis*, Rome,
Iacobus Mazochius, 1521. Fol. Brown calf, tooled in gold and decorated
with black, red and white paint; with the arms of Cardinal Granvelle
(Blacker sale 44). British Library, C.48.h.10.

Colour plate 8. Embroidered binding by May Morris, bound by T. J. Cobden-Sanderson, 1891. William Morris, *Love is enough*, London, 1873. Silk, with gold and coloured threads, pearls and garnets. 251 × 169 × 34 mm. Bancroft Library.

INDEX